I0816928

When Claiborne Bridged the Chesapeake

When Claiborne Bridged the Chesapeake

The Rise and Fall of the Ferry Era

Martin J. Bollinger

Maryland Center for History and Culture

Baltimore, Maryland

Library of Congress Cataloging-in-Publication Data

Names: Bollinger, Martin J., 1958– author.
Title: When Claiborne bridged the Chesapeake : the rise and fall of the ferry era / by Martin J. Bollinger.
Description: Baltimore, Maryland : Maryland Center for History and Culture, 2025. | Includes bibliographical references and index.
Identifiers: LCCN 2025033802 | ISBN 9780984213597 hardback
Subjects: LCSH: Ferries—Maryland—Claiborne—History | Claiborne (Md.)—History | Maryland—Politics and government—1775–1865 | Maryland—Politics and government—1865–1950.
Classification: LCC HE5783.M3 B65 2025 | DDC 386/.609752—dc23/eng/20250909
LC record available at https://lccn.loc.gov/2025033802

ISBN: 978-0-9842135-9-7

Jacket cover: steamer *Gov. Emerson C. Harrington, unknown photographer, 1947. Courtesy of the Chesapeake Bay Maritime Museum*

Author's photograph by Vivian Marie Doering

Cover and book design by Mayfly book design
Printed in the United States of America. First printing: 2025

To my wonderful neighbors in Claiborne.

Contents

Maps and Figures

Maps

Figures

Steamers, Ferries, and Transportation Companies

Steamers and Ferries Serving Claiborne

SS *Balloon*

SS *Olive*

SS *Thames River*

SS *Tockwogh*

SS *Groton* (never placed into service)

SS *B.S. Ford*

SS *Tangier*

SS *Helen*

SS *Maggie*

SS *Cambridge*

SS *Tred Avon*

SS *Joppa*

SS *Atlantic*

SS *City of Milford*

SS *Texas*

SS *York River*

SS *Gov. Emerson C. Harrington*

SS *Gen. Lincoln*

SS *Majestic*

MV *Gov. Albert C. Ritchie*

MV *John M. Dennis*

MV *Gov. Harry W. Nice*

SS (later MV) *Gov. Emerson C. Harrington II*

MV *Gov. Herbert R. O'Conor*

MV *Eastern Bay / B. Frank Sherman*

Transportation Companies Serving Claiborne

Baltimore and Eastern Shore Railroad Company (B&ES)

Baltimore, Chesapeake and Atlantic Railway Company (BC&A)

Chesapeake Bay Ferry System (CBFS)

Claiborne-Annapolis Ferry Company (CAFC)

Claiborne-Annapolis Ferry Inc. (CAFI)

Eastern Shore Development Steamship Company (ESDSC)

Transportation Companies Serving Areas Outside of Claiborne

Annapolis and Baltimore Short Line Railroad (ASL)

Baltimore and Eastern Railroad (B&E)

Baltimore and Eastern Shore Ferry Line (B&ESF)

Baltimore and Ohio Railroad (B&O)

Bay Bridge Ferry Corporation (BBFC) (never entered service)

Bay Ridge and Annapolis Railroad (BR&A)

Chesapeake Beach Railway (CBR)

Delaware Railroad (DRR)

Maryland Bay Company (MBC) (never entered service)

Maryland, Delaware and Virginia Railway Company (MD&V)

New York, Philadelphia and Norfolk Railroad (NYP&N)

Peninsula Ferry Company (PFC)

Pennsylvania Railroad (PRR)

Philadelphia, Wilmington and Baltimore Railroad (PW&B)

Queen Anne's Ferry and Equipment Company (QAF&E)

Queen Anne's and Kent County Railroad

Queen Anne's Railroad (QARR)

Tolchester Steamboat Company (TSC)

Washington, Baltimore and Annapolis Electric Railway (WB&A)

Wicomico and Pocomoke Railroad (W&P)

Acknowledgments

The endeavors of those who seek to explore the history of the Chesapeake Bay are blessed by a large number of dedicated individuals and organizations. They are the keepers of the history, committed to keeping alive the rich heritage of this region and holding that in trust for future generations. I am the fortunate recipient of their eagerness, expertise, and knowledge which helped shape this book.

In particular, local history societies remain the foundation for much of this archival work, and their collections and assistance remain invaluable. This includes the Talbot Historical Society (Peggy Morey, Kayla Weber), the Kent Island Heritage Society (John Conley, Linda Collier, Carol Mylander), and the Greater Harrington Historical Society (Doug Poore, Royden Powell). Similar assistance was provided by Becki Riti of the Talbot County Free Library in Easton, Maryland. Pete Lesher and Gabriella Cantelmo of the Chesapeake Bay Maritime Museum provided access to the museum's appreciable collection of artifacts, photographs, and records that informed my research. The image collection of the Newport News Mariners' Museum and Park also proved invaluable in this effort. Staff at the Hagley Museum and Library, the Maryland State Archives, and the US National Archives and Records Administration rendered great assistance to this project.

Others have written extensively on the history of steamboats and railroads in the Chesapeake, or have otherwise sought to document the history of that era, and this work follows in their wake. In particular, ephemera collector John Conley, local maritime author Jack Shaum, and legendary railroad guru John Hayman provided great support for this project.

While writing *When Claiborne Bridged the Chesapeake*, I was fortunate to connect with individuals who had direct contact with this history, either via their own personal experiences, or that of family members who worked on or rode the ferries to Claiborne. In particular, Margaret Bryan, the daughter of long-time manager of the Claiborne-Annapolis Ferry Company (later the Chesapeake Bay Ferry System) graciously provided valuable information about her father, B. Frank Sherman. She also opened up her personal collection of photographs and artifacts. Her sons Mark and Chris were also quite helpful. Daniel G. Higgins III made available the records of his grandfather and two great-uncles, all of whom were captains of Claiborne ferries. Similarly, Jackie Price provided me with the papers and archival material about other members of the famed Higgins family. Judge John C. North Jr., whose grandparents ran the Sea Gull Inn at the Claiborne wharf in the 1920s and early 1930s, shared anecdotes and photographs from that time. Trudy Guthrie shared stories of her grandfather, former Maryland Governor Emerson C. Harrington, who was the driving force behind the formation of Claiborne-Annapolis Ferry Inc.

I would be remiss if I failed to recognize the support of the wonderful Claiborne community. Many of its members seek to keep alive the history of this hamlet. Priscilla Morris provided a tour (via rowboat, with Priscilla pulling the oars) of historical Tunis family sites on Tilghman Creek. Mike and Jeanne Kuperberg shared their archive of photos of the old ferry terminal in Claiborne, which was later turned into a residence. Renny Johnson, Suzanne Todd, Bill Sewell, Flo Burdett, Frank Ferrell, Barbara Haddaway, Kirke Harper, and Jim Richardson—among many—provided insight and encouragement along the way, sharing what documents they had accumulated over the years.

Jack Shaum and John Conley, in addition to supporting my research, reviewed early drafts of the material and provided helpful feedback. Claiborne resident Paul Cooper did herculean work to copyedit the final draft, applying his considerable professional skill to the effort, with Rebecca Kerins providing additional copyediting via my publisher.

Special thanks to J. Elliott Russo of Snow Hill Solutions for her indexing expertise, and Maple Press for printing my maritime love letter to Claiborne. The composition of this history of ferries in Claiborne would not be possible without the creative team at Mayfly Design: Molly Mortimer, Julie Scheife, and Ryan Scheife. Thank you for the brilliant cover design and book layout. To my publisher at the Maryland Center for History and Culture, under the leadership of Katie Caljean, and the editors—Dr. Martina Kado and Chris Redwood—who wholeheartedly believed in this project, thank you for giving this book legs and the chance to walk the earth.

Finally, I would like to express great appreciation and admiration to my wonderful wife, Maura, whose skills in genealogical research appear unparalleled. So much of the history of this small community is tied up with family histories, and she was instrumental in untangling this complex subject. In addition, Maura found valuable information buried in century-old land records that shed new light on the operation of ferry companies. Her continuing encouragement and fair-minded critical appraisal are very welcome, in both my writing efforts and my life overall.

M. J. B.

Notes on Terminology and Sources

Terms familiar to most Marylanders may not make sense to readers unaccustomed to the local culture. It is therefore worth a moment to review the geography of the region and to introduce other terms and sources that will be used extensively in the pages that follow.

Maryland is almost completely divided north–south by the Chesapeake Bay. That portion of Maryland to the east of the Chesapeake Bay is called the *Eastern Shore* and runs from the Chesapeake to the Atlantic Ocean. When broadened to include Delaware and the equivalent eastern part of Virginia, that expanded area is known as the *Delmarva Peninsula*, the simple conjunction of abbreviations for Delaware, Maryland, and Virginia. The other side of Maryland is known as the *Western Shore*.[1]

The eastern side of the Delmarva Peninsula borders the Atlantic, while the western side borders the Chesapeake Bay. What can become confusing is when someone who lives on the Delmarva Peninsula's western coast refers to themself as living on the Eastern Shore, perhaps even mentioning the fantastic sunsets that the shore offers. The easiest way to understand this is to recognize that the Chesapeake Bay is so central to the state's identity that the two shores are defined by the Chesapeake, *not* by the Delmarva Peninsula nor the Atlantic Ocean.

Any discussion of the Bay inevitably involves reference to boats, and here too terminology can confuse. Ships powered by steam are technically referred to as *steamships*, often abbreviated as "SS." These would often be called *steamers* in common vernacular. Smaller steamers might be called *steamboats*, often reserved for inland vessels powered by paddlewheels or sidewheels instead of propellers. Vessels powered by internal combustion (typically diesel) engines are called *motorships* ("MS") or *motor vessels* ("MV").

By convention, steamboats or motor vessels engaged in the transport of passengers, freight, *and* other vehicles from one transportation hub to another are referred to as *ferries*. Whether such a vessel is a ship or a boat is cause for an endless and generally irresolvable debate, so we will use each and not agonize over it.

Names of boats can also confuse. Is it *General Lincoln* or *Gen. Lincoln*? Is it *Governor Emerson C. Harrington II* or *Harrington*? The pages that follow will use, as a primary reference for boat name and other particulars, the annual publication *Merchant Vessels of the United States*.[2] For the purposes of this history, it will be considered the definitive source.

Beyond *Merchant Vessels of the United States*, other sources of information have proven most useful in this effort. *Poor's Manual of Railroads* presented detailed financial information of relevant rail operations on an annual basis up through 1923. The annual reports of the Maryland Public Service Commission (PSC) contain records of filings and orders, which proved most useful given that the PSC regulated the steamboats and railroads during the relevant periods here. The reports for 1911 through 1932 also contain detailed financial accounts of regulated companies, including those covered in this book.

By a strange turn of fate, detailed records of the Claiborne-Annapolis Ferry Company from 1919 to 1940—including minutes of shareholder, board, and executive committee meetings—were preserved when the company was taken over by the State of Maryland in 1941. Most often such records are lost to history, but since they then fell under Maryland state archival policies, they have been preserved. Court records stored in the Maryland State Archives also provide useful insights into the many legal battles that extended across the ferry companies and railroad enterprises operating at this time. Several of these court cases went all the way to the US Supreme Court. The US National Archives and Records Administration holds other important records, including those of the US Steamboat Inspection Service.

Finally, this work makes extensive use of contemporary reporting in the newspapers of the day, especially *The Sun* (Baltimore, MD) and *The Evening Sun* (Baltimore, MD), *The Easton Star-Democrat*, *The Cambridge Daily Banner*, *The Afro-American* (Baltimore, MD), *The Denton Journal*, *The Evening Capital* (Annapolis, MD), *The Salisbury Times*, and various incarnations of *The News Journal* (Wilmington, DE).[3] Even small communities enjoyed vibrant newspapers during this period. If nothing else, one learns to appreciate the past vitality of local journalism—and the records left behind.[4]

Notes

1. Locals often do not capitalize *Western Shore* even when they do capitalize *Eastern Shore*, since the latter is a defined region and the former is more amorphous. We will capitalize both here.
2. From 1869, this is an annual compilation of data on the US merchant fleet, expanded in 1920 to include yachts. It was prepared by a variety of US government agencies over time: the Department of the Treasury (1829–1902), the Department of Commerce (1903–1942), back to the Department of the Treasury (1943–1966), and then the US Coast Guard (1967 to the present.) Importantly, each merchant vessel is assigned a unique number, one that persists through all of the potential name changes and structural reconfigurations (e.g., steamer to scow to barge) that a vessel might undergo during its existence.
3. It is contemporary reporting that is most important. There are many cases in later decades of newspaper articles "remembering" the early days of the ferries. Alas, many of the recollections in these later articles are incorrect. A classic case is the article written by B. Frank Sherman for *The Sun*, (Baltimore, MD), printed on July 27, 1952, relaying the stories of the ferry's early days. It is filled with errors: the founder's name was not J. P. Mehaham (it was Hampden D. Mepham), the initial subsidy was not $50,000 (it was $48,000), Sherman did not become general manager in 1924 (it was 1925, at least as officially recognized by board resolution), the company did not go into bankruptcy in 1921 (it avoided bankruptcy when Harrington bought out the original investors), *Gen. Lincoln* was not damaged in a storm in 1923 (it was 1922), and the passengers aboard were not rescued by the steamer *Talbot* (it was the *Lancaster*, with *Gov. Emerson C. Harrington* standing by if needed). Arguably, *Gov. Emerson C. Harrington* was not the "first cross-bay ferry" from Annapolis to Claiborne (that was *Atlantic* in 1912, or even *Tockwogh* in 1890, if Bay Ridge is included). To be clear, *Gov. Emerson C. Harrington* was the first *car* ferry. Finally, the incident described with Captain Daniel Higgins on the *Majestic* in 1923 may be a case of mistaken identity (the captain was, most likely, Thomas Woolford, but this is not certain).
4. For simplicity, references to these papers will use the name in common use for most of the period covered in this history. Not surprisingly, many newspaper names have changed over time. *The Sun* (Baltimore, MD) became *The Baltimore Sun* in 2008. *The Easton Star-Democrat* was *The Easton Star* until 1896 and was renamed *The Star-Democrat* (Easton, MD) in 1961. *The Evening Capital* (Annapolis, MD) was renamed *The Evening Capital and Maryland Gazette* between 1910 and 1922, resuming its former title until being

renamed *The Capital* (Annapolis, MD) in 1981. The *Salisbury Times* became *The Daily Times* (Salisbury, MD) in 1964. *The News Journal* (Wilmington, DE) traces its origins back to 1888 as the *Evening Journal.* It became the *Journal-Every Evening* in 1932, and in 1960 reverted to its original name of *Evening Journal* before being renamed *The News Journal* in 1989.

Introduction

The small community of Claiborne sits off the Chesapeake Bay on the Eastern Shore of Maryland, separating the Chesapeake's appendage of Eastern Bay from Tilghman Creek, the first side inlet one encounters when entering the Miles River. The waters are well known to local watermen and sailors. Coming from the north, down the Chesapeake, one rounds Bloody Point at the southern tip of Kent Island and then enters Eastern Bay. If desired, one can proceed from there directly to Broad Cove, the body of water in Eastern Bay that sits alongside the modern village of Claiborne.

Alternatively, a sailor can execute a quick tack—more likely a gybe in the summertime—and adjust course to the northeast, which then brings you around Tilghman Point and into the Miles River. For most sailors, their destination is farther east to the historic tourist town of St. Michaels, the self-proclaimed "drinking village with a sailing problem." Some sailors, seeking peace and quiet rather than boisterous diversions, instead round Tilghman Point at the tip of Rich Neck and from there head south through the channel into Tilghman Creek. Many, after passing through the channel markers, seek to anchor in the first cove to the right, unnamed but inside a shoal nicknamed "Wreck Point" by the adjoining landowners, who often are entertained by sailboats running aground there.

If it is peace and tranquility you seek, Claiborne is your place. It is, today, an isolated community of about eighty homes, mostly

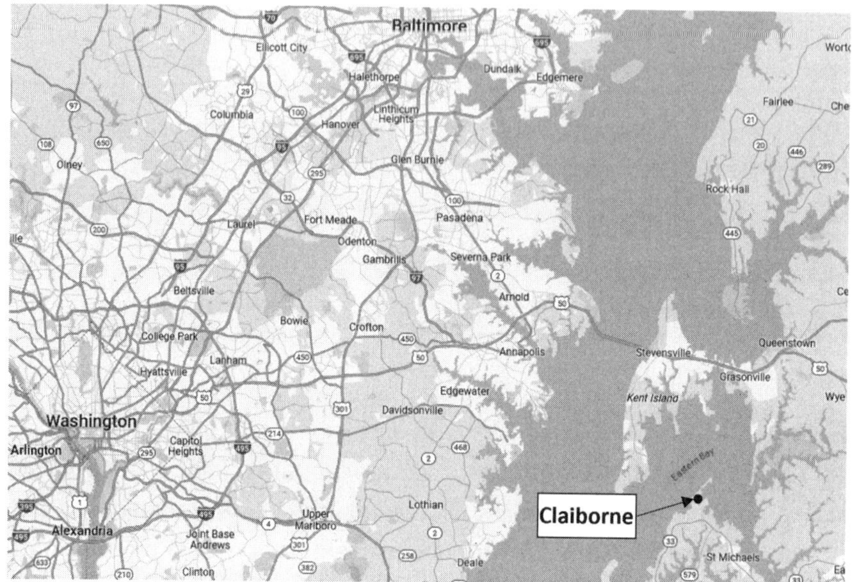

Map 1. Contemporary map illustrating the location of Claiborne. Source: Base map is from US Geological Survey, detailed and annotated by the author.

built in the one hundred years after the Civil War. The residents carry varied stories. Some work as watermen, harvesting the crabs, oysters, and rockfish (striped bass) for which this part of the United States is famous. Others work nearby in the tourist-frequented town of St. Michaels, or farther afield in Easton, the seat of Talbot County. Several are local artists or apply their talented hands in any number of crafts. Others are building contractors, working with stone or wood. Many are retired, having relocated from the cities or suburbs to this small village.

Claiborne is generally a quiet community. From March to November, the solitude is punctured by the cries of the ospreys as they circle the waters before diving for their catch of the day. Summer is a time of trolling "bay boats," laying and servicing trotlines that bring up the highly valued blue crabs. Autumn silence is occasionally disturbed by the shotgun blasts of hunters looking to fill the freezer with their allotted quantity of duck or goose. In the winter, one often hears only the wind rushing through bare trees as battalions of Canada geese parade along the shore in column formation.

Claiborne is quiet in another way as well. There are no shops or commercial activities in town. No one really goes through Claiborne to get anywhere else these days. It is just a small gathering of homes with community life centered on the Village Hall, a converted church that serves as a meeting place, a mailbox location, the venue for potluck dinners, and as an occasional spot for musical entertainment. The village is home to a number of talented woodworkers, artisans, and retired home builders, and thus the old Village Hall is maintained in impeccable condition. A number of retired nurses have moved into town in recent years, which brings a sense of comfort, perhaps mitigated by the new presence of an automatic external defibrillator in the Village Hall, a reminder that many of us are indeed well past mid-life.

If you leave the village heading east and wander down Cockey Road—yes, members of the Cockey family still live there—you will reach the top of Tilghman Creek. A few powerboats and workboats are tied up at wooden piers here. Off to one side are the decaying skeletons of long-abandoned workboats. A small squadron of sailboats occupies moorings out in the creek. It is a quiet, calm place that perfectly mirrors the town to which it abuts. The scene is precisely what you expect to see.

But a quick walk to where the town meets Eastern Bay, at Broad Cove on the western side, suggests quite a different past for this small village. At the water's edge, the eye is drawn to a long, straight, and narrow jetty formed of wooden bulkheads, large rocks, and packed earth. Decaying wooden pilings stand like sentries beyond, suggesting that at one time a large structure and platform extended over the water at the far end of the jetty. The whole thing seems to be whispering "look at me—I'm really old." This structure appears long-retired, seeking only calm and quiet in its old age—like many village residents.

Next to this structure is almost its opposite—a short, squat platform built of concrete and asphalt. It exudes modernity. Enormous pilings are wrapped in heavy steel cables, as if to challenge boats to try and push them aside. This pier looks ready for a fight. There is a launching ramp for small boats midway along, which seems miniscule next to the large docking apparatus at the far end. Why would such a small and isolated village have such a large pier at all? And why would it have two?

The locals know their history and will gladly share it. These structures were once both the end of the line—several lines, in fact—and a vital connection point. These are the remnants of Claiborne's earlier history as the major transportation hub linking Baltimore, Washington, Annapolis, and other cities on the Western Shore with Easton, Cambridge, Salisbury, Ocean City, and the broader Eastern Shore of Maryland. Claiborne is where the ferry ended and the train line started, or, to think about it differently, where the ferry line began and the train line ended.

There were many towns along the Chesapeake and its tributaries that were well served by steamboats during the age of steam. But none can match Claiborne for the length and criticality of the transport operations it supported. Five different ferry companies employed Claiborne as their major hub on the Eastern Shore, including a couple of periods where competing ferry lines operated concurrently. Claiborne was *twice* the focal point of an effort, promoted at the highest levels of Maryland government, to tie together the state's Eastern and Western Shores, first by rail and then by automobile. This little community served as the western terminal for rail service across the Eastern Shore for almost thirty-five years. It then served for three decades as a vital link for the subsequent car ferries, including a time when automobiles might be waiting in a mile-long line to ride the ferry.

The evidence of this storied history is all around us. Two of the homes in the village, now relocated from their earlier sites, once served duty as ticket offices and waiting rooms. An anchor from a legendary ferry leans gently alongside the exterior block foundation of the Village Hall, which itself is decorated inside with photos of old sidewheel steamers and more modern diesel ferries. The village seems to be calling out to both residents and visitors to acknowledge that this little gathering of homes used to be something more significant. Perhaps, like some of the villagers, it is recalling a past time when it was important and industrious, appreciating its current quiet life while remembering the former one.

Questions naturally arise for the curious. Why the two ferry wharves? Why are they in Claiborne, which is, after all, twice as far from the Western Shore's major population centers as many other Eastern Shore towns? Why would anyone come here? Who built the wharves? How were they used? And why did it all come to an end? In the beginning, it all started with a badly flawed business plan that collapsed after only eight months but that nonetheless set the stage for the next forty years—until geography finally struck back.

A study of this hamlet's history reveals several recurring themes about how transportation in the United States worked in the period between the Civil War and the Cold War. First, decisions that had a major impact on Claiborne—including the fact that the community came into existence—were almost never made locally. Rather, the fate of the community was determined by power brokers in political circles across the Chesapeake Bay in Annapolis (Maryland's capital) and Washington, DC, or by financial titans far away in Philadelphia or New York. Second, even though many of these decisions proved to be seriously flawed, the implications of those actions—wise or otherwise—had staying power for decades beyond. It was easier to build upon someone else's poor choices than to start again from scratch. Third, once a transportation network and its corresponding assets had been created, owners would take every possible measure to maintain a monopoly, using political and financial power to stifle competition. Finally, those monopolies would fall not so much to market forces, but to generational technological change, adopted by those willing to be bold and daring.

We will see three distinct cases where technical revolutions disrupted transportation monopolies. The first was the transition from sailing vessel and steamboat to land-based steam railroads (Chapters II through IV). This is what put Claiborne on the map in the late 1880s. Two efforts were made to undermine this rail-based monopoly. The first, which failed in 1916 (Chapter V), employed fast steam yachts. The second, which built upon that failure in 1919 and succeeded (Chapters VI through VIII), exploited the technical disruption of the automobile. With this disruption, one monopoly was soon replaced by another. This transition also led to Claiborne's "Golden Era." Various challenges sought to undermine this car-ferry monopoly (Chapters IX and IX), and even though these were unsuccessful, they forced responses that ultimately brought Claiborne's dominant position to an end. The final revolution was the state takeover of the ferry system (Chapter XI) and replacement of ferries with the Chesapeake Bay Bridge (Chapters XII and XIII), which returned Claiborne to the quiet, off-the-track backwater it had been before this all started.

When Claiborne Bridged the Chesapeake

I

Evolution of the Maryland Eastern Shore

Maryland's Eastern Shore is, and almost always has been, a bit of an outlier from the rest of the state. Even today, the population of the entire Eastern Shore is barely half that of the state's principal city, Baltimore. The Eastern Shore shares little in common with the forested mountains of the state's western counties or the twin metropolises of Baltimore and Washington on the other side of the Chesapeake. Not surprisingly, it has evolved differently from those regions. The one thing it has in common with the bulk of the state's population is proximity to water, notably the Chesapeake Bay and its many tributaries.

The First European Settlers

The Chesapeake Bay was first discovered by persons unknown at least twelve thousand years ago, just as the last Ice Age was releasing its frozen grip on North America. Those Native Americans settled the region, enjoying the bounty of the Bay and adjoining arable lands. The first Europeans to visit the region arrived one hundred centuries after it had been inhabited. Giovanni da Verrazzano of Florence briefly visited the coastal areas of Maryland in 1524 as part of a long trip up the eastern coast of the continent. He was followed by Lucas Vázquez de Ayllón in 1525 and then by Diego Gutiérrez, whose map, published in 1562, is the first to show the Chesapeake Bay. More detailed information on the region was revealed by English explorer and artist John White, who visited the region and published drawings between 1585 and 1593 from his visits to what is now Virginia.[1]

The name "Claiborne" becomes associated with the region in 1631, when fur trader William Claiborne set up a trading post on Kent Island, across the Miles River from what became his namesake community. Disputes over the control of this territory emerged among the English settlers, mirroring divisions back in England itself. Competing claims were made, and conflict arose between Claiborne and his followers and the followers of George Calvert, the First Lord Baltimore. In the end Calvert's supporters took control, and William Claiborne retreated to Virginia, leaving behind only his name.

Europeans were not the only new inhabitants of the region. Maryland was a slave-owning state, and the Eastern Shore, in particular, comprised a number of large slave plantations. Annapolis was one of many destinations for ships bringing enslaved Africans to the region. One of several local legends suggests that Bloody Point, the southern tip of Kent Island, was named as such because it is where slave ships discarded the bodies of those who had died en route before arriving into port. (There are competing stories about how Bloody Point earned its name.[2])

War came to this region in both the American Revolution and the War of 1812. St. Michaels, the largest town near Claiborne, was attacked by a raiding party on August 10, 1813, supplemented by an artillery duel. Additional destruction would no doubt have ensued if a party of British soldiers and marines, landing on August 26 not far from what would later become Claiborne, had not been blocked by the Bay Hundred militia, formed from the citizens of that region of Talbot County bordering Eastern Bay, known even today as Bay Hundred.[3]

Maryland or Delaware?

When peace returned to the region in 1814, the United States was being transformed by the Industrial Revolution. Major enterprises were emerging in transportation, manufacturing, shipbuilding, and textiles, and Maryland was part of that revolution. However, the benefits of the Industrial Revolution were not evenly shared between the urban centers, such as Baltimore, and the agricultural regions of the Eastern Shore. While Baltimore, Annapolis, and Frederick enjoyed an economic boom driven by the miracles of the industrial age, the Eastern Shore remained mired in a plantation economy more indicative of rural Mississippi than the rest of Maryland.

The diverging fates became even more apparent when the results of the 1830 census were published. Population across the state of Maryland was up almost 10 percent since the 1820 census, but the population on Maryland's Eastern Shore had actually fallen by 2 percent in that same period. The Eastern Shore accounted for over a third of the state's residents in 1790. By 1820 it was just over a quarter, and that percentage dropped further by 1830.[4]

Differences also emerged on the nature of the population in each region, reflecting inherent distinctions in the economy of each part of the state and the resulting use of enslaved labor. The Eastern Shore had a higher percentage of Black residents (44.1 percent)—mostly enslaved but some free—than the rest of the state (32.7 percent). The odious institution of slavery was deeply connected to the plantation economy of the Eastern Shore—especially tobacco—at least in the early decades of European colonization. When the United States became progressively divided between pro-slavery and anti-slavery contingents, the uneasy partnership between the Eastern Shore and the rest of the state became increasingly stressed.

The disconnect between the Eastern and Western Shores of Maryland led to ongoing debates over whether the former was, in fact, more aligned culturally and economically with Delaware than with the rest of Maryland. The fear of the Eastern Shore becoming disconnected from the rest of the state, and becoming more associated with Delaware (and Philadelphia), would become a recurring theme that drove many decisions on transportation. These outcomes would have a direct impact on the formation and evolution of the village of Claiborne.

In fact, some on the western side of the Chesapeake would have been happy to see the Eastern Shore leave the state. The Eastern Shore was granted unusual political influence that outweighed its population: one of the two US senators from Maryland was reserved for the Eastern Shore. (This was before the direct election of senators.) The counties on the Eastern Shore were also overrepresented in the state legislature, given how the delegates and state senators were apportioned.

On the other side, the state of Delaware saw an opportunity to expand its reach by absorbing Maryland's Eastern Shore into a Greater Delaware. Such was proposed in 1833 by the governor of Delaware, Caleb Prew Bennett. The Maryland House of Delegates then formally proposed that the Eastern Shore counties of Maryland should have the authority to set their fate: stay in Maryland or join Delaware. (The assumption was that those counties would vote to join Delaware.) In the end, the Maryland Senate discarded the House's proposal—by one vote—and Maryland remained united. But the stark differences between Western and Eastern Shores, and the fragility of the Eastern Shore's connection to the rest of the state, was laid bare. The fracturing relationship between the two shores had not been resolved.

For the next one hundred years, the desire to reinforce the bonds between the two sides of the Chesapeake drove many of the initiatives to improve transportation between Baltimore and the Eastern Shore. These efforts would become even more acute as the development of railroads—and the highways that followed—threatened to shift the orientation of Maryland's Eastern Shore more toward Philadelphia than Baltimore. The bugaboo of Philadelphia displacing Baltimore would be called upon to justify major new transportation initiatives in 1886, 1916, 1930, and 1938. In each case, the action that followed had a major impact on the steamboat and ferry operations in the small village of Claiborne and on the village itself.

Early Steamboat History on the Chesapeake

The state of Maryland is blessed by the Chesapeake Bay and its tributaries, not just as a source of seafood and visual charm, but also as a boulevard of transportation and commerce. On the Eastern Shore, the waters of the Bay extend far inland in the form of navigable rivers such as (going from north to south) the Bohemia, Sassafras, Chester, Miles, Choptank, Tred Avon, Little Choptank, Nanticoke, Wicomico, Manokin, and Big Annemessex. In the early 1800s these rivers allowed boats to reach far inland from the Chesapeake, connecting remote communities on the Eastern Shore with the commercial metropolis of Baltimore. The city of Baltimore prospered and grew and was ranked in the 1830 census as the second-largest city in the United States, behind New York and just ahead of Philadelphia (but only because Philadelphia had yet to absorb some of its surrounding suburbs).[5]

The Chesapeake Bay and its rivers provided a thoroughfare for commerce between Baltimore and the dispersed communities on the Eastern Shore. For the first two centuries after Europeans settled in the region, transportation by boat on the Chesapeake meant harnessing the wind for power. For decades this meant schooners and sloops, standard designs that were relatively fast and maneuverable. Boat builders on the Chesapeake also generated a series of custom designs, including bugeyes and skipjacks, to allow watermen to harvest the bounty of the Bay and to connect various communities.

Steam-powered transportation first appeared on the Chesapeake on June 13, 1813, when the small steamboat *Chesapeake* made a trial voyage from Baltimore to Annapolis. Confidence in the steam engine and paddlewheel remained limited, and *Chesapeake* thus retained a mast and sail—just in case. The entrepreneur behind the construction of *Chesapeake*, Edward Trippe, saw promise in the design and proceeded to form the Union Line, headquartered in Baltimore. The era of steam on the Chesapeake was underway.

Soon, the graceful Chesapeake sailboats would be covering waters already crisscrossed with the wakes of steamboats, the latter belching smoke and noise from steam engines and paddlewheels. While the romance of a voyage under sail might have been lost, it was offset by the reliability and predictability of steamboat operations. As one simple measure, before the arrival of steamboats, schedules for sailing craft only noted the time of departure, not a time of arrival. Subject to the wind (or lack thereof), it was hard to predict an arrival time. Now that mechanical power was being harnessed, and (except in extreme conditions) voyage times were independent of the winds, schedules could show both departure and arrival times.

There was also a kind of mystique in being on a steamboat, which might seem odd today given our fondness for the romance of sailing. The use of steam power was a novelty for most people, and a voyage on a steamboat allowed them to participate in a clear demonstration of human achievement. This was the Victorian Age, and the measure of progress was often linked to steam.

Steamboats of the era were also machines that displayed their mechanical power openly for all to see. A "walking beam" engine atop the boiler extended far beyond the upper "hurricane" deck, and its repetitive motion was clearly visible to passengers. Its rhythmic motion, simultaneously hypnotic and awesome, made transparent how mechanical motion was created from steam. Until propellers became more common, the very means of locomotion—sidewheels—were also partially exposed for all to see. However, it was probably the sense of sound and feel that most impressed early steamboat passengers. Rather than a quiet and graceful voyage on a schooner or sloop, a trip on a steamboat came with amazing and novel sounds: the thumping of the engine, splashing of paddlewheels, deep-note vibrations in the decks themselves, grunts of men loading coal into the furnaces, and the sound of whistles. Then there was the smoke and ash, conveyed high into the sky by tall smokestacks.

Sailboats and steamboats both left wakes in the water, but only steamers created these aerial wakes of smoke. Steamboats were not carried across the waves; they pushed the waves aside. They did not skate over the Bay; they conquered it. Riding on one was quite an experience in that era. It was a clear representation of the future.

Thus began a century-long love affair between the Chesapeake and steamboats, centered on the Light Street wharves in Baltimore's Inner Harbor. Many variations of these steamboats appeared. Excursion boats would bring holiday-seeking passengers on short voyages to the bevy of amusement parks that emerged across the Bay. Some excursion boats performed double duty as short-range transports, bringing passengers and freight to nearby locations best accessed via the Bay and its rivers. Most magnificent, perhaps, were the large overnight packets that connected Baltimore with far-flung regional cities such as Norfolk, with their salons, dining rooms, and cabins offering luxury to those who could afford it. Smaller overnight packet steamers—*packet* is derived from *packette*, an old word for mail—connected Baltimore with less populous towns down the Chesapeake, such as Crisfield and Salisbury.

A distinct class of steamers, perhaps less deserving of romance than those above, emerged in the late 1800s. These transports, which are the focus of this book, performed utilitarian duties, shuttling passengers from Baltimore to points across the Bay, where those passengers might connect to rail hubs and continue their journeys to their final destinations. Tending to sacrifice luxury for speed and reliability, the ultimate form for these steamers would be the double-ender, diesel-powered car ferries of the twentieth century, a design "which, with few exceptions, earned the scorn of true steamboat aesthetes."[6] Aesthetics aside, these ferries were important contributors to the local economy and made movement around the region easier for large segments of the population. For steamboats as well as sailboats, the Chesapeake and its rivers were the arteries that linked the Eastern Shore with the population and industrial centers across the Bay.

Steamboats on the Miles River

Steamboats inevitably made their appearance on the Miles River. In 1840, the steamboat *Maryland* conducted regular service connecting Baltimore and Annapolis with destinations up the Miles River, including St. Michaels. In the 1850s such service became relatively common, and steamboats of the Eastern Shore Steamboat Company, including *Osiris*, *Hugh Jenkins*, and *Champion*, ran scheduled services on the Miles River. During and after the Civil War, steamboat traffic on the Bay increased further with the emergence of the Maryland Steamboat Company. Steamboats, such as *Pioneer*, *Highland Light,* and *Samuel J. Pentz,* were often seen on the Miles River or docked at St. Michaels.[7] By acquiring the assets of other companies, the Maryland Steamboat Company soon had control of steamboat traffic on the Miles River.

All of these steamboats sailed past Claiborne, however, at that time just a small collection of homes at the tip of Tilghman Creek surrounded by family farms and large estates. The resident population was not seen as sufficiently dense, or the local economy sufficiently vibrant, to warrant its own steamboat landing. The nearest economic hub was centered on St. Michaels, five miles to the southeast, or the larger town of Easton, another ten miles to the east. In the 1860s there was not much of a call for tourism or expeditions to Claiborne. But what the community lacked in attractions, it sought to make up with aspirations.

A Steamboat to Claiborne

The desire to maintain—or break—transportation monopolies has had a large impact on the community of Claiborne, and the first example emerged just after the Civil War. Steamboat traffic between the Miles River and the Western Shore was already well served by the monopolistic Maryland Steamboat Company, making it difficult for new competitors to emerge. One way to break the established monopoly was to find alternative destinations, ones less popular and thus not yet served by existing steamboat companies. This pattern will emerge many times in this chronicle.

This was the strategy of disruption pursued by Captain Samuel Ogle Tilghman, and it led to the first scheduled steamboat operation to Claiborne—or more properly what is now called "Old Claiborne." In March 1867, Captain Tilghman purchased the tired sidewheel steamboat *Balloon*, which had been serving St. Michaels earlier under the flag of the Individual Enterprise Steamship Company, and began to run his own service from Baltimore to various destinations on the Miles River.[8] *Balloon*, built in Brooklyn in 1839, was an aging vessel by that point, having seen service out of Philadelphia in its early years and then on the Chesapeake during the Civil War.[9]

Eager to bypass the fortress hubs of existing steamboat companies, Tilghman sought to expand his reach by creating new landings in areas he believed were ripe for emerging resort communities, ones designed to appeal to city dwellers looking for "recreation and refreshment, and [who] desire it amid delightful scenes, pure air and invigorating salt-water bathing."[10] In addition to a new landing at Bruff's Island, at the entrance to the Wye River, Tilghman built a new wharf on Tilghman Creek . . .

> . . . at Bingham's Mineral Spring Grove, in Talbot, where a company of Northern capitalists are preparing to fit up a first-class watering place, which, containing as it does 324 acres of beautiful wooded land open to the sea, with springs of magnesia, sulphur, and iron, may ultimately become a popular summer resort.[11]

This new wharf, at the tip of Tilghman Creek, became known as "Bingham's Wharf" or "Bingham's Steamboat Landing."[12] *Balloon* would arrive from Baltimore every Tuesday and Saturday.[13] For a fare of $1.50 (about $34 in 2024), passengers were offered transit on *Balloon* to the promised pleasures of Bingham's Mineral Springs, a sulfur spring recognized as the "most important mineral spring of the county" in a 1926 geological assessment of Talbot County.[14] For the first time, Claiborne was linked by steam to the rest of the region.

Alas, the sale of the property for Bingham's Mineral Springs fell through, and the resort never emerged.[15] Tilghman's steamer business collapsed after just one summer season. He was sued by unpaid shipyard operators the following year and was forced to sell many of his own personal properties in 1871.[16] Without scheduled steamboat service, the village of Old Claiborne had to rely again upon sailing vessels or special arrangements made with steamboat lines running up and down the Miles River.[17]

Others attempted to succeed where Tilghman had failed, and as before, Claiborne was a beneficiary. A new company emerged in 1876 to challenge the dominant Maryland Steamboat Company on the Miles River. The upstart was founded by Richard S. Dodson of St. Michaels. The steamer chosen by Dodson for this service was *Olive*, a small but relatively up-to-date steamboat built in 1869 in Norfolk by John Luke Porter, who years before had been involved in the design of many Confederate warships, including CSS *Virginia*.[18] A screw-driven and wooden steamship, *Olive* was only one-half the size of the steamships that would soon connect Claiborne directly with Baltimore.[19] Dodson's David was going to take on the Maryland Steamboat Company's Goliath.

Under the command of Richard's uncle, Captain Edward N. Dodson, *Olive* was placed into service in April 1876 on the route between Baltimore and the Miles River, with its primary destination the steamer wharf in St. Michaels located within a stone's throw of Dodson's home.[20] The steamer left Baltimore for the Miles River on Tuesdays, Thursdays, and Saturdays and made the return journey on Mondays, Wednesdays, and Fridays. At the time, Claiborne was bypassed.

However, in May of the following year, the schedule was expanded and a new destination was added: "Tilghman's Creek," later relabeled as "Claiborne." Dodson sent *Olive* up Tilghman Creek and dropped off and picked up passengers and cargo at what is now Old Claiborne, alongside the property of the Maple Hall estate, using a new wharf constructed across Tilghman Creek from the old location of Bingham's Wharf.

Why was Claiborne added in 1877? The expansion of service was most likely connected to grand efforts underway to expand the Claiborne community under the direction of ambitious property owner Joseph T. Tunis. Tunis, whose family owned Maple Hall, had lofty expectations for his little community, which up to that point had been centered on lumber and oyster harvesting. His lumber company had already taken the trees from most of his property, so he was looking for another use for the land. The plan was to turn his now-treeless fields into a large town, complete with a grid pattern of streets and a central town square. The new wharf had been constructed alongside a sawmill, gristmill, and an oyster-packing facility already present on the family property. Tunis's marketing campaign, it is said, centered on the simple directive: "young man don't go West, but to Claiborne."[21]

In March of 1877, Tunis held a drawing for one hundred new property lots, an effort to kickstart the growth of this nascent community. Tunis was hoping that an influx of additional residents would ignite a boom in Claiborne, and reliable steamboat service would support those aspirations. Dodson responded to this opportunity by adding Claiborne to his Miles River route. Expectations for Claiborne were high, as illustrated in an editorial in the *Easton Star-Democrat*:

> Why shouldn't Claiborne flourish. It only needs population and capital to bring it out. One hundred families planted there will soon attract another hundred; two hundred will attract two hundred more, and so on to the end. As it grows, new packing houses will be established; new school houses and churches built; stores will multiply; the mechanical trades will flourish; and it will furnish a grand market for the fruits and vegetables, and poultry, and bacon and lard, and wood, and beef and mutton, and hogs of the surrounding country.[22]

Olive's three-times-per-week service to Claiborne continued for about a decade, with occasional interruptions. But once again, the predicted boom in Claiborne's economy and population did not happen, and the tiny backwater community at the tip of Tilghman Creek remained small and remote. In 1887, after the Tolchester Steamboat Company began to serve St. Michaels from Baltimore with the large steamer *Emma Giles*, Dodson gave up the competition and abandoned his own struggling service, listing *Olive* and its route for sale in January of 1888.[23] In April of that year, the small steamer was sold to Thomas M. Green, who evidently had no interest in the Miles River service and instead put *Olive* into service as an excursion steamer between Baltimore and Sparrows Point, Maryland.[24]

Once again, Claiborne was devoid of scheduled passenger steamboat service. But this was about to change, and the impetus did not originate from local property owners. This time Claiborne would sit at the center of a major campaign orchestrated by senior leaders across the Maryland government. This campaign would be driven not by boats on the water, but by railroads on the land. Moreover, *Olive* would soon return to Claiborne and play a brief but pivotal role in that campaign.

Notes

1. White became governor of the doomed colony on Roanoke Island in 1587. However, he escaped whatever fate confronted the colonists there because he had traveled back to England that same year. Upon his return to the Roanoke colony in 1590, he discovered it had been long deserted. White's daughter, Elinor White Dare, gave birth to Virginia Dare, the first child of English descent known to have been born in the British North American colonies.
2. See, for example, Christina Gardner, "Bloody Point," *CBM Bay Weekly*, n.d., bayweekly.com/bloody-point.
3. Following long-standing English tradition, communities in the area were organized into administrative units of one hundred residents. The community on the peninsula west of St. Michaels, ranging from Claiborne in the north to Tilghman Island in the south, constituted one such unit: the Bay Hundred. The name stuck and has become associated with the region itself, long after the administrative structure was abandoned.
4. David W. Guth, *Bridging the Chesapeake: A 'Fool Idea' That Unified Maryland* (Archway Publishing, 2017), 89.
5. Campbell Gibson, "Population of the 100 Largest Cities and Other Urban Places in the United States: 1790 to 1990," Working Paper No. POP-WP027 (US Census Bureau, June 1998), Table 6: Population of the 90 Urban Places for 1830.
6. David C. Holly, *Tidewater by Steamboat: A Saga of the Chesapeake* (Johns Hopkins University Press, 1981), xvi.
7. See various chapters in Robert H. Burgess and H. Graham Wood, *Steamboats Out of Baltimore* (Tidewater Publishers, 1968).
8. "Steamboats Sold," *Sun* (Baltimore, MD), March 6, 1867.
9. Tilghman himself had seen adventure during the war, having been arrested for treason in a raid on the Eastern Shore by Union forces in 1861 and jailed for much of that conflict. See "Arrested," *Chicago Tribune*, July 10, 1861. See also "Locked Up in Military Prison," *Sun* (Baltimore, MD), January 1, 1864.
10. "New Enterprises," *Sun* (Baltimore, MD), June 17, 1867.
11. Ibid.
12. The identity of Bingham remains uncertain, except for a reference in 1867 that the property in question was to be sold by owner Edward Covey to "Col. Bingham of Washington." This is most likely Colonel Judson D. Bingham, then operating in Washington in the Quartermaster Corps of the US Army. See "Sale of Lands in Talbot County," *Sun* (Baltimore, MD), May 7, 1867.
13. See various advertisements in *The Sun* (Baltimore, MD), for example, June 19, 1867.

14. *Maryland Geological Survey: Talbot County* (Johns Hopkins University Press, 1926), 87.
15. There was never a transfer of title from Covey to Bingham. The stream is still called the "Mineral Springs Branch" of Hemmersly Creek. The adjacent estate is known today as "Mineral Springs Farm." One is hard-pressed today to see any evidence of a therapeutic spring emerging in this area.
16. "Proceedings of the Courts," *Sun* (Baltimore, MD), June 11, 1868. See also the advertisement of the sale of Tilghman's Point Farm in *The Sun* (Baltimore, MD), May 19, 1871. He also lost ownership of *Balloon*, which survived only a brief period itself before being destroyed in a fire in 1872. Nevertheless, as was reported at the time, "the loss is not so much deprecated because she was of late years considered rather a dangerous boat for passengers." See "Notice," *Sun* (Baltimore, MD), January 27, 1870, and "Steamer Burned," *West-Jersey Pioneer*, November 11, 1872.
17. There are reports of one such steamboat, *Thomas Collyer*, making periodic visits to Claiborne in the 1870s. There is a potential first-hand account in a diary of a member of the Tunis family of such a voyage, and *Thomas Collyer* is referenced in several secondary sources. See, for example, Elizabeth Hughes, "Founded on Steam: A History of Claiborne, Maryland," *Weather Gauge* no. 28 (Fall 1992): 19–20. However, while *Thomas Collyer* was operating on the Chesapeake at the time, this author has been unable to document any specific visits to Claiborne. Confusingly, there are multiple steamboats named *Thomas Collyer* operating at this period, all built by the same shipyard. The *Thomas Collyer* referred to here is the steamboat built in 1850 in New York and later renamed *City of Brunswick*.
18. It is often written in error that *Olive* was built in Philadelphia, and one source erroneously places its origin as North Carolina. The probable site of construction was the Atlantic Iron Works shipyard. This is surmised. First, Porter ran the shipbuilding business of Atlantic Iron Works in Norfolk until it was discontinued in 1871, and we know that he was building ferries there. Second, there are references in August 1869 to a newly constructed steamer, under the command of a Captain Slacum, initiating the Norfolk to Washington (NC) route through the Albemarle and Chesapeake Canal. This steamer was identified as having been built at Atlantic Iron Works but is not named. There are multiple other references to a newly built steamer, identified as *Olive*, under the command of Captain Slacum, running the Norfolk to Washington (NC) route through that same canal in the second half of 1869, although these do not identify the place of construction. No other steamers on this route in 1869 have been identified. It is logical, therefore, to assume that these references

refer to the same steamer. It is possible that Porter built the steamer using the facilities of the Atlantic Iron Works, but that the Atlantic Iron Works itself did not execute the contract.

19. Some accounts of *Olive*'s size are also inaccurate. Some sources report that *Olive* measured 987 gross register tons (GRT). In reality, it started its career at 181 GRT and was later rebuilt to 288 GRT, at which point the maximum capacity was three hundred passengers, although it rarely operated with such a large passenger load.
20. Beyond St. Michaels, these local destinations included "Tunis' Wharf" (up Leeds Creek near Tunis Mills), "Trimble's Wharf" (most likely the property of David C. Trimble in Wye Heights), and "Wye Landing."
21. The quote is provided by Margaret Barton Driggs in "Claiborne: The Resort Whose Charms Live On," *Easton Star-Democrat*, November 5, 1982. For the record, this author has not been able to locate contemporary evidence of that quote being used in 1877.
22. "A Big Thing: Grand Scheme to Improve the County," *Easton Star-Democrat*, February 6, 1877.
23. The advertisement was posted in *The Sun* (Baltimore, MD), January 26, 1888.
24. See "Port Paragraphs," *Sun* (Baltimore, MD), April 12, 1888.

II

Enter the Railroads

It was the era of steam railroads.

A recurring theme in the history of Claiborne is the role played by technological disruptions to existing transportation networks and how decisions made in distant political and financial power centers influenced this small community. Nowhere is this more evident than in the 1880s when these factors, quite literally, put the modern community of Claiborne on the map. Another theme is that decisions that turned out to be seriously flawed, and which led to quick failure, nonetheless had staying power that influenced the region for decades afterward.

Steam transformed transportation on the water, and around the same time, steam-powered locomotives emerged on the land, running on rails. The same sounds, belching smoke, and raw power witnessed at sea were seen as well on solid ground. There was, however, a fundamental difference from the standpoint of economics. Steamboats, while expensive to build and operate, were nonetheless flexible and could be redeployed easily to meet evolving market conditions. Yes, they would need wharves or piers to be built for loading and unloading, and at times harbor entrances might need to be dredged, but the Chesapeake Bay itself was a free surface for movement, and the cost of these piers would be shared with all kinds of vessels. If a route proved unprofitable, it was no great feat to simply redeploy the steamboat on another route.

In contrast, locomotives required dedicated rails, and these could not easily be relocated once laid down. Creating a railroad required vast amounts of capital that would be tied up for decades. It became as much about finance as it was about operations. If steamboats attracted seafarers, railroads attracted bankers. But once tracks were laid, railroads provided a fast and relatively inexpensive way to transport people and freight because they were much faster than steamboats. Communities that had rail access often thrived, whereas those lacking such access, even if in the same county, often waned. Everyone wanted a nearby rail station. It was a sign that your town had reached the big leagues. It was a vote of confidence in the future. Some entire communities, such as Delmar, straddling the east-west Delaware/Maryland border, emerged solely because it made sense to have a railroad stop there. Claiborne would be another such community.

Both steamboat and railroad lines emerged in the area of steam, but there was a fundamental difference between them when it came to transport around the Chesapeake region. Whereas the Bay was a boulevard for steamboat commerce between Baltimore and the Eastern Shore, that same body of water became a barrier when steam-powered transportation shifted from water to land. We have seen earlier how Baltimore felt insecure in its relationship with the Eastern Shore, especially relative to Philadelphia. This insecurity would be magnified in the railroad era, and Claiborne would be the beneficiary.

Laying Tracks on the Delmarva Peninsula

The United States had been in a railroad-building frenzy for decades before the Civil War, and the construction only intensified after its end. The Delmarva Peninsula was no exception. In the two decades after the Civil War, hundreds of miles of tracks were laid on the eastern side of the Chesapeake Bay. This made perfect sense since the area was rich in agriculture but had limited population density.

Therefore, the markets for the produce of the Eastern Shore resided not in local communities but rather in distant cities along the Atlantic seaboard. At the same time, the towns on the Eastern Shore were far apart, at least by the standards of the day. A network of railroads was the perfect means to tie these towns together and to bring their produce to market. Finally, the land was flat, and while some marshes, rivers, and creeks dotted the landscape, none presented the major hurdles one encountered, for example, in laying track across the towering Rocky Mountains or the wide Mississippi River. Railway enthusiasts and investors, often supported by local politicians, sought charters to lay tracks across the Delmarva Peninsula, since such a charter effectively allowed the holders to build what they hoped would be a monopolistic transport system.

Through the early 1880s, the major railroad system on the Delmarva Peninsula emerged first not in Maryland but in Delaware. This was pioneered by the Philadelphia, Wilmington and Baltimore Railroad (PW&B), parent company of the Delaware Railroad (DRR). Prior to the Civil War, DRR had acquired the rail network of the pioneering New Castle and Frenchtown Railroad and extended its lines to create a north-south railroad running the length of Delaware, a state taller than it is wide, down to the new station of Delmar, on the Delaware-Maryland border. The DRR network was taken over by the PW&B in 1877.[1]

PW&B continued on a building and buying spree, centered on Wilmington and its short link to Philadelphia. It developed a branch that ran from the major station of Clayton near Smyrna to the Maryland town of Massey. PW&B reached deeper into Maryland when it acquired the assets of the Kent County Railroad, which had built a line from Massey to Chestertown. Another branch in Maryland had been built by the Queen Anne's and Kent County Railroad, running from the small inland community of Massey to Centreville; this was also acquired by PW&B. Next was the Dorchester and Delaware Railroad, running from Seaford, Delaware, to Cambridge, Maryland. This joined the PW&B family in 1882. The Maryland and Delaware Railroad, operating tracks from Clayton to Easton and thence to Oxford, was also part of the PW&B empire.

There were only a couple of railroads operating on the Delmarva Peninsula not under PW&B control. The Wicomico and Pocomoke Railroad (W&P) built an east-west line from Salisbury to Berlin (1868) and on to Ocean City (1876). In 1872, the New York, Philadelphia and Norfolk Railroad (NYP&N) began extending the PW&B lines south to Virginia, incorporating the line from Delmar via Salisbury to Crisfield, built for the Eastern Shore Railroad.[2]

In short, by 1880, much of the Eastern Shore was already served by railroads. The Maryland towns of Ocean City, Salisbury, Easton, Cambridge, Oxford, Chestertown, Centreville, Federalsburg, and Queen Anne were all part of an interconnected web of rail lines.

There was only one problem. None of them were linked directly to Maryland's Western Shore. They were all coupled to Wilmington, and beyond, to Baltimore's rival city: Philadelphia. With the exception of the W&P, all ran north-south. While several major communities with steamboat lines were served by these railroads, none of these provided a convenient way to get to the far Atlantic Coast of the Eastern Shore, much less link that Atlantic Coast to Baltimore or Annapolis. The fear that Baltimore would lose its economic connection to Maryland's Eastern Shore, and be displaced by Philadelphia, emerged once again.

The Pennsylvania Railroad Takes Over

That fear was magnified when the mighty Pennsylvania Railroad (PRR) began to exploit its dominant position in Philadelphia. PRR, then one of the largest corporations in the United States, was a company driven to maintain monopolies on its various routes, and it tenaciously defended these monopolies from emerging threats.

One investor sought to circumvent—literally—that control. The New York financier Jay Gould aspired to build a competing rail line to the PRR, with this new line running from New York to Baltimore. This new line would run through New Jersey and the Delmarva Peninsula, bypassing Philadelphia entirely.[3] The line would cross the Delaware River and upper Chesapeake Bay by rail-transfer

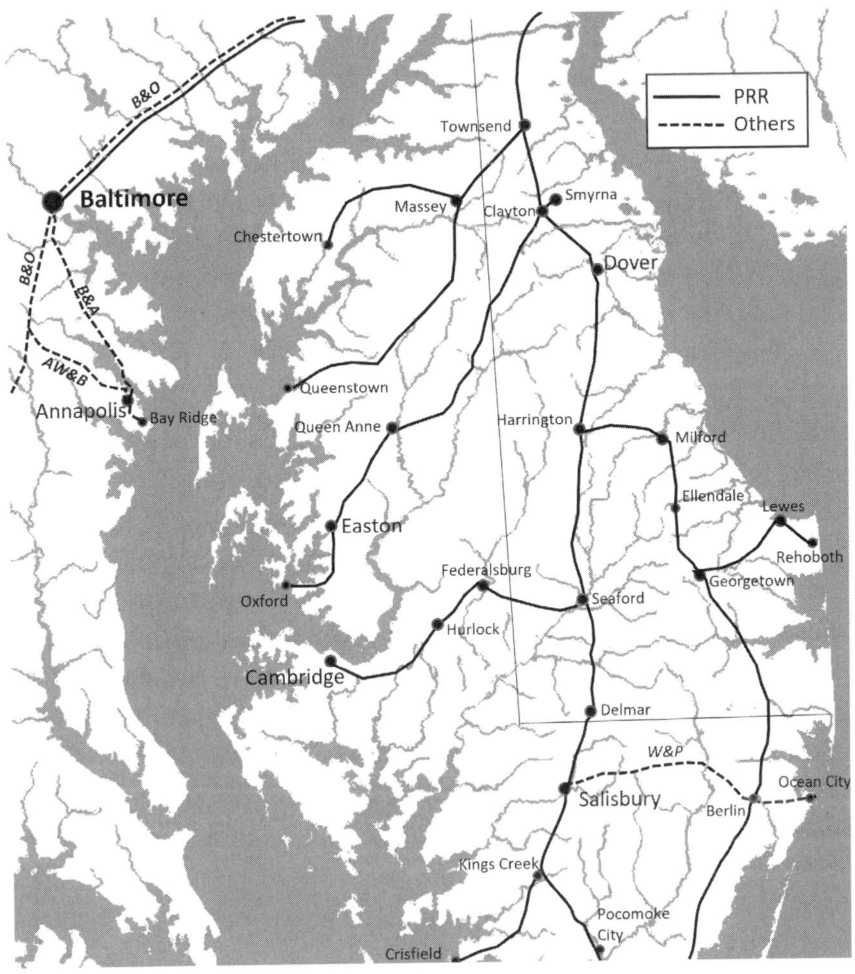

Map 2. Railroad networks on the Delmarva Peninsula by 1885. Source: Base map is from US Geological Survey, detailed and annotated by the author.

ferry. While this effort was abandoned following the financial crash of 1873, and when Gould's interests shifted to other areas, it also signaled to PRR the need to protect its flank by dominating rail traffic on the Delmarva Peninsula. In an example of how a failed enterprise can still have lasting impact, this aborted effort by Gould would, indirectly and a decade later, play a role in the major development of Claiborne. The first railroad ferry intended to serve Claiborne was originally built for Gould's aborted plans.

In 1881, yet another major competitor, the Baltimore and Ohio Railroad (B&O), made moves to acquire railroads on the Eastern Shore via the direct acquisition of PW&B, the parent of most Delmarva lines. PRR, understanding the threat this constituted to its Philadelphia hub, responded instantly to these moves and preempted B&O by taking over PW&B first.[4] Thus, by 1885 the entire rail network on the Delmarva Peninsula—with the exception of the small W&P—was under control of PRR. All lines running north to Philadelphia and Wilmington were now controlled by PRR.

There were other economic reasons for PRR to seek to dominate the transportation links on the Eastern Shore. Most immediate was the desire to harness the demand for transport of agricultural products from the region. The Delmarva Peninsula had become a veritable fruit basket for the US East Coast, leading in the production of tomatoes, strawberries, and peaches. Supplementing this were the oysters and blue crabs caught along the Chesapeake shore. There was also a growing demand for travel to ocean resorts on the peninsula, including Rehoboth in Delaware and Ocean City in Maryland. Another motive was more strategic in nature; control of the railroads on the peninsula would also allow PRR to duplicate Gould's strategy, this time by bypassing B&O's rail fortress at Baltimore. A route down the Delmarva Peninsula could be connected via steamboats to Norfolk, Virginia, and would thus allow PRR to expand its reach into Virginia and points south, completely bypassing the B&O Railroad hub.

This effort to control rail traffic on the Eastern Shore threatened Baltimore. Baltimore itself was no idle participant in the railroad arena and had, indeed, launched the era decades earlier with B&O. But the great B&O Railroad network mainly ran west from Baltimore, by design, to bring the produce of that region to the port of Baltimore. The realities of the existing railroad network on the Delmarva peninsula meant that the only way to move passengers and freight by rail from Salisbury to Baltimore would be to first go north to Wilmington through a hub controlled by PRR. At that point, the passengers and freight might very well prefer to continue on to nearby Philadelphia rather than turn around and head back south down the Western Shore to Baltimore.

Baltimoreans, on the other hand, *could* travel and move freight from their home city to cities on the Eastern Shore, including to the emerging resort town of Ocean City, all without leaving the state of Maryland. For example, one could catch the daily Eastern Shore Steamboat Company steamer (*Tangier*, *Maggie,* or *Helen*) from Baltimore, ride overnight all the way south to Crisfield, transfer to the Eastern Shore Railroad for a ride back north to Salisbury, then connect at Salisbury to the W&P train for the final leg into Ocean City.[5] This trip started in Baltimore at 5:30 p.m. and brought you to Ocean City at about 9:30 a.m. the following day. Alternatively, there was a simpler, thrice-weekly service by the Maryland Steamboat Company. Its steamer, *Enoch Pratt,* left Baltimore at 4:00 p.m. for an overnight journey down the Bay and up the Wicomico River to Salisbury, connecting the following morning with an early train to Ocean City, arriving there at 8:30 a.m.[6]

These treks would take sixteen hours or more. Marylanders asked for a better solution.

Notes

1. See the March 28, 1877, entry in Christopher T. Baer's "PRR Chronology: A General Chronology of the Pennsylvania Railroad Company Predecessors and Successors and Its Historical Context," available at prrths.com/newprr_files/Hagley/PRR1877%20Jun%2006.pdf.
2. See the March 15, 1872, entry in Christopher T. Baer's "PRR Chronology: A General Chronology of the Pennsylvania Railroad Company Predecessors and Successors and Its Historical Context," available at prrths.com/newprr_files/Hagley/PRR1872.pdf.
3. Gould's plan included rail transport ferries across the Delaware River and the Chesapeake Bay and is covered in more detail in Chapter III.
4. See the April 7, 1931, entry in Christopher T. Baer's "PRR Chronology: A General Chronology of the Pennsylvania Railroad Company Predecessors and Successors and Its Historical Context," available at prrths.com/newprr_files/Hagley/PRR1931%204_15_15.pdf.
5. See advertisement by the Eastern Shore Steamboat Company in *The Sun* (Baltimore, MD), August 4, 1882. Note that this Eastern Shore Steamboat Company is different from the one serving the Miles River in the 1850s, which went out of business in 1861.
6. See advertisement by the Maryland Steamboat Company in *The Sun* (Baltimore, MD), July 9, 1884.

III

Maryland Reacts: The Baltimore and Eastern Shore Railroad

The expanding transportation links from Maryland's Eastern Shore to Philadelphia troubled local leaders in both Baltimore and Annapolis. Trade and commerce follow lines of transportation, and the merchants, bankers, and politicians in Maryland saw the increasing ties of the Pennsylvania Railroad (PRR) to the Eastern Shore as a threat to their economic status. Baltimore had dropped from second to seventh place in the ranking of US cities since 1830, and by 1880 the city was less than half the size of Philadelphia.[1]

Leading the charge was Joseph B. Seth, the new speaker of the Maryland House of Delegates. His quest to connect the Eastern and Western Shores of the Chesapeake Bay would begin in 1886 and would persist well into the next century. Seth would be a player in steamboat and ferry operations across the Chesapeake for the next thirty-five years, and he would play some kind of role in all five different companies serving Claiborne over the decades. It was virtually a lifetime obsession.

Joseph B. Seth

Joseph B. Seth was born on November 24, 1845, on Maryland's Eastern Shore, in that part of Talbot County known as Bay Hundred. This was a region of agriculture and thus, in Maryland before the Civil War, of slave-owning estates, including the one on which he was raised off Broad Creek. Seth's formative years took place during the last two decades of slavery. An autobiography, drafted later in his life when Seth was a major apologist for the Confederacy and a promoter of the Lost Cause myth, suggests he had a highly revisionist view of the institution of slavery. He writes that enslaved workers "lived under a paternal, kindly rule. It is, therefore, not strange that we have had no bitter race feeling between the whites and the negroes, and have been able to live together in peace."[2]

Seth spent the years of the Civil War not serving in the military (on either side) but in school studying law. He was admitted to the Maryland Bar in 1867 and practiced for a while in Baltimore before returning to his native Talbot County in 1870, establishing a law practice focused on estates, trusts, and conveyances. At this point, there was nothing to suggest he would play such a critical role in the region's history.

However, it seems clear that Seth was a driven man with high aspirations. His father had once served in the Maryland House of Delegates, and Joseph dutifully followed in those footsteps. He ran for office in 1873 as an Independent Democrat, someone who supported the broad agenda of the Democratic Party but did not want to be too strongly associated with the misbehavior associated with that party at that time. Elected to represent Talbot County, he served only one two-year term starting in 1874. He lost reelection in 1875 and suffered another loss when his wife died unexpectedly in 1881.

He regained his seat in the 1883 election, rejoining the House of Delegates for the 1884–1885 term, and won reelection to another two year-term in 1885.[3] It was around this time that people began to take notice of Joseph B. Seth. He was described as a . . .

> . . . ready and forcible debater, quick and aggressive, and has already become quite prominent in the discussions in the House. At home he enjoys a large law practice, and had Judge [John M.] Robinson been elected United States Senator would have been a candidate for the democratic nomination for associate judge [of the Maryland Second Judicial Circuit Court]. He takes a lively interest in agriculture, and is the owner of some fine registered Jerseys.[4]

It was also around this time that Seth acquired the title of "general," one that he would use the rest of his life. This had nothing to do with military service, in the Civil War or anywhere else. Rather, he was appointed by Maryland Governor Robert M. McLane to the post of Judge Advocate General of the Maryland "Oyster Navy," a unit of state government patrolling the oyster beds of the southern Chesapeake Bay against illegal harvesting.[5] Seth assumed and used the title of brigadier general.[6]

Having served as the clerk of the House in his prior term, Seth was a logical candidate for the powerful position of speaker of the Maryland House of Delegates and was awarded that position in early 1886.[7] He was joined in this term of the Maryland Legislature by his Talbot County neighbor, Theophilus Tunis, himself elected for the first time to the Maryland State Senate. Tunis was part of the important Tunis-Cockey family that dominated economic activity in Claiborne at the time. His brother, Joseph T. Tunis, had proposed the great but ill-fated expansion of Claiborne a decade earlier.

A Railroad Connecting Baltimore and the Eastern Shore

As we have seen earlier, many Marylanders were concerned about the strength of the linkages between communities on the Eastern and Western Shores of the Chesapeake, especially after railroads began to dominate transportation on the eastern side. Seth was certainly among them, and one of his objectives was to strengthen the economic relationship between Maryland's Eastern Shore and the city of Baltimore by improving those transportation links. If only there was a way to build a new railroad network that ran from the Eastern Shore west to Baltimore, rather than north to Philadelphia. Although the Chesapeake Bay was in the way, that might be crossed using special rail-transfer ferries. Importantly, Seth was thinking first and foremost of railroads. The ferries were just a necessary link in the chain.

Within mere weeks of stepping into his new role as Speaker of the House of Delegates, Seth introduced legislation to create a new rail link from Baltimore to the Maryland counties on the Eastern Shore. In a March 1886 address to the Merchants and Manufacturers Association of Baltimore, he laid out his case for this new link. As reported by *The Sun* in Baltimore:

> Mr. Seth said that unless something is done at once Philadelphia will obtain a grip upon the trade of the Eastern Shore that Baltimore will never be able to break. All of the present [rail]roads on the Eastern Shore are feeders of the Pennsylvania Railroad system. With the exception of the water-borne traffic all of the grain, berry vegetable and fruit business of the Eastern shores goes to Philadelphia, as well as a large per cent of the travel, including the shopping trips of ladies. If the new [rail]road is built it will bring the largest part of this trade to Baltimore, which will be brought closer to the peninsula than Philadelphia.[8]

The legislation included a provision for funding the new railroad, authorizing the City of Baltimore to "endorse" (guarantee) $500,000 in bonds issued for that purpose. In return, until such point as that endorsement had lapsed and the bonds had been redeemed, 51 percent of the stock of the new venture would be held in trust for Baltimore by the Mercantile Trust and Deposit Company. The backers of the new railroad hoped similar arrangements could be worked out with Talbot, Wicomico, Dorchester, and Caroline counties to the tune of $50,000 each.[9] In aggregate, this would raise $700,000 in funds, which almost matched the expected cost of constructing the railroad, at least as envisaged at the time. The final passage of Seth's proposal was achieved on April 10, 1886, when it was approved by the Maryland Senate. Seth himself took the role as president of the new venture.

It looked as if Seth had pulled off a master stroke: he was going to get his railroad, and taxpayers would have to accept the risk. The upside would go to the owners of the railroad, while any downside would be socialized with the taxpayers of Baltimore and the four Eastern Shore counties.

There was an important caveat embedded in the legislation: the voters in Baltimore and the four counties would have to affirm this commitment via referendums. Most expected this approval to be a formality. Baltimore's leading newspaper of the era, *The Sun*, endorsed the proposal in July 1886:

> It is practically certain that in the course of time all of the land between the Chesapeake and Delaware bays and the Atlantic will be one vast garden. The trade with such a community, thrifty, industrious and prospering, must be of great value to any city, and Philadelphia has already taken time by the forelock by reaching down into the peninsula in every direction, while Baltimore, as the Eastern shore has grown and prospered, has been compelled to see her trade with that section drift to a large extent into other channels.[10]

It was settled. The State of Maryland would endeavor to build a railroad across the Chesapeake, linking Baltimore to locations on the Eastern Shore. Since a bridge across the Chesapeake was impractical at the time, special rail-transfer ferries would shuttle the railcars across the Bay itself. These ferries would have railroad tracks laid on their decks and could carry around a dozen railcars at a time, linking two shoreline rail terminals.

Here is where Jay Gould returns to the picture, albeit indirectly. His plan from the early 1870s to build a rail line from New York to Baltimore, bypassing Philadelphia entirely, required rail-transfer ferries to cross the Delaware River and upper Chesapeake. It was for this purpose that Gould engaged shipbuilder Henry Steers in Brooklyn, New York, to construct a large rail-transfer ferry, which Gould named *Charles J. Osborn* after his personal broker and financial agent. The ferry was launched on September 9, 1873, to great fanfare.[11] Nine days later, the stock market crashed and Gould's venture unraveled.

The *Charles J. Osborn* was eventually launched but not finished. It sat idle in the Steers Brooklyn yard until 1876, when a new buyer emerged. The ferry, renamed *Groton*, headed north and made its way to Long Island Sound to carry railcars across the Thames River in Connecticut. Few would have predicted at the time that *Groton* would, thirteen years later, return to play a pivotal role in the development of the Chesapeake ferry system.[12]

A New Company Is Born

Back in Maryland, Joseph B. Seth was interested in more than just advocating for the new railroad from his position as house speaker. He wanted to run it and profit from it personally. Jay Gould's failure thirteen years earlier did not dissuade him. The new Baltimore and Eastern Shore Railroad (B&ES) was established on April 1, 1886, with Seth as president. Serving as treasurer was Elihu E. Jackson, the equally powerful president of the Maryland Senate, a long-term resident of Salisbury on the Eastern Shore, and the man who would become governor of Maryland two years later. The corporate secretary was state Senator Theophilus Tunis, a resident of Claiborne. A number of other Democrat legislators and power brokers rounded out the board of directors for the new company.[13]

The new company faced three immediate challenges: raise the capital needed to build the railroad, establish the route for the railroad, and develop a plan for crossing the Chesapeake Bay.

The railroad was estimated to cost $728,000 to build, covering the railroad as well as the rail-transfer steamer and associated wharves.[14] The first step was to obtain the required voter endorsement of $700,000 in bond guarantees. The bonds would only pay interest when redeemed in twenty years—hence the need for such guarantees. If the railroad failed and the bonds became worthless, it would be Baltimore and the four countries that realized that loss, not the owners of the railroad.

The remaining sum of $28,000 would be raised privately by Seth, Jackson, Tunis, and other investors. In this way, they would own the B&ES Railroad while committing their personal capital for less than 4 percent of the investment cost.

Baltimore Derails the New Company's Plan

Here things began to unravel quickly. Seth's financing plan depended upon the support of the City of Baltimore and presumed that city's willingness to guarantee $500,000 in bonds. This required a referendum to be put to the voters, after approval by the City Council and the mayor. The Baltimore City Council did pass an ordinance to put the question of $500,000 in bond endorsements to the voters of that city. Then, in October 1886, Baltimore City Mayor James Hodges vetoed that ordinance—there would be no referendum, and no bond guarantee. Seth's plan was starting to fall apart six months after it was launched and before any tracks were laid.

Why did Hodges issue his veto? On the Eastern Shore, it was speculated that Mayor Hodges was heavily influenced by Enoch Pratt, a principal owner of the Maryland Steamboat Company, a line that would have to compete with the new rail and ferry system. As was the case many other times, owners of dominant transport networks would seek to undermine new competition, using political connections to do so. As editorialized by a newspaper on the Eastern Shore: "Mr. Pratt is deadly hostile to the proposed railroad and was not willing to allow the people of Baltimore to vote on it."[15]

Whatever political machinations were in play, it also appears that the Eastern Shore promoters did not fully appreciate what was happening in Baltimore at the time. A generation earlier, that city had launched a major effort to create prosperity though the development of railroads, as opposed to, for example, manufacturing. Considerable investment capital and guarantees had already been issued to the Baltimore and Ohio Railroad (B&O) and the Western Maryland Railroad. Yet by the mid-1880s, the tide had turned. Baltimore's leadership had concluded that the focus on railroads had been to the detriment of the city's development of manufacturing industries, and many of those small manufacturing concerns that did arise in Baltimore did so after regional competitors had already achieved scale. Baltimore saw many of its embryonic businesses acquired and then reduced to "branch offices" by the likes of Jay Gould and John D. Rockefeller. One of the consolidators was the New York-based Sugar Trust, about which we shall hear more shortly.[16]

Meanwhile, the investments previously made by Baltimore in the railroads were not providing the prosperity that had been hoped for. The B&O had stopped paying dividends and indeed would enter receivership as a failed business within a few years. Baltimore City leaders were already looking for ways to unravel its investment in the troubled Western Maryland Railroad. This was not the time for Seth to put forward yet another investment opportunity in rail transportation, yet he seems to have failed to grasp this.

Mayor Hodges made clear his opposition to yet another effort by railroads to seek Baltimore's capital as he issued his veto:

> . . . the general sentiment of the community is now and has been for many years strongly opposed to the policy of lending the credit of the city to railroad enterprises. I believe it safe to say that the public mind, which has passed through a costly experience, is now thoroughly educated up to that point.[17]

Despite the failure in Baltimore, Seth continued his crusade within the four counties on the Eastern Shore in an effort to salvage the other $200,000 in bond guarantees. Here, again, problems soon emerged. In September 1887, the commissioners of Talbot County agreed to add a referendum in the upcoming statewide November election for voters to approve the decision for the county to endorse its $50,000 share of the bonds.[18] That same month, the commissioners of Caroline and Dorchester Counties similarly agreed to submit referendums to voters, but only for a reduced amount of $30,000.[19] Likewise, voters of Wicomico County attending a public meeting convinced the county commissioners to submit for approval a reduced amount of only $25,000.[20] In aggregate, if approved by all four counties, the total amount of the endorsement would be only $135,000 versus the targeted $200,000.

The results of the November election were mixed. In Talbot County, the referendum passed by a strong majority of 3,407 in favor and 777 opposed. It passed unanimously within the Bay Hundred district, which would be home to the new railroad and ferry terminal. Wicomico County voters supported the referendum by the barest of margins. The referendum in Dorchester County was approved by a larger majority of votes cast, 1,709 for and 882 against. However, the referendum in Caroline County was voted down by a strong majority.[21] A special election held in Caroline County in May 1888 affirmed their opposition when the endorsement was again voted down with 1,002 opposed and only 771 supporting.[22]

But in the end, the effort to have the bonds underwritten by the four Eastern Shore counties was for naught. As written, the legislation enabling these votes made any endorsements from the Eastern Shore counties (the "Second Mortgage") contingent upon Baltimore City endorsing its own $500,000 bond issue (the "First Mortgage"). The directors of the B&ES would have to proceed without these endorsements, instead raising funds through capital-stock sales and bond sales, employing normal market mechanisms. There would be no government subsidy for those bonds. This would have a decisive and negative impact on the success of the operation, as we shall soon see. Failure to achieve the bond guarantee from Baltimore effectively guaranteed the eventual failure of the B&ES business.

Where Should the B&ES Route Go?

Meanwhile, the B&ES leaders had to find the optimum route for the new rail line. It is important to recognize that, at the end of the day, B&ES was about building a railroad, not a steamboat line.

The railroad dominated the planning, fundraising, and route selection. Only once the railroad route had been defined would it be possible to figure out how to connect the opposite points on the Chesapeake Bay.

That choice was now heavily influenced by the lack of guaranteed bonds. Given the inability to raise the needed capital as originally planned, it had become vital that the route chosen should minimize the expenditure for laying new rail tracks, since that would require the most capital. The land and rails on which trains run have to be acquired and built. The water on which steamboats run is free. This reaffirmed the need to think railroad first and steamboat second.

Selecting the bulk of the rail route on the Eastern Shore itself was straightforward. The easiest step was to acquire the existing Wicomico and Pocomoke rail line between Salisbury and Berlin on the way to Ocean City. This would already cover about one-quarter of the distance needed on the Eastern Shore. The acquisition was completed in 1888.[23] Work then began on upgrading the line from Berlin to Ocean City.

The next question was where the line should go next heading northwestward from Salisbury (where B&ES treasurer Elihu Jackson lived) toward the Chesapeake. This was also uncomplicated. It was clear the line had to connect to Easton, the second-largest community in the area, the county seat of Talbot County, and a major transfer point for passengers and cargo heading north on the competing railroad—and where B&ES president Seth lived. This, and a similar stop at Hurlock, might divert some Eastern Shore traffic away from Philadelphia and toward Baltimore. So, the Easton-to-Ocean City route was set.

Meanwhile, on the Western Shore, the only realistic choices were Baltimore, Annapolis, or the small community of Bay Ridge, south of Annapolis. The leaders of B&ES saw significant advantages to Bay Ridge, a town set right on the banks of the Chesapeake. First, a new rail line had recently been built from Annapolis to Bay Ridge, the Bay Ridge and Annapolis Railroad. This 4.5-mile line meant that passengers and cargo could now travel by rail

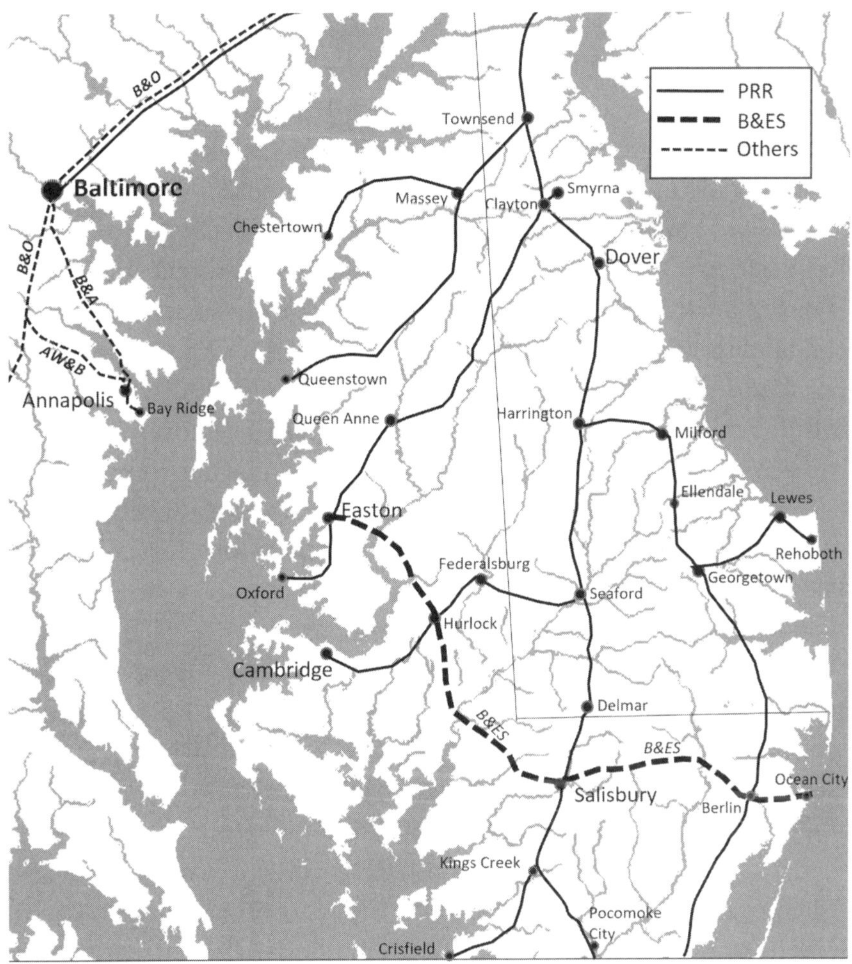

Map 3. First stage of route planning for the Baltimore and Eastern Shore Railroad. Source: Base map is from US Geological Survey, detailed and annotated by the author.

from Baltimore via Annapolis all of the way to within spitting distance of the Chesapeake at Bay Ridge. Second, the connection to Annapolis from Baltimore had just been streamlined via the new Annapolis and Baltimore Short Line Railroad, which meant a faster journey than before. Third, Bay Ridge was an emerging resort town itself, with existing steamer service, hotels, and other attractions. Finally, the rail terminal at Bay Ridge was the closest geographically to Easton. The combined rail and ferry distance would be minimized.

Now the challenge became how to connect Bay Ridge and Easton. Certainly, an additional rail line heading toward the Chesapeake Bay would be required. But where? One option would be to head north from Easton, connect to Queen Anne and Queenstown, and run west until you reach the Chesapeake Bay shore of Kent Island. But that distance was about twenty-eight miles, and laying that amount of rail would add significant costs, costs that capital-deprived B&ES could not now afford. A shorter route would be to run directly west from Easton to Broad Cove, where Eastern Bay meets Bay Hundred. The ground distance covered on that route would be less than half that of the Kent Island route, saving precious capital. True, the distance over water from Bay Ridge to Broad Cove was twice as long as that from Bay Ridge to Kent Island, but unlike the rail track, additional distance over water did not require more capital.

Hence it was decided that the train line on the Western Shore would terminate at Bay Ridge, and its peer on the Eastern Shore would run from Ocean City to Broad Cove, with a major stop at Salisbury, intersecting with the main Delaware Railroad (DRR) running north to Wilmington. Additional intersections with the DRR would take place at Hurlock (the DRR branch to Cambridge) and Easton (the DRR branch to Oxford). The chosen location on Broad Cove was given the name "Bay City," but almost as soon as that was done, it became known as Claiborne.[24] It also happened to be, conveniently, within walking distance of the home of B&ES Secretary Theophilus Tunis.

One senses that the location for the ferry route was chosen even before the land survey was conducted. Within only a few months of the start of the company, the ferry route on the Eastern Shore was made public.[25] It may have been that the route would always have terminated at the water in Talbot County. It is also possible that politics and personal gain influenced this choice.

For one thing, the politicians involved were dominated by those from Talbot County, including Seth and Tunis. Political support from

Talbot County was especially critical since the B&ES founders still hoped that the county would underwrite $50,000 of the required investment through bond guarantees. Moreover, the founders never even requested any bond guarantees from Queen Anne's County (location of Kent Island), so it seems unlikely that Kent Island was ever in serious contention.

Personal interests may also have played a role. Seth, the president of B&ES in 1886, was raised in Bay Hundred. Tunis, the secretary of the new company, was from Talbot County and was brother to Joseph T. Tunis, a major entrepreneur with business interests in Claiborne. Both Seth and Tunis (directly or via their families) already had substantial property interests in Claiborne. As soon as the new B&ES company was formed, they proceeded to acquire even more land around Claiborne.[26] The development that might follow the new rail and ferry terminal could only enhance the potential value of their holdings. The location would also without doubt simplify their working commutes from their Eastern Shore homes to the state capital in Annapolis.

Work on the railroad began immediately. By August 1890 everything was completed. There was for the first time a continuous rail line running east-west across Maryland's Eastern Shore, from the Chesapeake Bay to the Atlantic coast.

Crossing the Chesapeake

So the question now was how to get the railcars, along with their passengers and freight, across the Chesapeake Bay. The simplest solution in theory would be to build a railroad bridge traversing the Bay, but such was beyond the technical or financial resources available at the time. A rail-transfer ferry was a far more viable option and one with which the region had experience. The first rail-transfer ferry in the United States operated just above the top of the Chesapeake, conveying railcars and passengers from Perryville to Havre de Grace across the Susquehanna River, and thus completing the line from Philadelphia to Baltimore. Until 1866, this was the only way to travel by rail between these two cities.[27] As such, rail-transfer

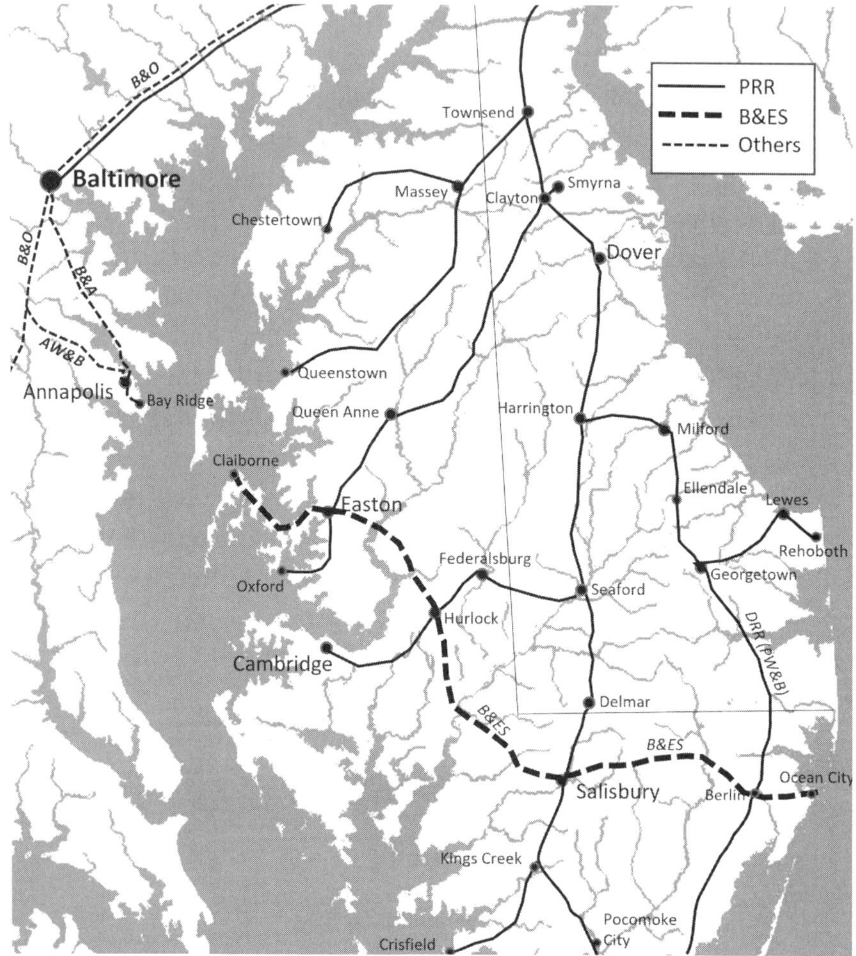

Map 4. The new B&ES rail line on the Eastern Shore in 1890. Source: Base map is from US Geological Survey, detailed and annotated by the author.

ferries were not a novel idea in the Chesapeake region, even if no longer in wide use by the 1880s. When it came time to look for specific solutions, including the acquisition of these specialized vessels, the leaders of B&ES turned north to Connecticut.

The Thames River in central Connecticut had long split the coastal rail links between New York and Boston. The only train bridge was far to the north and resulted in a long diversion. To move traffic more directly across the river, the railroad employed specialized rail-transfer ferries. These were steam-powered vessels using side paddlewheels for propulsion. Their decks were laid with train rails and they were "double-enders," open at either end so they could load and unload without turning around. Somewhat bulky and ungainly, these rail-transfer ferries nonetheless worked effectively at linking railroad terminals separated by bodies of water.

The concept was simple. An eastbound train would bring the railcars to the terminal in New London, on the western side. The railcars would be uncoupled from the locomotive and then shuffled onto rails laid on top of the ferry's main deck. The passengers would rest in comfort in the upper deck lounge for the short voyage, perhaps sipping a drink or enjoying a snack along the way. The ferry would cross the river and arrive at the terminal at Groton, on the eastern side. There the railcars would be shifted onto the regular tracks and hitched to another locomotive that would speed them on their way to Boston. This had worked well in Connecticut for many years, and a similar model had been employed in many other places around the world.[28] It seemed a workable model for Maryland's approach to linking the eastern and western sides of the Chesapeake by rail. This approach certainly appealed for train-centric managers who tended to think of rail as the best way to move people and freight, and the leaders of B&ES were first and foremost trying to build a rail line. The ferry link itself was an expedience to deal with the water that divided the Western Shore and Eastern Shore sections of the rail line.

For B&ES, the plan was straightforward and emulated what they saw in Connecticut: bring railcars to a new terminal in Bay Ridge, load them onto a rail-transfer ferry, convey them to the new terminal at Claiborne, and then return them to the tracks on their way to Easton, Hurlock, Salisbury, Berlin, and Ocean City.

So began the construction of a rail station and wharf in Claiborne, at that time a sparsely inhabited area of marsh, forest, and farmland. A 450-foot earthen jetty was constructed, and beyond that, a ferry wharf and rail terminal were built on pilings. Extending beyond was a long stone jetty, designed to protect the new harbor from rough waters and the accumulation of sediment. Meanwhile, on the far side of the Bay, a new rail and ferry wharf was constructed in Bay Ridge adjacent to the Bay Ridge Hotel, near what is today the intersection of Bay Drive and Mayo Avenue.[29]

All that was required now were the rail-transfer ferries to form the cross-bay connection between Bay Ridge and Claiborne. By a stroke of good fortune, Connecticut once again provided the answer. The primary rail-transfer ferry operating in Connecticut, *Groton,* had just been put out of a job by the newly built Thames River Railroad Bridge, completed in September 1889.[30] The smaller and older back-up ferry, *Thames River*, was also laid up. This meant both ferries were available to Marylanders, and both were acquired in November 1889.[31] It is for certain that *Thames River* was purchased for use by B&ES. In the case of *Groton*, contemporary accounts are unclear about its intended role, and the historical records on this are lacking. One newspaper account at the time suggested *Groton* was to be used to ferry railcars across Baltimore harbor, at least for a short time, perhaps before being assigned to link Bay Ridge and Claiborne once that operation was up and running.[32]

Groton was certainly an appropriate choice for the Claiborne mission. It was the same ferry that had been launched as *Charles J. Osborn* and left idle when, as described earlier, Jay Gould's railroad venture collapsed in 1873. It was eventually purchased by the New York, Providence and Boston Railroad (NYP&B) in 1876 and renamed *Groton*. That same railroad had already picked up *Thames River*, also built at the Henry Steers shipyard a few years before *Charles J. Osborn*.

Groton was also large. At 264 feet in length and 1,421 gross register tons (GRT),[33] it was the most commodious ferry *ever* considered for use out of Claiborne, larger even than the diesel-powered car ferries of the Claiborne-Annapolis Ferry Company in the 1930s. NYP&B had spent $42,000—a small fortune in 1885—to completely rebuild *Groton's* hull, transforming the ferry, having then been in use for about a decade, into "practically a new boat."[34] *Thames River*, by comparison, was less than two-thirds the size of *Groton*. It was older, prone to breakdown, and had not been upgraded. But a backup was required for those days when *Groton* would be offline for service and inspection, and the B&ES leaders assumed *Thames River* could fill that periodic role.

And now *Groton*, having recently been rebuilt, was available for service on the Chesapeake, along with *Thames River*. Both ferries had been designed from the ground up to carry railcars. Both were, for the time, modern steam-powered vessels, and *Groton* was in top condition. They could accommodate hundreds of passengers in comfortable lounges above the railcar deck. The planets were in alignment. The gods were smiling on the B&ES investors. What could possibly go wrong?

Groton never made it.

After being purchased, *Groton* and *Thames River* departed for Baltimore with a stop at Staten Island, New York. The steamers were accompanied by the tug *Cyclops*, with the operation under the command of Captain J. Fred Tribble. At that point, the good luck ran out. On November 30, 1889, the small convoy was slowly making its way along the Atlantic coast off Assateague Island in Virginia. Suddenly, flames emerged at the base of *Groton's* tall smokestack. Strenuous efforts were made to extinguish the blaze, but they all failed, and the flames spread uncontrolled. Fearing for their lives, the crew of twenty abandoned ship, scrambling over to *Thames River*, which had come alongside for the rescue. With all of *Groton's* crew members aboard, *Thames River* moved a safe distance away, and all aboard watched in shock as *Groton* burned itself to the waterline. Some thirty minutes later it was all over. *Groton* was gone. *Thames River* had no choice but to soldier on with *Cyclops* to Baltimore.[35]

The loss of *Groton* was consequential. It would have been the primary ferry for this Chesapeake Bay route. The older, smaller rail-transfer ferry *Thames River* had been relegated to backup service for the larger, newer *Groton*. B&ES was now down to only one ferry—and the smaller, less reliable one at that. A replacement rail-transfer ferry could not be found, certainly not in time.

B&ES had little choice except to persevere. After arriving in Baltimore, *Thames River* underwent modifications and repairs to prepare it for its primary role as the rail-transfer ferry. The work would take many months. After a rebuild by shipbuilder William Skinner & Sons, *Thames River* was taken to Locust Point and loaded with coal on September 30. The following day it entered the Bay and made a trial run to Bay Ridge to assess the docking facilities there, returning to Baltimore that same day.[36] Things must not have gone well, because *Thames River* was then dispatched to the Charles Reeder & Company machine works in Baltimore to have its engines repaired, yet again, and to be painted.[37] This was a forewarning of its life to come.

A Problematic Start

Meanwhile, B&ES could not wait for repairs to *Thames River*. The company was heavily in debt, accumulating mounds of unpaid invoices, and needed cash infusions immediately. They were still working to upgrade the line from Berlin to Ocean City, and this was depleting their remaining resources.

Therefore, while awaiting final repairs to *Thames River*, B&ES had initiated the route on August 25, 1890, chartering the new passenger steamer *Tockwogh* for the portion over the Chesapeake.[38] But *Tockwogh*, a classic steam-powered, sidewheel passenger steamboat, could not accommodate railcars. The entire model of seamless railcar movement from Baltimore to the Eastern Shore had to be temporarily abandoned.

By autumn 1890 the routine had begun to settle, with *Tockwogh* making two daily trips across the Bay Ridge-Claiborne route, except on Sundays.[39] However, the company had still not implemented the rail-transfer operation. According to a report in a local paper, on November 11, an excursion of Baltimore businessmen set out from their home city to Salisbury on a trip, organized by the railroad, to introduce the new route to these merchants and bankers and to inaugurate the new rail-transfer steamer.[40] Evidently, *Thames River* was still not ready for service and the trip across the Bay took place on *Tockwogh* instead.[41]

The first actual revenue voyage on the route by *Thames River* itself apparently was not until November 18, 1890.[42] But its operation on the route barely lasted two weeks. On an evening voyage from Bay Ridge to Claiborne on December 3, one of the sidewheels failed, and *Thames River* was left crippled, with its passengers "in distress." It had to be taken out of service until repairs could be made back in Baltimore.[43] Since *Tockwogh* had been released to other duties, another solution was required.

B&ES was again forced to charter a different replacement steamboat, in this case *Olive*, the same small, propeller-driven steam passenger vessel that had previously served Claiborne via Tilghman Creek.[44] (In this, *Olive* became the only steamer ever to serve Claiborne by both waterways, Eastern Bay and Tilghman Creek.) But like *Tockwogh*, *Olive* could not carry railcars, and once again the original rationale of ferrying entire railcars across the Bay had been undermined.[45] The whole business model of B&ES was flailing.

In the end, *Thames River* proved extremely unreliable, and constant maintenance was required. Evidently B&ES was not reimbursing shipyards, because a series of liens was placed on the steamer by Charles Reeder & Company (engine works) and William Skinner & Sons.[46] B&ES appeared to be running out of vendors willing to repair *Thames River*, at least on credit.

Nonetheless, *Thames River* was not yet finished with frustrating the lives of B&ES managers and passengers. Service was again disrupted on May 9, 1891, when *Thames River* suffered a major boiler failure.[47] B&ES must have had difficulty finding a suitable repair facility because it was not until June 20 that the steamer arrived for repairs at yet another shop, James Clark & Company.[48] In response, the steamer *Tangier* was chartered for temporary use on the route, introducing yet another passenger vessel unable to move railcars. *Thames River* appears to have re-entered service in July.[49] But again, the return was brief. August found *Thames River* undergoing major repairs at another shipyard, this time Peoples Works.[50]

The constant disruptions in service dented confidence in the operation as a whole and almost certainly affected ridership. One can imagine the number of times when families looking forward to a holiday were forced to wait instead in Bay Ridge for a steamer that never arrived. Merchants missed meetings. Farmers and watermen seeking to move their products to markets in Baltimore saw their catches lose freshness in the summer sun. Many must have wondered whether the complex Baltimore-Annapolis-Bay Ridge-Claiborne setup was worth it.

The whole point of using the terminal in Bay Ridge was to permit railcars to be moved on transfer steamers across the Chesapeake Bay, and in this B&ES had failed miserably. Company President Joseph Seth had himself diagnosed the problem as early as February 1891 and was willing to abandon *Thames River* and the whole rail-transfer scheme after only six months:

> The popularity of the line depends considerably upon the character of the passenger steamer which makes the connection between Bay Ridge and Claiborne. An effort has been made to get a steamer which will inspire confidence in the traveling public and the board authorized steps to be taken at once to make the purchase.[51]

There was a reason that B&ES had to keep jumping from shipyard to shipyard to have *Thames River* repaired. B&ES had not been paying its bills, and it had run out of cash. The cash-flow challenge was not an unforeseen development. Rather, it was inevitable given the way in which the company had been set up and funded. The business plan for the B&ES had been seriously flawed from the start.

The first flaw in the plan was basing the financial plan on the assumption that local jurisdictions would underwrite the bonds. The original plan to fund $700,000 via endorsements by Baltimore and four Eastern Shore counties had fallen through in 1887. B&ES decided to try again, this time asking the four counties to acquire capital stock in B&ES, as opposed to endorsing bonds. Talbot County was asked to kick in $25,000. Dorchester and Wicomico were asked to put in $20,000 each. Caroline County was to invest $10,000. Rather than raise $700,000 using the financial resources of local jurisdictions, B&ES was now trying to raise $75,000. The proposals to acquire stock in B&ES went down in crushing defeats.[52]

The second flaw was in the estimation of the costs of the new railroad. The original plan was to raise $728,000 to fully fund the railroad. It proved far more expensive to lay the rails and build the ferry terminals. By the end of 1890, the cost of constructing the new rail and ferry system had reached $1,495,000 (about $51 million in 2024), 92 percent of which was in the railroad and rolling stock. Investors had subscribed to $300,000 in stock, but the bulk of funding came from interest-bearing bonds sold to subscribers.[53] Moreover, costs were still growing. By the end of 1891, a total of $1,969,000 was committed to the venture, including $1,469,000 in bonds earning 5 percent interest. Unlike the original plan for guaranteed bonds—which would not require cash outlays for twenty years—the new bonds required interest payments every six months. The cost of servicing that debt was $73,000 per year, far more than B&ES was likely to be able to earn in revenues.

The problem was not an absence of customers. Over 82,000 passengers traveled on the line in the fiscal year ending June 30, 1891, covering the first ten months of operation, or about 270 per day. Nor did the rail and ferry operations themselves fail to adequately cover their costs. A small operating loss that first fiscal year was reversed in the second year ending June 30, 1892, in which B&ES generated an operating profit of over $21,000 carrying 137,420 passengers (about 375 per day).

The problem was the burden of the financing costs. The $21,000 in operating profit the business might generate in good years was far below the $73,000 in interest costs that had to be paid on the bonds. It did not take long for B&ES to run out of cash to pay its bondholders, or even its suppliers, such as the shipyards needed to maintain the continuously failing *Thames River*.

One such supplier—and creditor—was Scranton Steel Corporation, which took B&ES to court to force payment of $82,000 it was owed for steel rails used in railway construction. The case was reviewed by the Circuit Court of the United States for the District of Maryland, and as a result of the court examination, B&ES was declared insolvent and placed under the control of a court-appointed receiver.[54]

Eight months after the first steamer had connected Bay Ridge and Claiborne, it was all over. Creditors had until July 1, 1891, to register with the court in the hope that, at some point, some portion of the funds owed to the creditors would be repaid from the assets of B&ES.[55] The courts were now in charge.

While the financial matters were being managed through the courts, B&ES still had a business to run. Every cent realized through ticket sales was vital. This responsibility now fell to the receiver appointed by the courts in April 1891, Captain Willard Thomson of Delaware.

Unlike the founders of the B&ES ferry and railroad, Thomson at the time had little in the way of attachment to Talbot County or Claiborne. The center of his world in 1891 was Wilmington—the very city that had been seen by Baltimoreans to be siphoning off the riches of the Eastern Shore. From that perch Thomson would exercise power over the Claiborne steamboat lines, in one form or another, from 1891 until his death in 1917.

End of the Bay Ridge Line and Rail-Transfer Operations

Willard Thomson was born in Maine in 1837, and after a young man's career at sea, he settled down in Delaware. He married well, taking as his wife Emma Harlan, the granddaughter of Samuel Harlan, one of the founders of Harlan & Hollingsworth, the prosperous Wilmington-based builder of passenger steamers and other vessels. Thomson was hired as a superintendent at Harlan & Hollingsworth and used his sea-going expertise to help evaluate new steamers over a period of many decades.

Thomson was, objectively, the ideal choice for the court to select as receiver. He had gained experience in Chesapeake Bay steamboat operations as an original stockholder (with Samuel Harlan) of the Eastern Shore Steamboat Company, headquartered in Baltimore. Thomson had served as general manager and ran the complex steamship operations connecting Baltimore with Chesapeake Bay destinations as far south as Crisfield. Thomson also

Captain Willard Thomson was appointed as receiver of B&ES in 1891, which had been declared insolvent after only eight months of operation. Photographer unknown, October 6, 1906. Courtesy of *The Baltimore Sun*

had experience running a railroad, having been appointed in 1869 as the superintendent of the troubled Eastern Shore Railroad, running from Delmar to Crisfield.[56] He was successful in that endeavor, overseeing the operation for fifteen years through a series of financial restructurings, and eventually selling the line to the New York, Philadelphia and Norfolk Railroad in 1884.

As a court-appointed receiver, Thomson took over all executive functions in the company, effectively sidelining Joseph B. Seth and the other Eastern Shore-based founders. It might not have seemed an enviable assignment. Upon his appointment in 1891, Thomson faced a series of immediate crises. *Thames River* was not a viable ferry for this route. No other rail-transfer ferry was available for lease, and he had no money to invest in new boats, facilities, or rail lines. The rail-transfer concept was proving unworkable. Nonetheless, he dove into the task of turning B&ES around, at first continuing the same rail-centric business plan of the prior leadership.

By September 1891, Thomson had seen and suffered enough. He was ready to try something new and had already begun looking for a conventional steamer to replace *Thames River*.[57] He presented a petition to the US Circuit Court overseeing the company to abandon the Bay Ridge service entirely.

> Mr. Thomson says the present method of transporting passengers and freight from Bay Ridge to Claiborne is, in his opinion, unprofitable and unadvisable. The company's steamer, the Thames River, is declared to be entirely unsuited for the service required and it would be necessary to secure another vessel if the present method of operating the [rail]road should be continued.[58]

Judge Thomas J. Moore approved the petition and authorized Thomson to switch the Western Shore terminal from nearby Bay Ridge to more distant Baltimore and to lease steamers better suited for that passenger service. The last voyage of *Thames River* was a week later, when it took the remaining railcars from Bay Ridge to Claiborne for the final time. It was taken out of service permanently and laid up on October 5, 1891. The rail-transfer operation was over.[59]

Thames River was out. Bay Ridge was out. The rail-transfer model was out. The logical question, then, is whether or not Claiborne should be out. Now that the new Western Shore terminal was in Baltimore, the original decision to put the Eastern Shore terminal in Claiborne could be rightfully questioned, since Claiborne's selection had been based in part on its proximity to the railroad terminal in Bay Ridge. With the new terminal in Baltimore, the sea route to Claiborne—over forty nautical miles—would be almost twice as long as a route to the northern part of Kent Island. The additional distance to Claiborne would add almost two hours to the trip. Since steamers were the slow link in the transportation chain, operating at only a third or a quarter of the speed of trains, this would make the total trip time to Ocean City much longer, even if partially offset by a longer train ride from Kent Island.

Certainly, there were those at the time who advocated dropping Claiborne as the eastern terminal and shifting the line instead to Kent Island. An editorial in *The Evening Capital* laid out this argument the same day the B&ES western terminal was relocated from Bay Ridge to Baltimore:

> ...the company should then change its route from Eastern [Bay] directly north to Kent Island, and thence by transfer boat to the terminus at Annapolis of the Short line. The route to St. Michaels and then to Bay Ridge across a wide expanse of the Bay, was a grave error and perhaps the cause in great measure of its present embarrassments. The new route would avoid delays and dangers from steamboat navigation across a wide expanse of the Bay, as that part of the Bay between Kent Island and Annapolis is so land-locked as to render connections at this city, safe, speedy and sure. The change of [rail] route would be comparatively small in outlay as the country is as level as a threshing floor and free of bridges. Besides, it would be so near the rail-road terminating at Centreveille in Queen Anne's county, that a short spur to that flourishing town would place the [Baltimore-to-Annapolis] Short Line in close connecting with all of the counties of the Eastern Shore . . .[60]

The proposal did not garner support, especially on the Eastern Shore. The existing rail line at Centreville, operated by the Delaware Railroad, and controlled by the Pennsylvania Railroad, connected to the main line running up to Wilmington and not (directly) to rail service to Easton, Salisbury, or Ocean City. Such a plan would have reinforced the role of Wilmington and Philadelphia over Baltimore and therefore was inconsistent with the underlying rationale behind B&ES.

One of the themes of this history is that even bad decisions could have implications that persist for decades. This is a perfect example. While the Bay Ridge-Claiborne route had proved to be a calamity, the concept of revisiting the selection of Claiborne was moot: there were no resources available for new rail lines. There was no existing rail line on Kent Island, and Thomson had no money available to lay new tracks. When he did try to obtain more funds, his efforts were thwarted. Legislation was introduced in early 1892 authorizing Baltimore City to once again put to the voters a proposal to assume responsibility for $900,000 in bonds at a reduced interest rate of 3.5 percent, in return for rights to $251,000 of company stock. It smacked of desperation and ended up going nowhere.[61]

The reality is that Claiborne had gotten there first, a recurring theme in the history of steamboat and ferry operations in this region. Claiborne was the terminus of the *only* rail line running east to west across Maryland's Eastern Shore. The next such line—connecting Queenstown and Love Point on Kent Island with Rehoboth on the Atlantic coast—would not be completed for a decade and terminated in Delaware, not Maryland. The flawed decision to build a rail-transfer operation from Bay Ridge to Claiborne drove decisions about cross-bay steamboat and ferry service for the next forty years, even though the original operation was a complete failure, was declared insolvent after eight months, and ended after just one year. The die had been cast.

Even with the relocation of the service from Bay Ridge to Baltimore, Thomson faced another challenge: he had no ferries to use other than *Thames River*, now lying useless at a pier in Baltimore.[62] Since B&ES was under strict financial restraints, it was unable to acquire its own steamer fleet. Moreover, it could only lease steamboats for a period of four months without returning to the court for permission for a longer lease.[63] Thus, its service for the first few years resembled a game of musical chairs as Captain Thomson attempted to redirect service from Bay Ridge to Baltimore and bring some sense of normalcy to the route.

Service from Baltimore started on an interim basis with the steamer *Olive*, a familiar sight in the waters around Claiborne from its days of service on Tilghman Creek from 1877 to 1887. Meanwhile, Thomson searched for suitable large steamers for this new and longer route from Baltimore to Claiborne. For this, he looked to his in-laws and found the answer in steamers produced over the years by Harlan & Hollingsworth, the company built in large part by his wife's grandfather.

The full service started on October 5, 1891, with the steamer *B.S. Ford*, chartered from the Chester River Line for four months. Its maiden voyage on the route took three hours and seven minutes, with the connecting train ride to Ocean City adding another three hours and forty-five minutes.[64] When that charter ended in late January 1892, B&ES chartered the steamer *Tangier* from Thomson's own Eastern Shore Steamboat Company.[65] Later, the steamers *Maggie* and *Helen* would take their turns moving passengers from Baltimore to Claiborne.

The four steamboats involved—*B.S. Ford, Tangier, Maggie,* and *Helen*—were cousins. These were stout and efficient vessels built in Wilmington, Delaware, by the Harlan & Hollingsworth Company. These iron-hulled, side-paddlewheel steamboats were constructed in 1869 (*Maggie*), 1871 (*Helen*), 1875 (*Tangier*), and 1877 (*B.S. Ford*). They ranged from 418 to 681 GRT in volume. All had operated for years on the Choptank, Chester, and other rivers in the region.[66] They were reliable steam-powered, sidewheel-propelled, passenger-carrying maritime Clydesdales.

Thomson's new business model worked well, at least at one level. Transport operations had stabilized. Vacationers were getting to Ocean City, and seafood was getting to markets in Baltimore. B&ES revenues almost doubled between 1891 and 1892. They rose again in 1893. Captain Thomson's turnaround magic had worked.

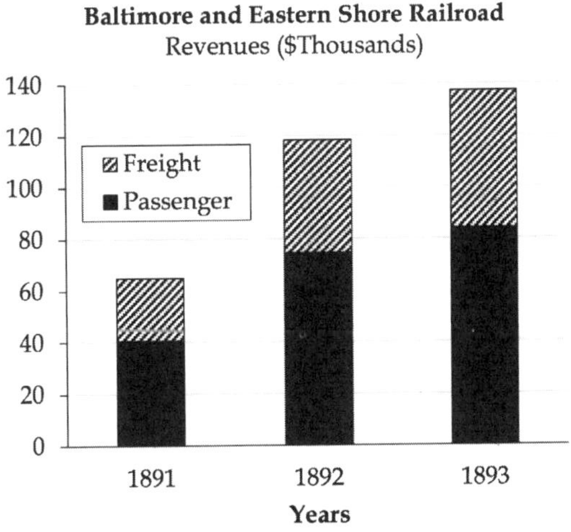

Operating profit also rose under Thomson's leadership. The operating loss in 1891 was reversed, and by 1893 the business was generating the level of operating profits originally envisioned when the business plan was created. But while the business was generating $30,000 in operating profit, that was still less than half the amount required to service its massive debt. The company needed over $73,000 in net operating cash each year just to pay the interest on the bonds, much less set aside a "sinking fund" to save up for paying off the principal when the bonds came due in ten years.

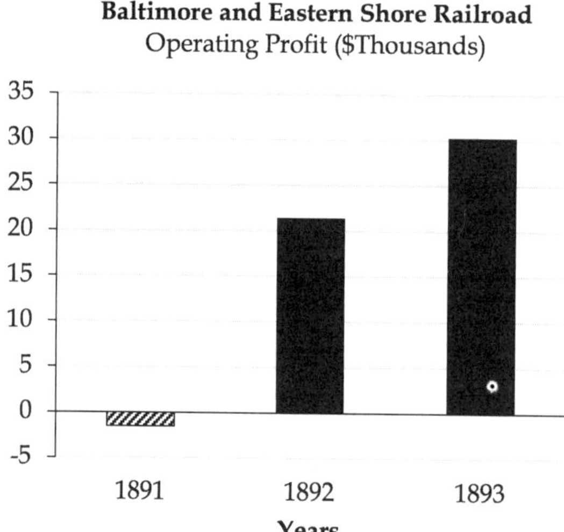

Then the US economy crashed in the Panic of 1893 with effects lingering into 1894. It was the final nail in the coffin for B&ES, and in the summer of 1894, the company was declared bankrupt and dissolved in a public auction of its assets. The grand plan of Joseph B. Seth to build a rail line across the Chesapeake had failed miserably.

But there was still a railroad terminal and a wharf in Claiborne, and a rail line running to Ocean City. These were valuable assets. Perhaps a better-funded company could make the operation viable. It was time for the professional monopolists to take the stage.

Notes

1. Campbell Gibson, "Population of the 100 Largest Cities and Other Urban Places in the United States: 1790 to 1990," Working Paper No. POP-WP027 (US Census Bureau, June 1998), Table 11: Population of the 90 Urban Places for 1880.
2. Joseph P. Seth and Mary W. Seth, *Recollections of a Long Life on the Eastern Shore* (Press of the Star Democrat, 1926), 10. He goes on to add: "The bulk of the slaves were devoted to their masters and their families, taking great interest in everything concerning them. They considered themselves a part of the family and their devotion was so great that they would run any risk to protect them. The families were equally devoted to the slaves and with the whole Southland had the tenderest affection for the faithful old Mammies and Uncles."
3. "Maryland Legislature," *Sun* (Baltimore, MD), January 7, 1886.
4. "From the Eastern Shore," *Sun* (Baltimore, MD), January 28, 1884.
5. Oswald Tilghman, *Maryland Manual, 1907–1908: A Compendium of Legal, Historical and Statistical Information Relating to the State of Maryland* (Wm. J.C. Dulany, 1907), 119: 300, accessed November 29, 2022, msa.maryland.gov/megafile/msa/speccol/sc2900/sc2908/000001/000119/html/am119--300.html.
6. He would end up leading the Oyster Navy in 1891. See John Wennersten, *The Oyster Wars of the Chesapeake Bay* (Eastern Branch Press, 1981), 86.
7. *Journal of the Proceedings of the House of Delegates of Maryland, January Session, 1886* (George T. Melvin, 1886), 5.
8. "Ocean City to Baltimore: The Advantages of Quicker Railroad Communication with the Eastern Shore," *Sun* (Baltimore, MD), March 22, 1886.
9. Notably, Queen Anne's County, in which Kent Island is located, was not considered as a potential source of funding. This suggests that, despite later suggestions, Seth never seriously considered the rail line reaching the Bay via Kent Island.
10. "The Baltimore and Eastern Shore Railroad," *Sun* (Baltimore, MD), July 17, 1886.
11. "Brooklyn," *New York Times*, September 9, 1973.
12. Christopher T. Baer, William J. Coxey, and Paul W. Shopp, *The Trail of the Blue Comet: A History of the Jersey Central's New Jersey Southern Division* (West Jersey Chapter of the National Railway Historical Society, 1994), 95.
13. "Baltimore and Eastern Shore Railroad," *Sun* (Baltimore, MD), April 14, 1886.
14. "Eastern Shore Railroad," *Sun* (Baltimore, MD), October 9, 1886.
15. "The Baltimore and Eastern Shore Railroad," *Easton Star-Democrat*, October 26, 1866.

16. Matthew A. Crenson has a detailed assessment of Baltimore's relationship with railroads in *Baltimore: A Political History* (Johns Hopkins University Press, 2017), 310–15.
17. Quoted in Matthew A. Crenson, *Baltimore: A Political History* (Johns Hopkins University Press, 2017), 314.
18. "Public Business—County Commissioners," *Easton Star-Democrat*, September 6, 1887.
19. "The Local department," *Denton Journal*, September 17, 1887.
20. "Items of Local Interest," *Easton Star-Democrat*, September 20, 1887.
21. "Officials Elected in Neighboring Counties Last Tuesday," *Easton Star-Democrat*, November 15, 1887. The affirmative votes in Wicomico and Dorchester County were questioned soon after the election. The enabling legislation required affirmation by a "majority of qualified voters," not a majority of votes cast. It was argued that while the referendums in those two counties received more than half of the vote cast, they fell short of receiving more than half of the vote of all qualified voters in the county. In the end, the endorsements were affirmed.
22. "The Railroad Vote," *Easton Star-Democrat*, May 29, 1888.
23. "Telegraphic Summary, Etc.," *Sun* (Baltimore, MD), June 29, 1888.
24. There already was a community at the top of Tilghman Creek called Claiborne. That community is now called Old Claiborne, and the new town on Broad Cove is Claiborne. The name Bay City was suggested because some of the founders hoped to create a resort town on Eastern Bay to match the resort town being developed on the other end of the rail line on the Atlantic Ocean that had been given the name "Ocean City."
25. "Route of the New Line," *Sun* (Baltimore, MD), July 17, 1886.
26. This is based on a review of Talbot County land records for the period in question.
27. The Baltimore and Port Deposit Railroad commissioned the building of a rail-transfer ferry in 1836, shortly before that railroad was merged into the Philadelphia, Wilmington and Baltimore (PW&B) Railroad. The PW&B line was interrupted by the Susquehanna River, between the stop of Perryville (northern side) and Havre de Grace (southern side). The steam ferry *Susquehanna*, built by Williamson & Richardson in the Fells Point neighborhood of Baltimore, started service in July 1837. *Susquehanna* was replaced in late 1854 by a new and larger ferry *Maryland*, built by Harlan & Hollingsworth in Wilmington. The PW&B line continued to rely upon rail-transfer ferries until the first bridge across the Susquehanna was completed in 1866.
28. A variation was already in use on the NYP&N line, connecting Cape Charles in Virginia's Eastern Shore with Norfolk. In this case, freight cars were loaded onto barges that were then towed or pushed across the Chesapeake.

29. Some have suggested the already-built steamer wharf in Bay Ridge was used as the rail-transfer wharf. In fact, the two were separate. The locations of both are clearly marked on an 1892 topographical map produced by the US Geological Survey. See *US Geological Survey, USGS 1:62500-scale Quadrangle for Annapolis, MD 1892,* US Geological Survey, sciencebase.gov/catalog/item/5a8a445be4b00f54eb3f42f5.
30. "Over the Thames River Bridge," *Hartford Daily Courant*, September 9, 1889.
31. The actual mechanism of transfer of ownership to B&ES remains a bit murky. Contemporary news accounts suggest that both ferries were acquired by the B&O Railroad in late 1889, with speculation as to their eventual use ranging from transporting cargo around Baltimore to ferrying railroad cars around New York. B&ES took formal title to the steamers in July 1890, at a B&ES stockholders meeting held at B&O headquarters in Baltimore. See "Through to Ocean City," *Star-Democrat* (Easton, MD), July 8, 1890. A likely scenario is that the B&O and the B&ES collaborated on this transfer, with the purchase in 1889 being made by the B&O on behalf of B&ES, with subsequent transfer to B&ES in July 1890 once that line became operational. However, definitive evidence that *Groton* was acquired at the outset specifically for use on the Bay Ridge-Claiborne route has yet to emerge in the sparse records surrounding its acquisition.
32. "The Railroad Ferry Boats," *The Daily* (New London, CT), November 22, 1889.
33. Gross Register Tons (GRT) is a measure of internal volume of a ship. Each register ton equates to 100 cubic feet. Despite the name, it is not a measure of weight. Other measures such as deadweight tonnage or displacement do measure the weight of a ship, but these were less commonly used in this era for commercial ships.
34. *Annual Report of the Directors of the New York, Providence, and Boston R.R. Co. for the Year Ending September 30, 1885* (G.B. and J.H. Steam Printers, 1885), 20–21.
35. "Ferryboat Burned at Sea," *Sun* (New York, NY), December 3, 1889. The plan was to rename the steamer *William Claiborne*, but that change never formally took place. However, in contemporary reporting, that is sometimes the name used instead of *Thames River.*
36. "B. & E. S. Transfer Steamer," *Evening Capital* (Annapolis, MD), October 1, 1890.
37. "A Gale in the Chesapeake," *Sun* (Baltimore, MD), October 21, 1890.
38. "Peninsula Points," *Morning News* (Wilmington, DE), August 26, 1890.
39. The morning train—the express to Ocean City—would leave Baltimore's Camden Station at 7:45 a.m., arriving in Annapolis about fifty minutes later for a short connection to Bay Ridge. Passengers would then ride the steamer to

Claiborne, at which point they would board the train and speed on to Ocean City, arriving by early afternoon. The evening train left Baltimore at 4:00 p.m. and connected on the other side to a Claiborne train that went only as far as Salisbury. The winter schedule over 1890/1891 was similar, with slightly altered departure times from Baltimore at 8:25 a.m. and 4:45 p.m. When summer returned, the morning express to Ocean City was moved earlier to a 7:00 a.m. departure. This is based on timetables as published in B&ES advertisements in various editions of *The Sun* (Baltimore, MD).

40. "Items of Local Interest," *Easton Star-Democrat*, November 11, 1890.
41. Several sources suggest this was the inaugural trip of *Thames River* on the route. See, for example, the excellent book by John C. Hayman, *Rails Along the Chesapeake: A History of Railroading on the Delmarva Peninsula, 1827–1978* (Marvadel Publishers, 1979), 91. However, contemporary news accounts hint that the trip was taken on *Tockwogh* and that *Thames River* was tied up in Claiborne, with its first service scheduled for the following week. See "Bring The Trade Here," *Sun* (Baltimore, MD), November 12, 1990.
42. "News of the Port," *Sun* (Baltimore, MD), November 18, 1890.
43. "Broke Her Wheel," *Evening Capital* (Annapolis, MD), December 4, 1890.
44. "News of the Ships," *Sun* (Baltimore, MD), December 6, 1890.
45. The gap in service during the period of repair in December 1891 was partially filled by two oyster-police steamers of the so-called "Oyster Navy." Under the direction of Elihu E. Jackson, then governor of Maryland and founding treasurer of the Baltimore and Eastern Shore Railroad, Captain James A. Turner of the *Governor R.M. McLane* and Captain Thomas C. B. Howard of the *Governor P.F. Thomas* carried passengers between Bay Ridge and Claiborne for several days that December, filling in for the crippled *Thames River*. They did not follow correct procedure in preparing their passenger manifests and were heavily fined for their efforts. Captain Howard would later serve as the general manager of the Claiborne-Annapolis Ferry. It is worth noting that B&ES President Joseph B. Seth was in the leadership of the Oyster Navy at that time and had requested this assistance. He escaped any punishment.
46. "Mechanics Liens," *Daily Record* (Baltimore, MD), April 11, 1891, and April 18, 1891.
47. "The Local Department," *Denton Journal*, May 9, 1891.
48. "Port Paragraphs," *Sun* (Baltimore, MD), June 20, 1891.
49. "Port Paragraphs," *Sun* (Baltimore, MD), July 7, 1891.
50. "Galveston in Commission," *Sun* (Baltimore, MD), August 25, 1891.
51. "Eastern Shore Railroad Projects," *Evening Capital* (Annapolis, MD), February 2, 1891.
52. It was defeated in Wicomico County (2,125 against versus 556 for) and in Dorchester County (3,496 against versus 248 for). It also failed in Caroline

County. It succeeded only in Talbot County (2,420 for versus 1,645 against). See "Maryland's Vote: Return of Counties in Detail," *Sun* (Baltimore, MD), November 6, 1890.

53. "Baltimore and Eastern Shore Railroad," *Poor's Manual of Railroads 1891*, (Poor's Publishing Company, 1891), 35–36. All of the financial data presented here is from the annual *Poor's Manual*.
54. This is standard practice in the case of insolvency. The receiver's job was to protect the remaining value of the assets in the company, minimize costs, and attempt to preserve what value could be salvaged by restructuring operations and/or finding a buyer.
55. Who were the creditors? The largest was Joseph Ricker & Company of Portland Maine, owed $286,000. Joseph S. Ricker was the president of the Annapolis and Baltimore Short Line Railroad ("Annapolis Short Line"), which connected Baltimore via B&ES' own Bay Ridge and Annapolis Railroad to the B&ES Bay Ridge ferry terminal. He and his fellow New Englanders Charles Goodrich and George Burnham Jr. had been major investors in B&ES, expecting no doubt to see the value of their own railroad rise in concert with the new connection to the Eastern Shore. The Atlantic Trust Company was owed another $120,000. Edwin L. Tunis & Company (owned by the younger brother of Theophilus and Joseph) was in for $76,000, and Maryland's then-serving governor, Elihu E. Jackson, an original founder of B&ES, had invested $60,000 in bonds.
56. The Eastern Shore Railroad was built from Delmar to Salisbury in 1860 and then, after the Civil War, from Salisbury to Crisfield in 1866. At that point it was financially stressed and defaulted on the interest on its bonds. While the Eastern Shore Railroad owned the tracks, the trains themselves initially were operated by the Philadelphia, Wilmington and Baltimore Railroad. In 1869 the owners of the Eastern Shore Railroad decided to operate the trains themselves and hence they needed a superintendent. Thomson was chosen for the role.
57. In September 1891, Thomson sought to charter the New York-based ferry *Sirius*. See "Baltimore & Eastern Shore Railroad," *Evening Capital* (Annapolis, MD), September 16, 1891.
58. "Baltimore and Eastern Shore R. R.," *Evening Capital* (Annapolis, MD), September 28, 1891.
59. "Discontinuance of the Eastern Shore Trains," *Evening Capital* (Annapolis, MD), October 5, 1891. *Thames River* was seized by US marshals in November. It was later converted to a barge.
60. "The Short Line R. Railroad's Opportunities," *Evening Capital* (Annapolis, MD), October 10, 1891.
61. "Eastern Shore Railroad," *Sun* (Baltimore, MD), February 25, 1892.

62. In 1896, *Thames River* was purchased by H. Clay Tunis—another member of the Tunis family—and converted into a lumber barge. It was sold and renamed *John R. King* in 1897 and converted again into a scow in 1900. Renamed *Virginia H. Hudson* in 1905, it was under that name that it was lost in a storm in the Atlantic Ocean near the Hereford Inlet, adjacent to Wildwood, New Jersey, on September 15, 1906. The crew was saved.
63. "Baltimore and Eastern Shore R. R.," *Sun* (Baltimore, MD), September 28, 1891.
64. "From Claiborne to Baltimore by Boat," *Sun* (Baltimore, MD), October 6, 1891.
65. "Summary of the News," *Sun* (Baltimore, MD), January 27, 1892.
66. *Maggie* had been built for the Chester River Steamboat Company, and the others were constructed for Thomson's Eastern Shore Steamboat Company.

IV

Transition to Black Cinders and Ashes

Claiborne had been put on the map by the Annapolis legislature, in an effort led by three Eastern Shore state legislators. Their plan had failed within months and was declared officially dead when the bankruptcy of the Baltimore and Eastern Shore Railroad (B&ES) was announced on July 28, 1894.[1] The railroad and steamboat assets of the company would be auctioned off at the courthouse door in Salisbury at 1:00 p.m. on August 29. This was a surprise to no one.

While the locals lamented the failure of B&ES, others looked upon the circumstances more favorably. The travails of B&ES had been acutely observed by a group of out-of-state investors who knew a good potential monopoly when they saw one. For them, the bankruptcy actually represented an opportunity. Rather than invest from scratch, it was far more efficient financially to pick up the assets of a bankrupt company at distressed prices. Claiborne's fate was about to be driven not by politicians across the Bay in Annapolis, but by financiers in New York, an example of how distant powers influence the destiny of small towns.

In the end, the auction was a non-event. The near-worthless bonds of B&ES had been acquired in July by a new company formed

In 1894, bankrupt B&ES' assets were acquired by the new Baltimore, Chesapeake and Atlantic Railway, another venture of sugar magnate Henry O. Havemeyer. Photograph by Aimé Dupont, ca. 1899. From *The Successful American: Volumes 1–2* (The Press Biographical Company, 1899)

specifically for that purpose: the Baltimore, Chesapeake and Atlantic Railway (BC&A). By purchasing the bonds for pennies on the dollar, BC&A took a controlling interest amongst all the creditors in B&ES. BC&A's takeover of the assets themselves was a formality: the deal for the takeover had been concluded before the bankruptcy auction even took place.[2] The shareholders would lose their investments, but the bondholders and others awaiting payment would recover at least some of their investments from the sale.

Moreover, the new BC&A was aiming big. In July 1894, while all this was happening, BC&A also acquired three major steamboat lines operating on the Chesapeake: the Maryland Steamboat Company, the Choptank Steamboat Company, and the Eastern Shore Steamboat Company. It now had access to a fleet of steamships crossing the Chesapeake and was soon to control a rail line across Maryland's Eastern Shore.[3] The new company would control fifteen steamboats and more than 110 wharf properties. It would absolutely dominate transportation across the Bay and onward to Maryland's Eastern Shore, and thus inevitably would challenge the Pennsylvania Railroad's (PRR's) dominance of Delmarva rail transportation.[4]

BC&A was not just a continuation of B&ES under a different name. This was a different company, led by different investors and pursing different objectives. Whereas B&ES was led originally by people with deep personal ties to Talbot and Wicomico Counties, the new BC&A leadership had none. The president (John E. Searles) and treasurer (Winthrop M. Tuttle) both hailed from New York City. Of the twelve members of the initial BC&A board of directors, five were from New York. Two were from Wilmington, including Captain Thomson. Only three were from Maryland, and none of those were from Maryland's Eastern Shore.[5] Joseph B. Seth, Elihu E. Jackson, and Theophilus Tunis were out.

While B&ES was, in part, about building the economy of the Eastern Shore and strengthening connections to Baltimore, BC&A was about building wealth and solidifying bank accounts for the New York-based owners. Their standard business model to date had been to create and defend monopolies. The jewel in their business portfolio was the Sugar Refineries Company—the "Sugar Trust"—that eventually controlled 98 percent of the US sugar market. (Their company, which would change its name to Domino Sugar in 1900, had already acquired and shut down local businesses in Baltimore.) It was widely expected that the same objective applied to the railroad and steamboat lines, as reported in *The New York Times*:

> John E. Searles, of New York, Secretary of the Sugar Trust, and associates have purchased controlling interests in a railroad and three steamboat lines, and will form a company to monopolize traffic between Baltimore and the Eastern Shore counties of Maryland.[6]

While the owners changed, several things remained the same. Captain Willard Thomson, who was receiver of B&ES as well as the head of the Eastern Shore Steamboat Company, was retained as general manager of BC&A and was appointed as vice president of the company. Ever the survivor, Thomson would continue to run the operation for more than two decades.[7] The wharf and terminal in

Claiborne would continue to be Baltimore's gateway to the Eastern Shore of Maryland. Why spend money building a closer steamboat wharf if it also meant adding (and funding) twenty-eight more miles of new railroad?

Some things did change. The new owners had reserves of cash, and they brought stability to the Claiborne transport system, finally freed from the heavy debt incurred five years before. The first step was to acquire the modern steamers that would provide stable and reliable service. Starting in July 1894, and proceeding for the next three decades, the primary steamer shuttling passengers between Claiborne and Baltimore would be *Cambridge*, "which had the reputation for being the fastest steamboat on the bay."[8] A similar steamer, *Tred Avon*, also worked the route, especially when *Cambridge* was taken in for maintenance or repair.[9]

These were not old-fashioned paddlewheel steamers. *Cambridge* and *Tred Avon* were newer and more advanced than the sidewheel steamboats that had served the route to date. They were also cousins—and local ones at that—both constructed in Baltimore by William E. Woodall & Company. *Tred Avon* was completed in 1884 and measured 677 GRT and 151 feet in length. *Cambridge*, built in 1890, was larger at 834 GRT and 165 feet in length. *Tred Avon* was of conventional iron construction whereas *Cambridge* was a "composite" vessel, with wood planking covering iron frames. Each had modern propulsion systems, using propellers instead of paddlewheels.[10] Author David C. Holly describes what a passenger might experience while traveling on *Cambridge* in this era:

> She was a graceful vessel, questionably reputed to be the fastest on the Bay, with a decided sheer and a rake to her funnel. On the top deck, a passenger could feel the pulsing of the triple-expansion engine far below and, most remarkably, note the flexing of her upper deck with each thrust of her propeller. Cutting through the water, out of the Patapsco and across the Bay, [they] stirred up a sensuous breeze across her open deck, a vacation in itself for the street-weary passengers from Baltimore.[11]

Speed, comfort, and reliability became the focus of BC&A management. The trip aboard *Cambridge*, described by author Holly as "fast but overrated," consumed a bit over three and one-quarter hours from Baltimore to Claiborne.[12] While on board, passengers could avail themselves of meal service, and the line soon built a reputation for good eating aboard. Passengers could also rest in a salon or, if more adventurous, ride up top to better feel the breeze, see the passing scenery, and anticipate their eventual arrival in Easton, Salisbury, or Ocean City.

The land portion of the rail line was also upgraded. In September 1894, BC&A introduced an express train between Claiborne and Ocean City, known locally as "The Flyer." The express train ride took only two hours, versus more than three hours on a regular train making local stops. Another ten to fifteen minutes was spent in transferring from steamer to train. Thus, one could step aboard the steamer in Baltimore and reach Ocean City in just under six hours if travelers caught "The Flyer" express train from Claiborne.

Once aboard the train, the pleasures of the water voyage were replaced by the less appealing railway experience of a crowded carriage behind a locomotive belching clouds of thick, black smoke. It was especially tough in the summertime. Passengers had a choice: either leave the railcar windows closed and suffer in the heat or, alternatively, open the windows and see why BC&A was nicknamed "Black Cinders and Ashes." For those passengers heading to Ocean City aboard the regular train, with its numerous stops along the way, the train ride seemed interminable. Some passengers told stories of dirty conditions in some passenger cars, including an atmosphere scented by infants who desperately needed to have diapers changed.[13]

Eventually, the rail trip ended, and the ocean breezes of Ocean City replaced less favorable conditions in the carriages. Baltimorean Emma D. Price explained that while the adults might be worn out from the journey . . .

> . . . we youngsters, widely excited, would be only hot, sticky, and dirty. The minute we set foot on the Boardwalk, stretching out before us, and not more than 50 feet from the

> ocean, the magical scene would make us forget everything else. We forgot the hot train ride, we forgot that we lived in a big city which we would have to return to. We just kept feeling a quickening of the pulse, a consciousness of glamorous adventure awaiting us.[14]

Under BC&A leadership, the connection between Baltimore and Ocean City via Claiborne soon settled into a routine. During the peak summer months, when residents abandoned Baltimore and Washington for Ocean City and other resorts on the Atlantic Coast, BC&A ran two departures each day. The morning steamer departed Baltimore at 7:30 a.m., connecting to a train that would bring holiday makers to Ocean City by early afternoon.[15] An evening steamboat departed at 4:10 p.m. and would connect to a train that arrived in Ocean City late in the evening.[16]

Notably, the Claiborne route was one of only several major steamboat operations from Baltimore under BC&A's management, a result of the merger of B&ES with several other steamer companies.[17] Despite once-daily or twice-daily service to Claiborne—more than any other steamer destination in the BC&A empire—there was no steamboat line identified with that service. There was, in other words, no "Claiborne Line." Rather, service to Claiborne was considered part of BC&A's Railway Division.[18] Claiborne was less of a steamboat destination than just a transfer point from steamer to railroad on the line to Ocean City. Some BC&A schedules did not even list Claiborne as a stop.[19]

From 1895 through the turn of the century, BC&A dominated cross-bay rail traffic and the connecting steamer service. Business was good. Ridership on the steamer service showed steady annual growth, and rail ridership took off after 1897, as the region's economy recovered from the Panic of 1896. Financial performance also improved from the lackluster B&ES days. Operating income more than doubled between the 1895/1896 fiscal year and the 1902/1903 fiscal year. This was the start of a prosperous era for BC&A in Claiborne.

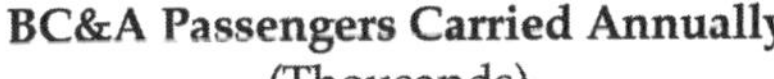
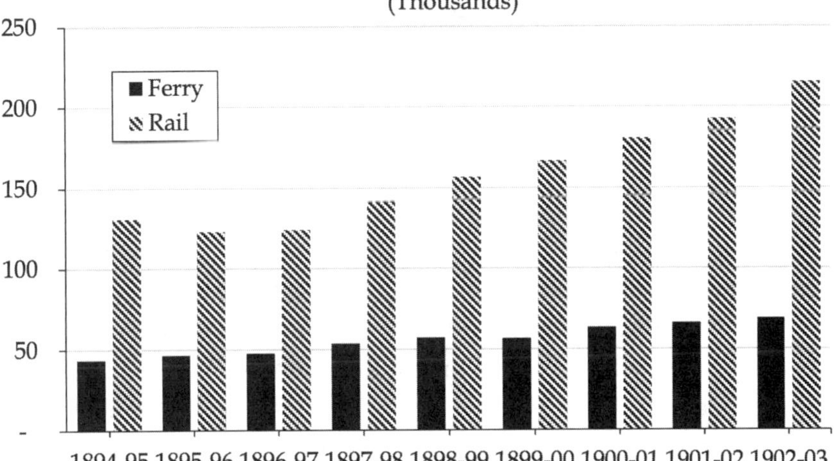

Claiborne Emerges

The small village of Claiborne expanded to accommodate this new service. When Broad Cove was selected as the site of the rail-transfer ferry terminal on the Eastern Shore, the community of Claiborne was just a set of farms and woodlots with the only substantial set of residences and commercial activity some distance away, in the com-munities of McDanieltown (McDaniel today) and the Tunis-Cockey hamlet at the tip of Tilghman Creek (Old Claiborne today). With the arrival of the steamers and railroad, a proper town would have to be built from scratch.

The initial hopes even involved constructing a twin parallel resort to the booming Ocean City. To be named Bay City, this project never emerged, and instead a small community of homes and businesses made its appearance between 1886 and 1905. Over time, the town would develop an impressive ability to repurpose existing structures for new uses. Because of this, many of these early structures are still evident today along Claiborne's main road.

Commercial development accelerated in July 1890, just as the steamer service began, when the manor house at Rich Neck Farm, located about one mile from the wharf, was repurposed as the Rich Neck Hotel. It offered pleasant accommodations to travelers arriving on the steamer from Bay Ridge.[20] This was soon supplemented in 1892 by the repurposed residence of the Cockey family, Maple Hall, located at Tilghman Creek. Maple Hall would go on to serve visitors to the community (on and off) up through the 1960s. A third residence, this one owned by Joseph T. and Helen D. Tunis and named Claiborne Hall, started advertising rooms to boarders in the mid-1890s. A bit farther away, starting in 1904, was Little Haven-on-the-Bay, a boarding home connected by a horse path to the new steamer terminal. Plans for a large new hotel in Claiborne, able to accommodate three hundred guests, were undertaken in 1902 but never reached fruition, with the investors losing large sums when the venture failed.[21]

A general store opened in Claiborne around this time, operated by the Horney family and later by Frederick Farlow. The store is known today primarily under the name "C.G. Jackson's General Store" after proprietor Clayton G. Jackson, who purchased the property in 1910.[22] The separate Claiborne Supply Company opened in or before 1903, run by merchant John E. Adkins.[23] It continued as a general store, post office, and local gathering place well into the 1980s.

The congregational needs of the growing community were supported at this time by the development of two new houses of worship. The first was Holy Innocents (Episcopal) Chapel, constructed in 1879 as a combined church and school on the grounds of Claiborne Hall, in what was then known as Claiborne and is now known as Old Claiborne. The new chapel was said to be "one of the prettiest churches in Talbot County."[24] Upon completion, the new congregation was formally established within the broader St. Michael's Parish as the "Chapel of the Holy Innocents, Claiborne."[25]

The Tunis family at Claiborne Hall evidently had greater aspirations for its religious chapel, and fundraising was undertaken in 1889 for a major remodeling, including the addition of a steeple and bell tower mimicking a similar steeple already present on Claiborne Hall, located near the chapel along Tunis Road.[26]

The Claiborne Methodist Episcopal Church was founded in 1902, when the local Methodist Episcopal congregation acquired property off Rich Neck Road and constructed a new church, a handsome structure with its own steeple and bell. The Methodist church operated in its religious capacity for many decades, winding down a few years after entering the twenty-first century. In 2010, the empty church was acquired by the local residents for use as a community center. It still stands today, in a secular capacity and lovingly renovated, as the Claiborne Association's Village Hall.

As the village emerged from the marsh and woodlots, some workers on the steamer system decided to call Claiborne home. Since the boat's crew would often live and eat aboard the steamer for days on end as it cycled between Baltimore and Claiborne, it was entirely practical for the workforce to live at either end of the line. Many preferred the Eastern Shore as a residence, either in Claiborne itself or farther east along the BC&A rail line to Easton and beyond. Notably, this included a number of BC&A steamboat captains.

In that era, steamboat captains were highly respected professionals entrusted with the care of hundreds of lives and an expensive vessel. Captains often served on the same route and the same boat for a decade or more and became familiar faces to those who regularly sought passage on the steamer. Their experienced, wind-beaten faces and commanding presence were also a source of comfort to some who might feel trepidation when voyaging in unsettled weather. Respect for the captains was earned not only by reliable operation of the steamer itself, but also through the many times their vessels saved the lives of others in dire circumstances on the Chesapeake. In dozens of cases over the decades, steamer and (later) diesel-ferry captains came to the aid of dismasted bugeyes, sinking schooners, grounded bay boats, or stranded steamboats. Many of the rescues were performed under challenging conditions. High winds, fog, sudden storms, shallow mudbanks, and frozen waters were all common hazards waiting to envelop unsuspecting captains, crews, and passengers on the Chesapeake.

One of the first of these legendary captains, and the first to assume residence in Claiborne, was Charles W. Spence, the master of the BC&A steamer *Cambridge*. Spence commanded his vessel on the route between Claiborne and Baltimore for almost a decade, from 1895 until his premature death in 1904 from kidney disease at the early age of forty-four. His reassuring countenance was well known to travelers on the BC&A line to Baltimore. Living in Claiborne, Spence would commute between steamboat wharf and his home with just a three-minute walk each way.[27] His presence in the town seemed to validate the emergence of Claiborne as a real community rather than a mere transit point.

The Pennsylvania Railroad Steps In

The success of the rail line and steamboat operation was welcomed in the community of Claiborne and by fellow residents of Talbot County. Others were watching from a distance as well, with perhaps different motivations. The prosperity of BC&A caught the attention of the primary rail and steamboat operator on the Delmarva Peninsula, the Pennsylvania Railroad Company (PRR). Through a complex set of crossholdings and linked management, PRR effectively controlled all of the major rail carriers in Delaware and on Maryland's Eastern Shore, with the notable exception of BC&A. PRR also owned several other steamboat lines operating in the Chesapeake, including the Chester River Steamboat Company (Rock Hall, Jackson Creek, Queenstown, Bogles, Centreville) and the Weems Steamboat Company (serving Washington, DC, and locations in Virginia). BC&A's rail and steamboat business was just about the only major independent operator on the Chesapeake not under the control of PRR. This would not last.

On September 2, 1899, it was rumored that a New York broker, Scott & Company, acting on behalf of a major BC&A investor, sold BC&A shares worth $2,250,000 to PRR. The sale apparently came as a surprise to at least one person: BC&A's president, John S. Wilson, who commented:

> Mr. John Searles of New York, who is the largest stockholder in the [rail]road, was in Baltimore yesterday but he

> said nothing to me about intending to sell his interest in the property. In any deal of any kind, he would naturally be a leading figure.[28]

The rumors were true, as confirmed by BC&A president Wilson just two days later. The sale had transferred enough shares for PRR to own a 60-percent stake in the company. BC&A was now under the control of (technically, "affiliated with") the PRR monopoly. Wilson, initially clueless as to what had been transpiring, was swept along with events, declaring:

> I think it exceedingly fortunate that the [rail]road has fallen into the possession of the Pennsylvania [Railroad], a company everywhere known for its broad and liberal policy. I do not anticipate any radical changes in either the management or the policy of the Baltimore, Chesapeake and Atlantic, unless the present owners are subject to such additional burdens as will make it necessary to advance rates. Should this condition of things transpire, it would, in my opinion, be more loss to the City of Baltimore than the amount of taxes it is proposed to collect even if they could be collected after a lawsuit.[29]

Wilson's overconfidence in the "broad and liberal" policy of PRR was matched by his earlier misreading of PRR's inclinations. Within weeks he was out of a job—discarded by the new owners and replaced by the new president, Sutherland M. Prevost. There was one survivor amongst the former management team, none other than the ever-present Captain Willard Thomson, who continued as vice president and general manager.

Why did the owners of BC&A sell at that time, when the railroad was earning good profits? B C&A s uffered a se ries of advance rulings on tax liabilities in a case that went all the way to the US Supreme Court.[30] The initial adverse ruling in this case was revealed on August 22, 1899, and less than two weeks later the owners of BC&A decided to sell.[31] BC&A's president, John S.

Wilson, speculated that the tax liability was behind the decision by original owner Searles to abandon his stake in BC&A after only five years. Wilson stated:

> My belief is that the late owners of the property arrived at the conclusion to sell rather suddenly, and their action was probabily stimulated by the recent declaration of the Baltimore Appeal Tax Court to tax the property. . . . The late owners had invested with the distinct and explicit understanding that the property was free of tax for 30 years.[32]

With the sale of a controlling interest to PRR, that railroad now controlled all of the rail traffic on the Delmarva Peninsula—but only for two years. The railroad version of whac-a-mole continued. A new railroad was emerging in Maryland, centered on the small town of Queen Anne. In a pattern mirroring the steamboat competition in the 1860s and 1870s, in which upstarts could challenge incumbents by taking service to smaller unserved communities, the investors in Queen Anne decided it was about time that Baltimore was connected to a closer railroad terminal on the Eastern Shore. In the 1860s and 1870s, Claiborne had been that smaller unserved community. Now it was the incumbent, about to be challenged.

Competition from Love Point

One might argue with merit, along with *The Evening Capital* way back in October 1891, that a steamboat service out of Baltimore to bring people to Ocean City should really have made landfall on the Eastern Shore at Kent Island rather than farther south in Claiborne. Kent Island is closer, and the slightly longer rail journey to destinations in eastern Maryland would be offset by a much shorter sea journey across the Chesapeake. The original logic of Claiborne as a rail-transfer ferry destination had been based on moving railcars from Bay Ridge, not people from Baltimore. Over time, the realities of the geography would begin to show. This began in the late 1890s as a new rail line began to emerge from Queen Anne, stretching east to the Atlantic and west to the Chesapeake. Where the rail line met the water, steamboats would congregate.

Steamboats had operated for years from Baltimore to destinations in Queen Anne's County (which includes Kent Island) and neighboring Kent County (which confusingly does not). But until 1900, none of these steamboat terminals connected with a railroad, and thus none promised an easy transit to any ocean resort. However, in 1898 the new Queen Anne's Railroad (QARR) started service on a rail line it had constructed connecting Lewes, Delaware, with the town of Queen Anne and on to Queenstown on the Chester River, not far from where the river reached the Chesapeake.[33] In November 1898, the QARR announced its intention to begin steamboat service from Baltimore to Queenstown, connecting passengers to the rail line to Rehoboth. The steamboat *Queen Anne* was launched in June 1899, followed by the purchase of the relatively new steamer *Endeavor* in November 1899. The larger *Queen Anne* would operate in peak travel periods, whereas the smaller *Endeavor* would operate in the winter. Thus was born the Queen Anne's Ferry and Equipment Company (QAF&E).

Service to Queenstown was problematic. Though closer to Baltimore than Claiborne, entrance into Queenstown's picturesque harbor was difficult and time-consuming. In the wintertime, ice often presented navigational challenges and risked damage to boats. Moreover, the QARR rail line did not extend to the major population centers on Maryland's Eastern Shore—one had to connect at Queen Anne and Easton to reach Ocean City or Salisbury. This was not an oversight—the primary orientation of QARR was to bring passengers to Lewes where they could connect on another QARR steamboat system using the steamer *Queen Caroline* and cross the Delaware Bay to Cape May, New Jersey (a route that still operates today).

Nonetheless, BC&A took the threat seriously. While BC&A promised a five-hour trip from Baltimore to Ocean City, the citizens of Baltimore could take a train directly to Atlantic City in only four hours. The emergence of a new convenient destination at Rehoboth would provide another, faster option for Baltimoreans seeking the pleasures of a seaside resort. One solution, which never materialized, was to once again shuttle passengers from Bay Ridge to Claiborne, not on a failing rail-transfer steamer as was the case in 1890, but on modern passenger steamboats.[34] This might cut an hour off the door-to-door travel time. In the end, no changes were made.

In 1902, however, the situation evolved in a way that presented a more immediate threat to BC&A, which means PRR started to pay attention. QARR extended their rail line from Queenstown west and then north up to Kent Island's tip, a location named Love Point. This reduced steamboat transit times from Baltimore by up to an hour, and the appeal of the QARR service increased as a consequence. Now there were two rail lines running east-west across the Delmarva Peninsula, both linking ocean resort destinations to terminals on the eastern side of the Chesapeake Bay. BC&A trains ran from Claiborne to Ocean City. QARR trains ran from Love Point to Lewes and, in the summer, to Rehoboth.[35]

Operations at QARR and its QAF&E subsidiary started to pick up. The steamboat line operated two steamers a day from Baltimore to Love Point, with connecting rail service to Rehoboth. The total trip time was about six hours. As had Claiborne, the town of Love Point suddenly emerged from next to nothing, with local hotels and restaurants accommodating travelers, including many who saw Love Point as their ultimate destination and thus never boarded the train. Especially notable was the grand Love Point Hotel, with three floors and fifty rooms and an idyllic location right at the tip of Kent Island, all within a leisurely walk from the ferry pier. It was a full-fledged holiday resort, with fishing, bowling, canoeing, and sporting clays amongst the attractions. Some two hundred diners could be accommodated for deluxe meals featuring the best produce, game, and seafood available from Maryland's Eastern Shore.[36]

Fortunately for rival PRR (and thus BC&A and Claiborne), in what appears to be an ever-recurring pattern, QARR ran into financial difficulty almost from the start. By February 1904, QARR was no longer able to pay the interest and principal on the bonds used to fund QAF&E, and the steamboat operation went to court to have a receiver appointed to oversee QARR.

At this point, PRR pounced to reestablish its dominance. In January 1905, at a foreclosure sale analogous to that of B&ES a decade earlier, PRR stepped in and acquired the assets of QARR. These assets were merged with those of the Chester River Steamboat Company and the Weems Steamboat Company, also owned by PRR, to form a new entity: the Maryland, Delaware and Virginia Railway Company (MD&V).[37]

So now the two steamer-rail systems across the Chesapeake and extending to Atlantic Ocean resorts were controlled by PRR. BC&A ran the line from Baltimore to Ocean City via Claiborne. MD&V, whose trains soon became known as "Many Dirty Visits" due to the soot produced, ran the line from Baltimore to Rehoboth via Love Point. To ensure that the two rail systems worked in harmony—rather than in competition—the operations of MD&V were subsumed within those of BC&A, a move that made MD&V, in essence, an operating subsidiary of BC&A.[38] Willard Thomson was established as general manager of both lines. The steamboat lines even posted joint advertisements and brochures listing both services. The lack of competition allowed them to keep prices high, while minimizing the need to invest in new steamboats or expanded services.

BC&A restructured the steamer operations at Love Point in an attempt to turn prospects around for MD&V. It dispensed with the relatively new steamers *Queen Anne* and *Endeavor* on the Baltimore-Love Point route. Instead, starting in June 1906, it deployed the 1884-built sidewheel steamer *Emma A. Ford,* upgraded and renamed *Love Point* the previous month. It also terminated the QARR steamer service across the Delaware Bay since it competed with existing PRR services, making the *Queen Caroline* surplus as well.

For the next seven years, from 1905 to 1912, BC&A's monopoly on steamer-rail connections across the entire Delmarva Peninsula generated attractive financial results for PRR. Business was solid, and BC&A for the first time was able to pay annual dividends to its shareholders, as revenue grew steadily and outpaced any growth in operating expenses.

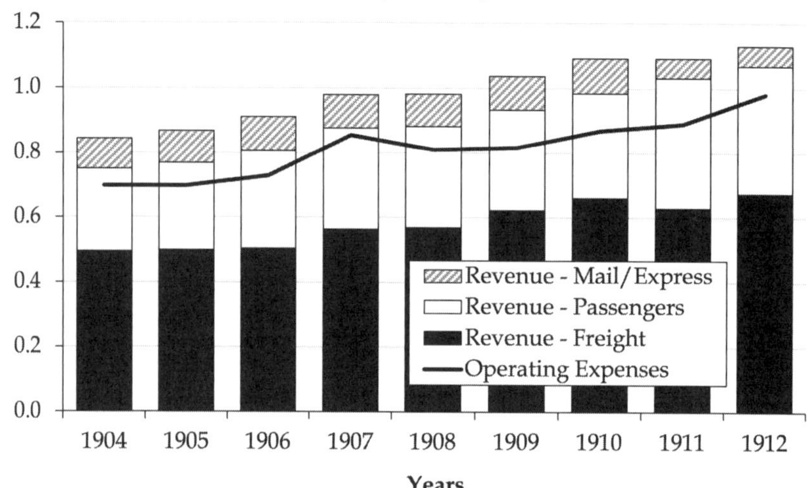

The prosperity of BC&A and its MD&V subsidiary did not escape notice. Both customers and employees began to criticize the company, and Willard Thomson himself, for being far more interested in dividends to parent PRR than in providing efficient and modern service across the Chesapeake. This would lead to a series of controversies that mirrored broader social and economic issues at the beginning of the twentieth century. There would be trouble on the line.

Notes

1. "Public Sale of the Baltimore and Eastern Shore Railroad," *Sun* (Baltimore, MD), July 28, 1894.
2. "The Deal Completed," *Sun* (Baltimore, MD), July 19, 1894.
3. "Steamboat Line Sold," *Morning News* (Wilmington, DE), July 12, 1894.
4. "Railroad Deal Completed," *Morning News* (Wilmington, DE), August 30, 1894.
5. Ibid.
6. "News of the Railroads: Alleged Important Deal by New-York Men," *New York Times*, July 20, 1894.
7. The town of Willard, Maryland, is named for him.
8. David C. Holly, *Steamboat on the Chesapeake* (Tidewater Publishers, 1987), 17.
9. It would also be used to supplement *Cambridge* on the route between 1914 and 1916 in an apparent attempt to weaken the business of a new competitor, the Eastern Shore Development Steamship Company.
10. One last steamer made a brief appearance. For a fleeting period in 1923, the old steamer *Joppa*—another Harlan & Hollingsworth steamer built in 1885—would be employed on the route after *Cambridge* was damaged in a collision.
11. David C. Holly, *Chesapeake Steamboats: Vanished Fleet* (Tidewater, 1994), 186. Alas, Holly confuses the route taken on this voyage, suggesting that Claiborne was connected to Rehoboth and that Love Point was connected to Ocean City, whereas it was the reverse until 1924 when Claiborne lost its connection entirely and Love Point became connected to Ocean City.
12. David C. Holly, *Tidewater by Steamboat: A Saga of the Chesapeake* (Johns Hopkins University Press, 1981), 108.
13. This account of a voyage was by a passenger as told to a descendant, Terri Fellinger. The account was obtained in an interview by the author with Fellinger on November 12, 2022.
14. The quote is from Emma D. Price in an unspecified article in *Eastern Shore Magazine*, as quoted by Mary Corddry, *City on the Sand: Ocean City, Maryland, and the People Who Built It* (Schiffer Publishing, 2012), 28.
15. Starting in 1900, the morning departure shifted to 6:30 a.m., and starting in 1916, it shifted to 6:25 a.m.
16. In 1903 the afternoon departure was changed to 3:50 p.m., and starting in 1904 it became 3:30 p.m. It was moved earlier to 2:30 p.m. in 1905 and stayed there until moved up to 2:15 p.m. in 1916 and 2:10 p.m. in 1922.
17. The Choptank River line brought passengers to Cambridge, Oxford, and Easton with daily service. Other lines operated only one, two, or three days per week. The Wicomico River line connected Baltimore with Wingate's Point, Deal's Island, and Salisbury (thrice weekly). The Nanticoke River line

operated to Deal's Island with connections to Seaford (thrice weekly). The Great Wicomico and Piankatank River line stopped at Dividing Indian, Dymer's Creek, Little Bay, Milford Haven, and Freeport (twice weekly). BC&A's Pocomoke River line went to Crisfield, Tangier Island, and Ononcock, with connections to Pocomoke City and Snow Hill (twice weekly). The Messongo River line and Occohannock River line had weekly service to various locations on the southern Delmarva Peninsula. The route structure and frequency of service is identified in BC&A advertisements in *The Sun* (Baltimore, MD).

18. The annual reports of the Maryland Public Service Commission include financial reports for various regulated utilities, including steamer lines and railroads. Most of the BC&A steamer lines are in the section of the report for steamer companies. However, the Claiborne operations (and later, Love Point operations) are embedded within the parent railroad company financials in the railroad section.
19. See for example, the advertisement in *The Democratic Messenger* (Snow Hill, MD), September 8, 1894. This advertisement for BC&A lists destinations on the line as Ocean City, Salisbury, Hurlocks (transfer point to the Delaware Railroad), Easton (another transfer point), and Baltimore.
20. See various advertisements in the local newspapers, including The *Easton Star-Democrat*, July 8, 1890.
21. "Hotel at Claiborne," *Sun* (Baltimore, MD), October 10, 1902; "Lost His Wife's $40,000," *Sun* (Baltimore, MD), December 1, 1904.
22. The first evidence of commercial activity appears in tax records for the transfer of the property and merchandise in 1905, though it is likely the operation began before then.
23. The first evidence of merchant activity appears in the tax records for 1903, but it is very possible the operation existed before then.
24. "Local Record," *Easton Star-Democrat*, June 3, 1879. The property transfer is recorded in a deed for the conveyance of lot 54 in Old Claiborne. See *Joseph T. Tunis and Helen D. Tunis, His Wife, to the Vestry of St. Michael's Parish*, property deed dated March 18, 1879, and recorded September 3, 1889, Talbot County, MD, Circuit Court Land Records, Plat Book 111: 46.
25. *Journal of the Thirteenth Annual Convention of the Protestant Episcopal Church in the Diocese of Easton* (John Cox [publisher], 1881), 436.
26. "Items of Local Interest," *Easton Star-Democrat*, June 4, 1889.
27. Other BC&A captains chose to live elsewhere. Following Spence as captains of *Cambridge*, for a short while, were Elmer "St. Elmo" Todd, who chose Easton for his home, and William H. H. Perry, who lived in Preston, until later moving to Baltimore. Each served as master for a brief period during the transition after Spence's death, before moving on to other commands. Spence's ultimate replacement was Samuel P. Stewart, former first mate on *Cambridge*

under Spence, and then captain of *Cambridge* starting in 1907. Stewart, who chose to live on the other end of the line in Baltimore, would go on to serve as master of *Cambridge* for more than fourteen years and became familiar to families and merchants transiting the Bay between Baltimore and Claiborne.

28. "News of the Railroads," *New York Times*, September 3, 1899.
29. "News of the Railroads," *New York Times*, September 5, 1899.
30. And what of the tax issue to which Wilson had referred? This was part of a long-running dispute between the owners of BC&A and various jurisdictions in Maryland in which it conducted business. BC&A argued that it was exempt from state and local tax in Maryland because of the way in which the bonds of B&ES were originally structured and approved by the state. The state and local taxing authorities argued that this original exemption had been overtaken by new legislation passed in 1896 and by virtue of the company's reorganization from B&ES to BC&A. BC&A protested and took two jurisdictions to court, losing on both occasions. See Baltimore, Chesapeake and Atlantic Railway Company v. City of Ocean City, 89 Md. 89, 42 A. 922. (1899); Baltimore, Chesapeake and Atlantic Railway Company v. Commissioners of Wicomico County, 93 Md. 113, 48 A. 853 (1901). They appealed this decision and lost in Baltimore, Chesapeake and Atlantic Railway v. Wicomico County Commissioners, 103 Md. 277, 63 A. 678 (Md. 1906). BC&A then took the case to the Supreme Court and lost again. See County Commissioners of Wicomico Mico County v. Samuel Bancroft Jr., 203 US 112, 27 S.Ct. 21, 51 L.Ed. 112 (1906).
31. "B., C. and A. Property," *Sun* (Baltimore, MD), August 23, 1899.
32. "Sale of a Railroad," *Sun* (Baltimore, MD), September 4, 1899.
33. Rights to use trackage from Lewes to Rehoboth, Delaware, were obtained from the Delaware, Maryland and Virginia Railroad (DMVR), which extended QARR's reach to that ocean resort.
34. "Fast Time to Ocean City," *Sun* (Baltimore, MD), December 9, 1897.
35. Had the QARR rail line existed a decade before, when Willard Thomson was attempting to save B&ES, it is entirely possible that service to Claiborne would have ended in 1891 when the Bay Ridge connection was terminated, and the eastern terminus of the new line from Baltimore shifted to Love Point.
36. As cars replaced trains, fewer people stopped at Love Point. When the ferry to Love Point ended in 1947, the hotel closed. It burned to the ground in 1965.
37. Why Virginia? While the rail line was confined to Maryland and Delaware, the steamboat operations included destinations in Virginia.
38. BC&A owned all of the common stock of MD&V and one-fifth of the preferred stock. See Poor's Manual of the Railroads of the United States, 1907 (*Poor's Railroad Manual Co., 1907*).

The steamer *Olive*, built in 1869, served Old Claiborne from Baltimore between 1877 and 1887, operating from a wharf at the head of Tilghman Creek. Photograph by Roger H. Burgess, n.d. Chesapeake Bay Maritime Museum, Robert H. Burgess Collection, 0000.1290.2952

Joseph B. Seth, while serving as speaker of the Maryland House of Delegates, founded the Baltimore and Eastern Shore Railroad in 1896. Unknown photographer, n.d. Talbot County Free Library, Maryland Room, binder 1, photo 111-A

Joseph B. Seth wanted to employ the large rail-transfer ferry *Groton*, moving it to the Chesapeake from the Thames River in Connecticut. It never arrived, instead burning and sinking en route. Photograph by Everett Augustus Scholfield, ca. 1890. Mystic Seaport Museum Digital Archives, 1933.174

B&ES had to rely upon the smaller, older, and unreliable *Thames River*. It lasted less than one year before being removed from service permanently. Unknown photographer, ca. 1890. Mariners' Museum and Park, Elwin Eldredge Collection, MS0091/03.01-24#008

An early aerial photograph of the BC&A rail line, terminal, and wharf in Claiborne. Along the right side is a partial image of Claiborne-Annapolis Ferry Inc.'s upgraded pier. Unknown photographer, 1920. Chesapeake Bay Maritime Museum, 0000.0731.0011

Service from Bay Ridge started with *Tockwogh* because *Thames River* was not ready in the summer of 1890. Unable to carry railcars, *Tockwogh* was an inadequate substitute for *Thames River*. Photograph by Wilfred Warren, n.d. Providence Public Library, Rhode Island Collection, VM013_GF5208

Olive replaced a failing *Thames River* in 1891. *Olive* was already familiar with these waters, having served Old Claiborne from Baltimore a few years earlier. Unknown photographer, n.d. Chesapeake Bay Maritime Museum, 0000.0173.0001

After the rail-transfer plan was abandoned in 1891, the steamer *B.S. Ford* began direct service to Claiborne from Baltimore, bypassing Bay Ridge entirely. Photograph by Samuel Ward Stanton, August 14, 1893. Mariners' Museum and Park, Regular Steamship Photographs Collection, P0001.003/01-#PB29231

Tangier served the Baltimore-Claiborne route from 1891 to 1894, alternating with *B.S. Ford*. Photograph by Samuel Ward Stanton, August 14, 1893. Mariners' Museum and Park, Collection of Samuel W. Stanton, MS0094/01-#0067

The elegant steamer *Cambridge* served the Baltimore-Claiborne route from 1894 to 1924. It was the longest-serving steamer or ferry connecting Claiborne to other parts of the Chesapeake. Photograph by Samuel Ward Stanton, August 31, 1896. Mariners' Museum and Park, Collection of Samuel W. Stanton, MS0094/01-#2521

Steamer *Tred Avon* would substitute for *Cambridge* during the latter's overhauls and complement it during busy summer periods. Photograph by Samuel Ward Stanton, August 29, 1896. Mariners' Museum and Park, Collection of Samuel W. Stanton, MS0094/01-#2412

BC&A created a fast steamer and rail service from Baltimore to Ocean City, MD, via the Claiborne hub. This revolutionized transportation to Ocean City. Courtesy of the Greater Harrington Historical Society

Passengers switched seamlessly from steamer to rail without ever leaving the BC&A Claiborne wharf. Photographer unknown, n.d. Courtesy of the Greater Harrington Historical Society

BC&A's express train, known as the "Flyer," speeds along the Eastern Shore from Claiborne to Ocean City. Photograph by H. Robins Hollyday, ca. 1920. Talbot Historical Society, H. Robins Hollyday Collection, 1981.019.001061

An early view of Claiborne village along Claiborne Road. Unknown photographer, ca. 1915. Courtesy of the Claiborne Association

Cambridge approaches Claiborne, alongside oyster shucking houses located on the breakwater from about 1890 to 1910. Unknown photographer, ca. 1895. Courtesy of the Maryland Center for History and Culture

This photo from 1920 shows the new Claiborne-Annapolis Ferry Inc.'s pier (center/top), built in 1912 and upgraded in 1919, alongside the longer railroad pier and breakwater. Unknown photographer, 1920. Courtesy of Flo Burdett

Atlantic, relocated from Maine, served only half a year on the Annapolis-Claiborne route before being removed from service in December 1912 after a major failure. Unknown photographer, ca. 1894. Mariners' Museum and Park, Elwin Eldredge Collection, MS0091/03.01-04#064b

Atlantic was replaced by the steam yacht *Texas* on the Annapolis-Claiborne route. *Texas* was purchased from the son of Henrietta Green, the "Witch of Wall Street" and arguably the richest woman in the world in 1916. Unknown photographer, 1912. Gift of the estate of H. Graham Wood, Chesapeake Bay Maritime Museum, 0000.0961.0103

From 1912 to 1916, two lines competed at Claiborne. Here, ESDSC's *Texas* (left) departs ahead of BC&A's *Tred Avon* (right). Unknown photographer, 1914. Gift of the estate of H. Graham Wood, Chesapeake Bay Maritime Museum, 0000.0899.0298

The small steamer *York River* was employed by ESDSC in 1915 after the other ESDSC steamers had all suffered failures; it was itself badly damaged in a collision shortly after entering service. Unknown photographer, 1915. From the Higgins Family Collection, courtesy of Daniel G. Higgins III

A meeting of key stakeholders in Claiborne-Annapolis Ferry Inc., including B. Frank Sherman (standing far left), Maryland Attorney General Albert C. Ritchie (seated far left), and Maryland Treasurer John M. Dennis (standing third from left), launched the company after Governor Emerson C. Harrington (seated second from right) signed the legislation that authorized the annual subsidy to the company, allowing it to begin operations. Unknown photographer, ca. 1919. From the B. F. Sherman Family Collection, courtesy of Margaret Bryan

The original 1912 ESDSC pier was expanded in 1919 for the new Claiborne-Annapolis car ferry. Hampden D. Mepham and two colleagues, standing toward the end of the pier, are inspecting the work. It was feared the three had perished during the return trip to Annapolis that evening, but they were later found safe after spending the night on the Bay in a small boat with a failed motor. Photograph by Harry Ogle Tunis, 1919. Private collection

The BC&A train rolls by in the background as workers complete the Claiborne-Annapolis car-ferry pier. Within five years the car-ferry service would render the train operation obsolete. Photograph by Harry Ogle Tunis, 1919. Private collection

Claiborne-Annapolis Ferry Inc. President Hampden D. Mepham chose steamer *Thomas Patten* as the first Claiborne-Annapolis car ferry. This decision also saved General Manager Charles B. Harrison from a failed investment. Photograph by Frederick J. Sedgwick, May 1905. Mariners' Museum and Park, Elwin Eldridge Collection, MS0095/02-#1215

Thomas Patten was renamed *Gov. Emerson C. Harrington*, after the then-serving governor whose efforts led to the creation of the new Claiborne-Annapolis Ferry Inc. Unknown photographer, ca. 1919. Mariners' Museum and Park, Elwin Eldredge Collection, MS0091-03-01-23-#65

The period between 1919 and 1924 was a golden era for Claiborne, with the small village served by a steamer/rail service (right) to Baltimore and car ferries (left) to Annapolis. Unknown photographer, ca. 1920. Gift of the estate of H. Graham Wood, Chesapeake Bay Maritime Museum, 0000.0960.0221

Gov. Emerson C. Harrington (left) and *Cambridge* (right) shared tight spaces in the turning basin in Claiborne. Unknown photographer, ca. 1920. Gift of the estate of H. Graham Wood, Chesapeake Bay Maritime Museum, 0000.0842.0057

The old sidewheel steamer *Gen. Lincoln* was added in 1920, but remained in service only two years before suffering a catastrophic failure in 1922. Unknown photographer, September 1916. Mariners' Museum and Park, Elwin Eldredge Collection, MS0091/03.01-72#058

The old and the new: a seaplane in front of a Claiborne train and terminal, probably in 1923. Unknown photographer, ca. 1923. Gift of Frank Ferrell, courtesy of the Kent Island Heritage Society

Cambridge made its last run to Claiborne in 1924, when BC&A finally abandoned the Baltimore-Claiborne route. Instead, Baltimore passengers headed to Ocean City would connect to a train at Love Point on Kent Island and then switch rail lines at Easton to bypass Claiborne entirely. Unknown photographer, n.d. Talbot Historical Society, 1981.019.020832

The old steamer *Gen. Lincoln* was ill-equipped to carry automobiles. It often proved easier to pick them up off the pier and carry them aboard the ferry. Photograph by B. Frank Sherman, ca. 1921. From the B. F. Sherman Family Collection, courtesy of Margaret Bryan

Majestic replaced the disabled *Gen. Lincoln*, starting service in 1923. It was taken out of service in 1926 when the first diesel double-ender ferry entered operation. Photograph by H. Robins Hollyday, n.d. Talbot Historical Society, H. Robins Hollyday Collection, 1981.019.014962

Delays in loading automobiles, as shown here on *Majestic*, often led to long turnarounds, resulting in fewer ferry trips per day and poor financial performance. Photograph by Percy E. Budlong, July 30, 1923. Chesapeake Bay Maritime Museum, Robert H. Burgess Collection, 0000.1290.3155

Majestic sank in the Baltimore Harbor in 1927, risking the lives of 970 passengers. All survived, but the resulting inquiry into the incident surfaced deep racial tensions in Baltimore. Unknown photographer, July 25, 1927. Courtesy of *The Baltimore Sun*

In 1926, the double-ender *Gov. Albert C. Ritchie* revolutionized the Claiborne car-ferry service, finally putting the company on a profitable footing. Photograph by H. Robins Hollyday, ca. 1935. Talbot Historical Society, H. Robins Hollyday Collection, 1981.019.001094

The Claiborne-Annapolis Ferry Inc. pier (upper right) had to be redesigned to accommodate new double-enders. The largely abandoned BC&A ferry pier remains visible in the center. Photograph by J. Victor Dallin, August 16, 1929. Hagley Digital Archives, J. Victor Dallin Aerial Survey Collection, 1970.200

Robert and Nodie North in front of their new Sea Gull Inn at the Claiborne wharf. Unknown photographer, ca. 1921. From the personal collection of Judge John C. North Jr.

The modern ferry *John M. Dennis* joined the fleet in 1929. It was largely taken off the Annapolis-Claiborne route after 1935, instead serving only the new terminal at Matapeake in Kent Island until the line ended in 1952. Photograph by Henry W. Gillen, ca. 1929. Mariners' Museum and Park, Museum Photography Collection, P0010/-#170

In 1930, the Claiborne-Annapolis Ferry Company opened a new, shorter route from Annapolis to Matapeake, allowing drivers to bypass Claiborne. Thus began the slow decline of Claiborne's commercial activity. Unknown photographer, July 11, 1930. *The Baltimore Sun*, BNK-773-BS

Busy days in Matapeake: *John M. Dennis* (left) and *Gov. Albert C. Ritchie* (right) load cars at this modern ferry terminal on Kent Island. Photograph by A. Aubrey Bodine, 1940. From the A. Aubrey Bodine Collection (aaubreybodine.com), ID 41-501

The new *Gov. Harry W. Nice* was placed on the Annapolis-Matapeake route in April 1938. It would dock at Claiborne only on rare occasions. Photograph by H. Robins Hollyday, 1938. Talbot Historical Society, H. Robins Hollyday Collection, 1981.019.001089

The grand opening of Kent Island's Romancoke wharf in 1938 meant the end of direct cross-bay service to Claiborne for the first time in almost five decades. The village's slow decline accelerated after this. Uknown photographer, 1938. From the B. F. Sherman Family Collection, courtesy of Margaret Bryan

The new Romancoke wharf on Kent Island was "bare bones," with any form of entertainment or commercial activity barred by the deed of sale. Unknown photographer, 1947. Chesapeake Bay Maritime Museum, 0000.0178.0004

The old coal-fired *Gov. Emerson C. Harrington* (far right) was removed from service in 1937. Photograph by B. F. Sherman, 1933. Chesapeake Bay Maritime Museum, 0000.0899.0061

Gov. Emerson C. Harrington was turned into a restaurant in Pocomoke City, Maryland, in 1938. It soon failed, was relocated to Annapolis as a hotel, and then failed there as well. Unknown photographer, ca. 1939, Chesapeake Bay Maritime Museum, 0000.0655.0002

The coal-fired *Gov. Emerson C. Harrington II* was acquired specifically for the new the Romancoke-Claiborne shuttle. However, it would be diverted to the Annapolis-Matapeake route when traffic on the route was heavy, leaving Claiborne without any service. Photography by H. Robins Hollyday, ca. 1941. Talbot Historical Society, H. Robins Hollyday Collection, 1981.019.014956

Daniel Higgins (right) was the senior captain of the Claiborne-Annapolis Ferry Company, and served aboard most of the system's ferries. He made his home in Claiborne. Unknown photographer, n.d. From the Higgins Family Collection, courtesy of Daniel G. Higgins III

The Higgins brothers, Gardner (left), Edward (Ned) (center), and Daniel (right), served for decades as ferry captains, as did several of their sons. Unknown photographer, n.d. From the Higgins Family Collection, courtesy of Daniel G. Higgins III

SHORTEST
CONNECTING
LINK BETWEEN
EASTERN AND
WESTERN SHORES
OF MARYLAND
SHORTEST
CONNECTING
LINK BETWEEN
EASTERN AND
WESTERN SHORES
OF MARYLAND
CLAIBORNE-ANNAPOLIS FERRY
JOHN M. DENNIS
ANNAPOLIS
CLAIBORNE
& MATAPEAKE
FERRIES
ANNAPOLIS
CLAIBORNE
& MATAPEAKE
FERRIES

ANNAPOLIS — MATAPEAKE
ROMANCOKE — CLAIBORNE
FERRIES

EFFECTIVE SCHEDULE
Subject To Change Without Notice

DAILY AND SUNDAY
Eastern War Time

Between Annapolis and Matapeake

LEAVE ANNAPOLIS	LEAVE MATAPEAKE
7:25 A. M.	7:25 A. M.
8:00 A. M.	8:00 A. M.
9:00 A. M. (c)	9:00 A. M.
10:00 A. M.	10:00 A. M.
11:00 A. M.	11:00 A. M.
12:00 Noon	12:00 Noon
1:00 P. M. (c)	1:00 P. M.
2:00 P. M.	2:00 P. M.
3:00 P. M. (c)	3:00 P. M.
4:00 P. M.	4:00 P. M.
*5:00 P. M. (c)	5:00 P. M.
6:00 P. M.	6:00 P. M.
7:00 P. M. (c)	7:00 P. M.
8:00 P. M.	8:00 P. M.

(c) Ferry service through to Claiborne for vehicles via prompt connection at Romancoke.
*Bus transportation furnished between Matapeake and Romancoke for pedestrians destined for Claiborne — Daily and Sunday.

Between Romancoke and Claiborne

LEAVE ROMANCOKE	LEAVE CLAIBORNE
10:00 A. M.	†9:00 A. M.
2:00 P. M.	1:00 P. M.
4:00 P. M.	3:00 P. M.
6:00 P. M.	5:00 P. M.
8:00 P. M.	‡7:00 P. M.

†Bus transportation furnished between Romancoke and Matapeake for pedestrians destined for Annapolis — Daily and Sunday.
‡Same as above note for pedestrians — SUNDAYS ONLY.
NOTE—All boats leaving Claiborne make connections with boats leaving Matapeake 1 hour later.

For Connecting Carrier Information, Consult:
Red Star Motor Coaches, Inc.
Salisbury and Baltimore, Md.
Baltimore & Annapolis R. R. Co.
Baltimore, Md.
Pennsylvania Greyhound Lines
Washington, D. C.

B. Frank Sherman, General Mgr.
Annapolis, Maryland

DESTROY ALL PREVIOUS ISSUES

USE MARYLAND'S
CHESAPEAKE BAY
FERRY SYSTEM

Save GAS TIRES and TIME

State Roads Commission
OF MARYLAND

Chesapeake Bay Ferry System
EFFECTIVE SCHEDULE

Between
Annapolis — Matapeake
Romancoke — Claiborne

For Further Information Write:
CHESAPEAKE BAY FERRY SYSTEM
F. P. LEITHISER, Advertising Director
108 East Lexington Street
Baltimore, Md.

Issued August 1, 1942

SHORTEST ROUTE to and from
THE EASTERN SHORE

In 1941, the Claiborne-Annapolis Ferry Company (CAFC) became the state-owned Chesapeake Bay Ferry System (CBFS). These two brochures reflect this change, with the CAFC brochure (page 108) changing to the CBFS brochure (this page) after the state assumed control of the company. The sale generated an attractive financial payout to former governor Emerson C. Harrington. Unknown graphic artist, n.d. Courtesy of John Conley

From 1919 to 1943, the car ferries' western terminal was located in downtown Annapolis. Photograph by the Baltimore Gas & Electric Company, 1929. Baltimore Museum of Industry, BGE.2399N

In 1944 *Gov. Albert C. Ritchie* failed a structural inspection and was scrapped. It was deemed impractical to try to repair the ferry during World War II. Unknown photographer, ca. 1919–1920. Maryland Center for History and Culture, H. Furlong Baldwin Library, Peale/Baltimore City Life Museum Glass Negatives Collection, MC6824

Claiborne's pier (bottom left) was condemmed in 1944 in a (failed) effort to shut down operations. Photograph by H. Robins Hollyday, ca. 1933. Talbot Historical Society, H. Robins Hollyday Collection, 1981.019.019642

In 1945, the coal-fired *Gov. Emerson C. Harrington II* was converted to diesel engines, leaving Claiborne without any ferry service for more than a year. Photograph by H. Robins Hollyday, ca. 1946. Talbot Historical Society, H. Robins Hollyday Collection, 1981.019.015009

Matapeake was upgraded in 1946 so that two ferries could operate simultaneously. The additional capacity was required to accommodate booming traffic after World War II. Photograph by H. Robins Hollyday, ca. 1946. Talbot Historical Society, H. Robins Hollyday Collection, 1981.019.002208

CBFS added *Gov. Herbert R. O'Conor* in 1947 to expand capacity on the line between Sandy Point and Matapeake. Photograph by H. Robins Hollyday, ca. 1948. Talbot Historical Society, H. Robins Hollyday Collection, 1981.019.010104

CFBS added *Eastern Bay* in 1948. It was soon renamed *B. Frank Sherman* after the long-serving general manager. Photograph by H. Robins Hollyday, ca. 1948. Talbot Historical Society, H. Robins Hollyday Collection, 1981.019.010107

John M. Dennis (left) *B. Frank Sherman* (right) at the upgraded Sandy Point terminal shortly before the line closed for good. Photograph by A. Aubrey Bodine, 1952. Mariners' Museum and Park, P0001.003.01-PB13046

The Romancoke-Claiborne line limped along for a few months in 1952 after the main Sandy Point-Matapeake line closed. It was served by the old *Gov. Emerson C. Harrington II,* shown here docking at Romancoke in 1947. Unknown photographer, 1947. Chesapeake Bay Maritime Museum, 0000.0178.0001

The new Chesapeake Bay Bridge, pictured in the background, rendered the ferries obsolete in 1952, terminating the role of ferry *B. Frank Sherman* with the company after only three years. Unknown photographer, n.d. Enoch Pratt Free Library, State Library Resource Center, mdph001998

For reasons that remain uncertain, ferry *John M. Dennis* rammed the Bay Bridge shortly before it opened in 1952. Unknown photographer, 1952. Chesapeake Bay Maritime Museum, 0000.0369.0008

General Manager B. Frank Sherman (left) and Maryland Governor Theodore McKeldin (right) bid a last farewell to *Matapeake*. Unknown photographer, 1952. From the B. F. Sherman Family Collection, courtesy of Margaret Bryan

The Claiborne ticket office was moved to its current location for use as a residence. The earlier ticket office had been moved and repurposed in 1932. Both are still serving as residences in Claiborne. Unknown photographer, ca. 1954. From the personal collection of Lorraine Renshaw, courtesy of Jeanne and Mike Kuperberg

V

Trouble on the Line

The first part of the twentieth century saw the United States engaged in political and social turmoil across a number of contentious issues, including labor rights, racial segregation, and abuses of corporate monopolies. Each of these both affected and were mirrored in the challenges faced by the Baltimore, Chesapeake and Atlantic Railway (BC&A) during this period.

The 1906 Captains' Strike

On March 6, 1906, Samuel Gompers, the president of the American Federation of Labor (AFL), published a letter to leaders in the US government outlining *Labor's Bill of Grievances*. It was a watershed moment in the national political agenda of the AFL, an organization founded the very year (1886) that Joseph B. Seth had first established the Baltimore and Eastern Shore Railroad (B&ES), the forerunner of BC&A. Just a few months after the AFL letter was published, labor turmoil reached BC&A itself.

Labor relations between BC&A (including the Maryland, Delaware and Virginia Railway Company [MD&V]) and its licensed masters, first mates, and second mates had already begun to erode over the years as BC&A was managed as a "cash cow" for the parent Pennsylvania Railroad. Tensions crested in October 1906 when virtually every licensed deck officer turned in their resignations to General Manager Willard Thomson and then walked off their steamboats. Close to thirty of the steamboats operated by BC&A were idled. For almost two weeks, the normally busy waters of the Chesapeake Bay seemed quiet. Steamboats, rather than churning up those waters, sat idle and rose and fell with the tide alongside empty wharves. Shellfish piling up on Eastern Shore wharves began to spoil, broadcasting their unique perfume across nearby towns. Fertilizer required for Eastern Shore farm fields, normally applied in the autumn, could not be delivered. Passengers were stranded, and much commerce was halted. How did this come about?

For three decades, across both the US Atlantic Coast and the Great Lakes, the officers directing the American fleet of steamships began to organize themselves, mirroring broader trends in the union movement. The Brotherhood of Steam Pilots was launched in New York City in 1887. It grew from that one harbor to others and expanded to include mates (other deck officers), changing its name in 1900 to the American Association of Masters, Mates and Pilots of Steam Vessels (MM&P). (The MM&P name changed again in 1954 to the present-day International Organization of Masters, Mates and Pilots.) Formed largely as a benevolent organization, at first defending captains charged with criminal neglect in accidents and supporting families of officers killed on the job, it later evolved into an advocacy group, pushing for better working conditions and higher pay.[1] It would eventually affiliate with the AFL, though not until 1914.

The Baltimore chapter of the MM&P was Rescue Harbor no. 14, and most deck officers at BC&A and MD&V were members. On June 29, 1906, the national leadership of MM&P dispatched a polite letter—their own version of Gompers's *Labor Bill of Grievances*—to BC&A general manager, Willard Thomson, laying out a series of complaints on the part of employees and articulating the case for higher wages. The letter suggested specific wage levels for deck officers for each of the BC&A and MD&V steamboat lines, including both Love Point and Claiborne. Some nineteen masters, twenty-one first mates, twenty-one second mates, and four quartermasters were identified by name in the letter as supporting this action. The letter did not mention or threaten any job action.[2]

Willard's response was immediate—and prickly. He simply and adamantly refused to engage in any discussion with the MM&P, period. There would be no dialogue, and his word was final. As he laid out his logic in a later letter to *The Sun* of Baltimore:

> We simply want to conduct our own business and not turn it over to outsiders. We want to deal with our own men if they have any complaints to make. We have told them we are willing to adjust their wages. They work for us, and we have no contract and no dealings with any organization, benevolent or otherwise.[3]

The situation stewed over the next three months. Finally, with growing impatience, the officers acted. At a late summer meeting the MM&P members decided to call Thomson's bluff. A resolution was passed affirming that if an agreement were not reached by September 20, all of the officers (except three, as agreed to by the union) would tender their resignations to BC&A and MD&V, effective October 1. The sixty-three officers acting in this way would leave their boats and idle the bulk of the fleet. The result . . .

> . . . was almost a complete cessation of traffic on the Chesapeake Bay; as these companies practically controlled some thirty boats and railroad connections on the Eastern Shore for the transportation of the cargoes carried by the boats from the City of Baltimore, or from the Eastern Shore to the city of Baltimore.[4]

Seeing the potential for major economic harm to the state's economy, the Maryland Bureau of Statistics and Information decided to intervene as arbitrator, using the powers recently granted to it by the Arbitration Act passed by the Maryland legislature in 1904. Their initial approach was amicable in tone, asking both parties to simply meet together with the Bureau to discuss the issues. The union responded at once, reciprocating the original letter's cordial tone, and indicating that it "will be glad to avail themselves of your offer." Thomson responded via his company's lawyer, who drafted a three-page letter reaffirming that the company did not intend to deal at all with the MM&P union and suggesting (albeit in legal language) that the Bureau should, in effect, keeps its nose out of other peoples' business.[5]

Thomson's view seemed unshakable and focused almost entirely on principle rather than practicality. It was probably hard for him to see his domination of BC&A challenged—he had been in charge for almost fifteen years at that point, and he was master of his empire of steamer lines and railroads. Tensions began to rise. Using the power granted to it by the legislature, the Bureau of Statistics and Information conducted a hearing, issuing summons for both the union representatives and Willard Thomson to appear. The striking officers showed up in force and made quite a scene for the public, as noted by an admiring observer: "The little room in which the investigation was held was crowded with men whose sun-browned visages and sturdy frames spoke of long years on the water."[6]

Thomson did not show, sending his lawyer instead, who simply reiterated the company's refusal to have any discussion with the national union representatives. They insisted they would only deal with their own employees, without national union involvement. As these tribulations were revealed daily in the press, and as traffic remained idled, anger against Thomson began to grow. Thomson was losing the battle for public opinion:

> The masters and pilots say they will win or starve, and Captain Thomson is reported as saying that he will take action to revoke their licenses. . . . The people along the route have learned to admire the officers on these steamers, and their sympathy is all with them.[7]

Meanwhile, the crabs and oysters piled up at wharves on the Eastern Shore continued to rot and the fields were left unfertilized. The local economy was starting to feel the pain.

Finally, after being stonewalled for a week, the Bureau of Statistics and Information issued a public report—reprinted as an advertisement in the local newspaper—that squarely placed the blame for the crisis on Willard Thomson alone. Chief of the bureau, Charles J. Fox, then dropped the hammer, deploying what later generations might call the "nuclear option":

> . . . in view of these facts and the arbitrary refusal to consider these questions of differences between employer and employe [sic], in an ordinary business manner, fully justify us in suggesting to the Governor of this State that he take such steps as may compel the corporations named either to perform the public service for which they were chartered or *vacate such franchise*. [Italics added.][8]

Thomson had met his match in Mr. Fox, a dedicated civil servant who would go on to run his bureau for another three decades. Faced with the elimination of the monopoly franchise that had been generating such attractive financial returns, Thomson capitulated, while insisting publicly he had done no such thing. The recommended wages were adopted (varying somewhat, according to the length of the routes involved): $100 to $125 per month for masters, $65 to $80 per month for first officers, $45 to $60 per month for second officers, and $35 per month for quartermasters. The MM&P would continue to represent the officers, even as Thomson maintained his insistence that he would have nothing to do with that association. On October 13, the steamers once again carved wakes across and down the Chesapeake, and commerce resumed.

Business at BC&A steadied for a while. For the next decade, *Love Point* and its successors churned the waters to Love Point while *Cambridge* (at times replaced by *Tred Avon*) did the same to Claiborne. The business continued to generate high returns for shareholders of BC&A. The only major glitch in operations was when *Love Point* burst into flames on March 18, 1909, and burned to the waterline.[9] Its hull and machinery sat there for all to see until it was removed later that year. BC&A, ever looking to minimize investment, placed the aging steamboat *Westmoreland*—even older than *Love Point*—on the route starting May 28.[10]

Race Relations

The ferry *Love Point* was not the only burning issue affecting BC&A and other ferry companies; Maryland had a legacy as a slave state before and during the Civil War. Exempt from the Emancipation Proclamation, which freed enslaved persons only in states then in rebellion, Maryland did not end slavery until a new constitution was ratified in November 1864. Although by the early 1900s, Black people in Maryland had been freed legally for almost two generations, racial segregation was still the order of the day. Efforts to institutionalize that separation expanded at the end of the nineteenth century with the broadened application of regulations known as Jim Crow laws, enforced when necessary, in their view, by white supremacist organizations such as the Ku Klux Klan. For example, in 1904, Jim Crow rules on railroads and steamboats meant that racial segregation, practiced informally beforehand, was officially enshrined in the Maryland Code of General Laws. How did this come about?

Black people had been guaranteed "full and equal" accommodations with whites when it came to "conveyances on land and water" in the Civil Rights Act of 1875. Over the following three years, a series of US Supreme Court decisions, especially Hall v. Decuir, 95 US 485 (1878), clarified, and in part voided, this act by embedding segregation into law and practice when it came to transportation on steamships and railroads. The court ruled that states were not permitted to require integration on the part of any business involved in interstate commerce, even if the trips involved took place only within that state's own borders. Homer Plessy, a mixed-race man in Louisiana, tried to test the laws on separation of races by sitting in a whites-only section of a railroad car. His case went all the way to the Supreme Court, yielding the infamous Plessy v. Ferguson decision of 1896, which allowed states to compel the separation of races in public transport.

Southern states took advantage of these new powers. Virginia passed legislation in 1900 *requiring* segregation of races on steamboats operating within its waters. Since many of these boats also operated in Maryland, segregation became effectively institutionalized in that state as well. The first case taken to trial under that new Virginia law was against BC&A Captain Wesley Thomas of Baltimore, master of the steamboat *Ida*. Observers at Queen's Point, Virginia, had seen both Black and white passengers sitting on the foredeck of *Ida*, and this commingling was seen as a violation of the rules for segregation. Captain Thomas was indicted and taken to trial. Fortunately for him, Thomas was acquitted with the help of his attorney, Albert C. Ritchie.

By 1904, Maryland's legislature followed Virginia and established segregation on steamboats and railroad cars, not just as an option but as a legal mandate. It is worth presenting the two main sections of the law in full:

> SECTION 1. *Be it enacted by the General Assembly of Maryland*, That it shall be the duty of any captain, purser or other officer in command of any steamboat carrying passengers and plying in the waters within the jurisdiction of the State of Maryland to assign white and colored passengers on said boat to the respective locations they are to occupy as passengers while on said boat: and that it shall be the duty of said captain, purser or other officer in command to separate, as far as the construction of his boat and due consideration for the comfort of the passengers will permit, the white and colored passengers on said boat in the sitting, sleeping and eating apartments; provided, however, that no discrimination shall be made in the quality and convenience of accommodation afforded passengers in said locations, and provided, that this Act shall not apply to nurses or attendants traveling with their employers, nor to officers in charge of prisoners, whether the said prisoners are white or colored, or both white and colored, or to prisoners in their custody.

> SECTION 2. *And be it enacted*, That any captain, purser of other officer in command of any steamboat as aforesaid who shall refuse to carry out the provisions of Section I of this Act shall be deemed guilty of a misdemeanor, and, upon indictment in any court having jurisdiction, and conviction thereof, shall be fined not less than twenty-five dollars, and not more than fifty dollars for each offense.[11]

BC&A, and its subsidiary MD&V, had to ensure its railcars, steamboats, and protocols were configured to make sure the law was fully executed on their rail and steamboat lines. "Separate but equal" was the law of the land for BC&A in Maryland.

Not everyone was content with the "equal" nature of the provisions made for Black passengers aboard BC&A steamboats and trains. In particular, a Black lawyer named William Ashbie Hawkins registered a complaint in 1911 about how first-class Black passengers were treated by BC&A, based on experiences aboard *Avalon* and *Joppa* on overnight trips from Baltimore to the Choptank River. Hawkins took his case to the Maryland Public Service Commission (PSC) with specific objections to the following:

> . . . only two staterooms are assigned for the use of colored passengers; that these are inside rooms, illy ventilated and the least desirable rooms on the boat; and that when these are sold no other rooms can be obtained by colored passengers.
>
> . . . no accommodation is made for serving meals to colored passengers, except at an hour when all white persons have been served.

The PSC reviewed the case in a hearing on December 4, 1911, and ultimately dismissed the complaint, but not without informing BC&A that it needed to reconfigure its accommodations to ensure that the "separate" accommodations were in fact "equal."[12] Nowhere was the separation of accommodations ever questioned.

The next year Hawkins filed another case with the Maryland

PSC, this time involving a BC&A railroad trip from Claiborne to Salisbury. On November 12, 1912, Thomas W. Turner, a Black man, was traveling with his wife when he observed that the conditions of compartments assigned to Black passengers were substantially inferior to those assigned to white passengers. Specifically, while compartments for white passengers were cleaned at the end of each train journey (remember, BC&A was also known as "Black Cinders and Ashes" due to the engine's steam entering the rear cabins), the cars for Black passengers were not. Moreover, the only accommodations for Black passengers were in a small section of the smoking car, with the rest of the car occupied by white passengers. There was no way for Black passengers to avoid the smoke. This small section reserved for Black passengers also lacked adequate toilet facilities, certainly in comparison with the facilities provided for white passengers[13]

As before, the Maryland PSC viewed this complaint only through the lens of "equal" rather than "separate." Its response reaffirmed the legality of requiring BC&A to provide separate accommodations for trains out of Claiborne, but also ordered BC&A to provide equal toilet facilities in each section of a divided car and to install a partition to separate smoking and nonsmoking passengers in the Black seating area.[14]

Segregation would remain the practice on Chesapeake ferries for another four decades, even when it had largely begun to disappear on other modes of transportation in Maryland. (Segregation in trolleys and streetcars in Baltimore ended in practice in 1871.[15]) It was not until March of 1951 that this practice would be banned on ferries in Maryland. Notably, one-quarter of Maryland's state senators, all but one of them from the Eastern Shore, voted *against* desegregation on ferries that year. Over one-third of the members of the House of Delegates—again primarily from the Eastern Shore—voted to retain racial segregation on the ferries. Given that the ferry system would come to a complete halt in 1952, the practical effect of this new statute was trivial.[16]

Customer Frustrations Lead to Demands for Competition

There were other controversies closer to home for BC&A, ones mirroring the national debate about antitrust and monopoly power. While the continued performance on the Claiborne and Love Point routes may have pleased the investors in BC&A—primarily PRR—the satisfaction of customers was becoming undermined by what those customers saw as high fares, old steamboats, and inadequate service. As one observer declared:

> It is hard to believe that those investors are shouting for joy when the company, in the face of immense offerings of freights at high rates, seems determined to carry as little as possible. The investor is hardly happy to learn that passengers and freights are delayed and that goods are left on the wharves through the sheer inability of the company to transport them.[17]

There was merit to this criticism. The BC&A and MD&V fleets were mostly comprised of old, tired steamers. At a time when steamboats were expected to have an average useful life in scheduled service of only about thirty years, a sizable proportion of the BC&A and MD&V fleet was already approaching that use-by date. *Westmoreland*, which would start on the Love Point route in 1909, would be twenty-seven years old at that point. *Cambridge*, serving Claiborne, was relatively new when put on the route in 1894, but would be nine-teen years old by 1909.

BC&A could apparently afford to upgrade its fleet but, under Thomson's leadership, had decided against it. One investor in BC&A explained the approach:

> . . . the company does not use the money it makes for the purpose of extending its business, but takes this money and lends it to the Pennsylvania Railroad Company at a low rate of interest, instead of building new steamers and

maintaining the older ones in their best state of efficiency to take care of the vast amount of business which it has monopolized on the Chesapeake.[18]

Locals wanted better service. Baltimore Mayor J. Barry Mahool called a summit to address the issues—and got an earful. Samuel C. Appleby, a reporter for *The Sun* newspaper in Baltimore who had studied the issue in detail, addressed the mayor:

> The hitches between the steamboats and the railroads, the long delays in handling freight and the inadequate steamboat service of the Baltimore, Chesapeake and Atlantic Railway and the Delaware, Maryland and Virginia Company, certainly demand your attention.
>
> . . . The conclusion the people down in [the Eastern Shore] have reached is that there must be an opposition line or lines or there must be threats of such a line or lines, and that a maximum and minimum freight rate must be fixed and that a State commission must enforce it, so that any opposition company will not be driven out of business by the ruinous cutting of rates by the Pennsylvania [Railroad].[19]

Another critic of BC&A's approach was a local Claiborne resident by the name of Albert Lowe, who alleged that BC&A was disadvantaging merchants who shipped by steamboat to Baltimore while favoring those who shipped by rail to Philadelphia. He explained that it cost him about the same to ship a calf by steamer to Baltimore as it did to ship a calf to Philadelphia, even though the latter was twice as far a journey.[20] Albert Lowe would emerge a few years later as a pivotal figure in an effort to take on the BC&A monopoly.

PRR, the ultimate entity controlling BC&A and MD&V, worked hard to maintain its effective monopoly on steamers to and railroads across the Eastern Shore. Competitors attempted to start new services on the Bay, but those efforts typically failed after BC&A would cut rates, temporarily, to drive them out of business. Willard Thomson is said to have exclaimed, after yet another independent line went belly up, that "The Pennsylvania does not mind losing $10,000 to teach an object lesson."[21]

Not everyone within BC&A agreed with Thomson's priorities: sending cash to PRR as opposed to improving service across the Chesapeake. The day after the mayor's summit, Tully A. Joynes, the BC&A superintendent overseeing all of the steamboat lines, resigned—at the insistence, he declared, of Willard Thomson. Joynes and Thomson had reached a fundamental point of disagreement on how much BC&A should spend to maintain and improve the fleet of steamers running on the Chesapeake.

> Captain Thomson is said to be a strict economist and favors making few and then only necessary repairs at times when they are imperative, but Mr. Joynes has the reputation of being in favor of a more liberal policy and has always favored spending sufficient money upon the boats to keep them at all times in good repair and make them last longer.[22]

Thomson seemed perfectly content to spend as little as needed to keep the boats operating and passing inspection. Thomson himself survived this criticism, despite rumors that he would follow Joynes out the door and onto the street. The old steamers kept churning.

But the BC&A monopoly was about to be challenged once again. In a recurring pattern, the new entrant would target an underserved market (Annapolis-Claiborne) using a new operating model (small but fast steam yachts). Once again, Claiborne would be the center of it, and would benefit as well.

Notes

1. Benjamin M. Squires, "Association of Harbor Boat Owners and Employees in the Port of New York," *Monthly Labor Review* 7, no. 2 (August 1918): 51.
2. The letter is reprinted in Charles J. Fox and J. G. Schonfarber, Annual Report of the Bureau of Statistics and Information of Maryland for 1906 (Kohn & Pollock, 1907), 92–93.
3. "Capt. Thomson Explains," *Sun* (Baltimore, MD), October 12, 1906.
4. Charles J. Fox and J. G. Schonfarber, *Annual Report of the Bureau of Statistics and Information of Maryland for 1906* (Kohn & Pollock, 1907), 94.
5. The communications between MM&P, BC&A, and the Bureau of Statistics and Information are reprinted in full in Charles J. Fox and J. G. Schonfarber, *Annual Report of the Bureau of Statistics and Information of Maryland for 1906* (Kohn & Pollock, 1907), 97–101.
6. "Masters Tell of Tie-Up," *Sun* (Baltimore, MD), October 9, 1906.
7. "Steamboats Still Idle," *Sun* (Baltimore, MD) October 4, 1906.
8. "Office of the Maryland Bureau of Statistics and Information," *Sun* (Baltimore, MD), October 11, 1906.
9. The steamboat had been tied up overnight at the Love Point wharf, and the crew barely escaped the fire, with the captain fleeing the vessel only half-dressed. Efforts were made to put out the fire, but the battle soon appeared hopeless. In order to at least save the wharf, *Love Point* was cut loose and allowed to drift toward shore where it ran aground and burned. See "Steamer Love Point Is Burned," *Denton Journal*, March 20, 1909.
10. "Storm Drenches City," *Sun* (Baltimore, MD), May 28, 1909.
11. Act of March 17, 1904, Ch. 110, 1904, MD Laws 209 (Misdemeanor for failing to maintain racially segregated quarters on steamboats). See Laws of the State of Maryland: Made and Passed (John Murphy Co., 1904; repr., Maryland State Archives, 2000), 209: 188. Citation refers to the edition in the Maryland State Archives, msa.maryland.gov/megafile/msa/speccol/sc2900/sc2908/000001/000209/html/am209–189.html.
12. "In the Matter of The Compliant of W. Ashbie Hawkins vs. Baltimore, Chesapeake and Atlantic Railway Company," *Annual Report of the Maryland Public Service Commission for 1912* (Sun Book and Job Printing Office, 1913), 415–17.
13. "Complaint of Thomas W. Turner vs. Baltimore, Chesapeake and Atlantic Railway Company," Case No. 522, *Annual Report of the Maryland Public Service Commission for 1913* (Sun Publishing Company, 1914), 101–3.
14. Order No. 1000, Case No. 522, in "Complaint of Thomas W. Turner vs. Baltimore, Chesapeake and Atlantic Railway Company," *Annual Report of the*

Maryland Public Service Commission for 1913 (Sun Publishing Company, 1914), 104–5.

15. David S. Bogen, "Precursors of Rosa Parks: Maryland Transportation Cases Between the Civil War and the Beginning of World War I," *Maryland Law Review* vol 63 (2004), 733.
16. "House Passes Repealer of 'Jim Crow' Act," *Sun* (Baltimore, MD), January 31, 1951.
17. "The Bay Trade: Baltimore, Chesapeake and Atlantic Has Made Much Money," *Sun* (Baltimore, MD), August 6, 1907.
18. "Can B., C. and A. Do It?" *Sun* (Baltimore, MD), August 12, 1907.
19. "Pennsy Scored," *Sun* (Baltimore, MD), August 1, 1907.
20. "Can B., C. and A. Do It?" *Sun* (Baltimore, MD), August 12, 1907.
21. "Pennsy Scored," *Sun* (Baltimore, MD), August 1, 1907.
22. "Says He Was Forced Out," *Sun* (Baltimore, MD), August 2, 1907.

VI

Eastern Shore Development Steamship Company

Poor Annapolis.

When the rail link across the Chesapeake was first established in 1890, the focal point of the system was Annapolis. The ferry left from nearby Bay Ridge, just a short rail hop away. Then, just a year after that service started, all that was set aside, and the Baltimore and Eastern Shore Railroad (B&ES) shifted its Western-Shore terminal to Baltimore, the big city to the northwest. New owners Baltimore, Chesapeake and Atlantic Railway (BC&A) continued that route. Now passengers and cargo in Annapolis heading to the rail line in Claiborne had to make the journey first to Baltimore—traveling in the opposite direction—and only then catch the steamer to Claiborne. Even the opening of the new steamboat line to Love Point in 1902 required a preliminary trek to Baltimore for any passengers or cargo originating in Annapolis. This was about to change, once again driven by outside forces and New York investors. In 1911, three ambitious entrepreneurs from the Empire State launched the Eastern Shore Development Steamship Company (ESDSC).

ESDSC is the "Rodney Dangerfield" of Claiborne steamer and ferry companies—it gets no respect. It is often ignored entirely by historians, especially in comparison to the much larger Claiborne-Annapolis Ferry Company that followed on its heels and benefited from its experience. While it lasted just a few years, ESDSC did pave the way for its far more successful follower. And it—not the Claiborne-Annapolis Ferry Inc.—is the reason there are two ferry wharves in Claiborne. Thus, its brief story is an important one.

A New Competitor Emerges

Leading the effort, and serving as the initial president of ESDSC, was Andrew J. McIntosh. Born in 1866 in Philadelphia, he relocated to New York. Described as a tall (six feet, three inches) thin man with a pointed chin, aquiline nose, and fair hair mixed with gray, McIntosh was determined to pursue his fortune, initially working, and faltering, in the feathers business, supplying down-filled quilts and cushions.[1]

A second and more successful venture was A.J. McIntosh Yacht Brokers, based in Manhattan. There he prospered as an agent in transactions involving expensive yachts being bought and sold across the large yachting community along the shores of Long Island. Meanwhile, working with his two brothers, John and Frederick, he entered the marina business, building the McIntosh Boat Basin in Brooklyn. That venture generated a good return when the property was acquired in 1906 by the Delaware, Lackawanna and Western Railroad for conversion into a freight terminal.[2] McIntosh had his substantial gain.[3] Now he was looking for somewhere to invest it. Feathers, quilts, and cushions were out. He was looking for something involving boats.

There is little doubt about the source of the wealth of McIntosh's co-investor, Bernard A. Sinn, a co-founder of the Wall Street banking firm Steinberger, Sinn & Company, a fixture on the New York Stock Exchange. Sinn would join the management of ESDSC as a vice president and later serve as president, retiring from his investment banking business in 1913. Born in Frankfurt, Germany, he had immigrated as a young child to the United States in 1879, settling in New York and building his fortune on Wall Street.

Entrepreneur Andrew J. McIntosh saw an opportunity to compete with BC&A, employing fast steam yachts to provide a faster and cheaper Baltimore-Claiborne service via Annapolis. Unknown photographer, July 28, 1916. Ancestry.com, US Passport Applications: 1795–1925, no. 204

The final partner was John W. R. Crawford, a businessman and son-in-law of the editorial cartoonist Thomas Nast. Originally from western New York State, he had relocated to Manhattan and made his way through the executive ranks in the oil industry, serving as a vice president of Standard Oil and later president of Union Oil Company of Delaware. In contrast to McIntosh and Sinn, Crawford does not appear to have ever taken an active role in the management of ESDSC, and indeed it was Crawford's legal action that led to the company's eventual dissolution.

ESDSC's original plan was to use Claiborne as its primary hub, with feeder lines—over both land and water—bringing passengers and freight to Claiborne from nearby communities around the Eastern Shore. ESDSC would then use modern fast steamers to connect his Claiborne hub with the Western Shore at Annapolis. As a yacht specialist, McIntosh appreciated the potential for fast steam yachts to transform the passenger experience. He was determined to provide a faster and cheaper service to Claiborne compared to the tired, old steamers run by BC&A from Baltimore. He was also convinced that he could make a profit while still pricing his services under what it currently cost customers in Annapolis or Baltimore to travel to Claiborne via BC&A services.

His approach made sense, and McIntosh was quite correct in his ability to create a faster and less expensive service between the Eastern and Western Shores of the Chesapeake. Yet his operation collapsed in short order. McIntosh's failure to sustain this new transportation service is a striking example of the power of entrenched monopolies to crush competing start-ups. Willard Thomson, the general manager of BC&A, was experienced in such tactics. ESDSC was about to become the target of one of Willard Thomson's "object lessons" in how aggressively BC&A would defend its monopoly.

For his plan to work, of course, wharf facilities had to be obtained in both Annapolis and Claiborne. While there were ample steamer venues to use in Annapolis, the only existing wharf in Claiborne was the rail and steamer jetty owned and operated by BC&A, the incumbent monopoly. BC&A was not especially keen to facilitate a new entrant, even if that upstart was bringing passengers to the rail line there. BC&A was still owned by the Pennsylvania Railroad (PRR), the monopoly-protection specialist. A battle was in the offing.

On the Eastern Shore, ESDSC looked for local assistance to Claiborne Wharf and Warehouse, a business incorporated in August 1910 by Claiborne locals Albert G. Lowe and Carroll C. Cockey.[4] Lowe, a recurring customer of BC&A, is the same person who in the past complained vociferously and publicly of poor BC&A service and high rates, and he had advocated for introduction of a new competitor. Cockey, his partner in Claiborne Wharf and Warehouse, would go on to be the local agent in Claiborne for ESDSC. The following month, that newly established business acquired waterfront property in Claiborne's Broad Cove, immediately adjacent to BC&A's own holdings. Mcintosh and his fellow investors appear to have been operating in stealth mode as they advanced their schemes, using Claiborne Wharf and Warehouse as their intermediary.

In 1911, Claiborne Wharf and Warehouse started erecting a new pier in Claiborne on its newly acquired property. However, if ESDSC was operating in stealth mode through Claiborne Wharf and Warehouse, it did not fool Willard Thomson, the general manager of BC&A. He was always on the lookout for new competitors. There was public speculation even in 1911 that the construction underway was to support a new steamer operation. BC&A, schooled in these methods by its PRR parent, jumped into action as soon as it saw construction begin.

The first thing BC&A did was demolish much of the work in progress, removing pilings, filling in ditches that Claiborne Wharf and Warehouse had constructed, and tearing up other structures. The confrontation became heated, leading an observer to comment that it was "causing much bitter feeling and may result in physical violence." Indeed, Claiborne Wharf and Warehouse, reacting to the destruction wrought by BC&A, as well as the ongoing harassment, suggested "there appears to be no way to stop it except by force."[5]

Things quieted down a bit and violence was averted, perhaps as a result of the glare of publicity. BC&A then shifted tactics. The railroad engaged the law firm of none other than Joseph B. Seth to file a complaint and request an injunction before the Circuit Court of Talbot County, arguing that:

> The Claiborne Wharf and Warehouse company, claiming to own a lot of ground adjoining the aforesaid property of [BC&A] on the south and fronting on the waters of said Broad Cove, disregarding the riparian rights of [BC&A] in [BC&A's] track of land, aforesaid, has entered upon and disseized [BC&A] of twenty feet more or less, of the front of his said lot, and has cut a ditch through [BC&A's] land and driven Piles, and commenced to dig a foundation and erect buildings thereon although [BC&A] has forbidden him to do so.[6]

The injunction was issued two days later.[7] Claiborne Wharf and Warehouse responded, telling the court that every one of BC&A's assertions was incorrect and that, more or less, their accuser should just go and pound sand.[8] It submitted a blueprint of its pier layout and associated structures that demonstrated that none of the construction work transgressed onto BC&A property or riparian rights.[9] As the legal battles continued, the pier was constructed.

That same Claiborne Wharf and Warehouse pier, built in 1911, is the origin of what today is called Claiborne Landing.

A second challenge for ESDSC was to find boats to use. Here, Mcintosh's experience as a yacht broker paid dividends. He had access to a large number of fast yachts and houseboats and could pick those most suitable for operations on the planned route.

Two boats would be needed at the outset. The initial plan was to connect Claiborne to Annapolis via a fast steamer and then run a short feeder service between Cambridge and the town of Bellevue using a small but speedy steam yacht. Then, from Bellevue, "large and fast automobiles" would bring those Cambridge-originating passengers the twelve miles to Claiborne, saving the time and cost of much slower thirty-three-mile water voyage down the Choptank River and around Tilghman Island.[10]

Claiborne thus became the hub of the operation, with connections to Annapolis on the Western Shore (via steamer), to various communities on the Eastern Shore (via BC&A trains), and to Cambridge (via a ground route to Bellevue and connecting steam yacht service from there). For the main Claiborne-Annapolis route, ESDSC chose the steamer *Atlantic*. For the feeder route between Cambridge and Bellevue, the company selected the steam yacht *Texas*. The vessels were quite different.

Texas was a fast steam yacht owned by wealthy entrepreneur (and playboy) Edward H. R. Green. Green was the son of Henrietta Green, the "Witch of Wall Street," who had turned a small inherited fortune into a large one through wise and careful investing. (Today she might have been labeled the "Sage of Wall Street," but those were different times.) Mrs. Green was reported to be both the richest woman in the world, as well as, according to the *Guinness Book of World Records*, the world's "Greatest Miser."[11]

Edward Green's *Texas* was a modern screw steamer, built by renowned yacht maker Herreshoff Manufacturing Company in Bristol, Rhode Island. Completed in 1889 as *Augusta*, the luxury steam yacht with graceful, sleek lines had a long history, operating from Bristol (as *Vivienne*), Boston (as *Toinette*), and New York (as *Laurita* and *Crescent*). Green had picked up the yacht around 1909,

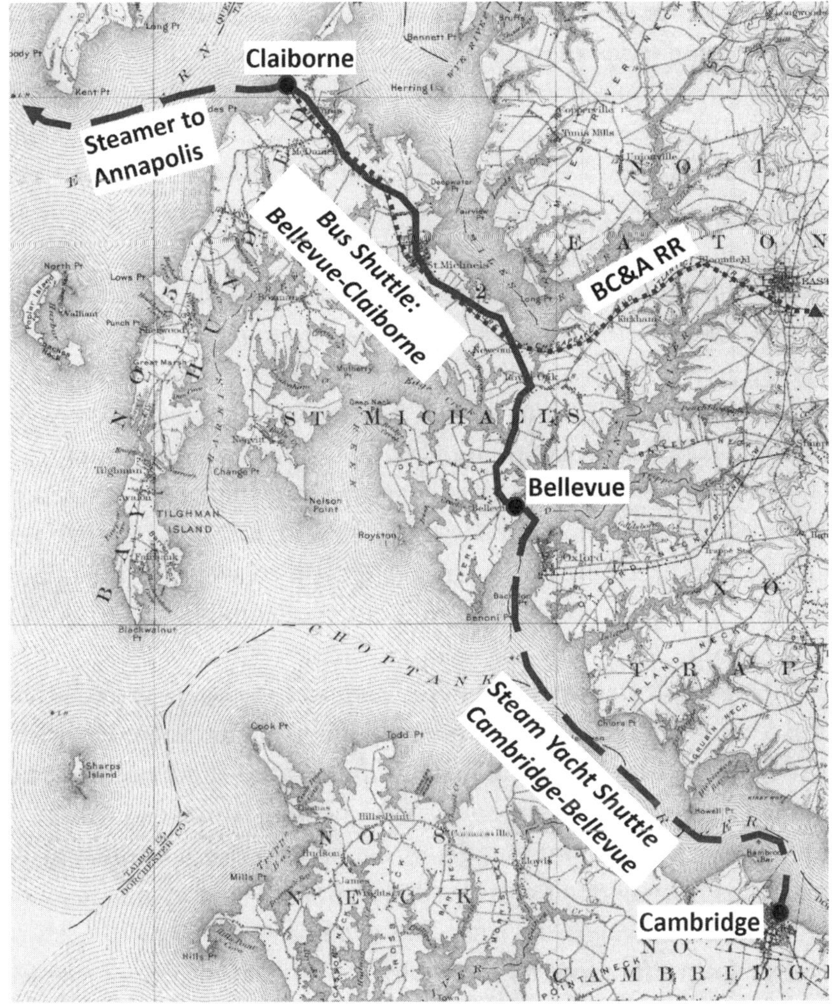

Map 5. Original ESDSC route map, overlaid on a 1908 US Geological Survey map. Source: Base map is from US Geological Survey, detailed and annotated by the author.

being the first person in Texas, then his residence, to own a steam yacht (as well as an airplane). McIntosh in turn acquired the yacht from Green and transferred it to his new steamboat company.

The other vessel, *Atlantic*, had been built as the steamer *Ruth* in Rockland, Maine, in 1894 by shipbuilder George A. Gilchrist. Compared to *Texas*, a thoroughbred in the fleet of steamboats, *Atlantic* was a draft horse. *Atlantic* was, at 103 feet, two feet shorter than *Texas* but had twice the net-register tonnage (a measure of internal volume not occupied by machinery and crew spaces) as did *Texas*. Still, *Atlantic* was a relatively modern screw steamer, reasonably fast, and well suited for cross-bay traffic. It had earned its stripes carrying passengers in the coastal waters of Maine, operating from Mt. Desert for many years.

A third vessel joined the fleet, managed by A.J. McIntosh Yacht Brokers. This was *Mermaid*, a gasoline-powered houseboat built originally for Mrs. Julia Armour Ferguson, heir to the Chicago meat-packing family. Constructed in 1906 by shipbuilder James M. Bayles and Son in Port Jefferson, New York, it had been employed, when not in the service of Mrs. Ferguson, as an excursion steamer for the boys of Adelphi Academy in Brooklyn. *Mermaid* was not intended (at first) for use in passenger operations, but rather was moored in Claiborne and served as the administrative offices for ESDSC.

Another critical element of the plan was to establish a relationship with one of the few remaining rail lines not dominated by PRR. ESDSC found the Washington, Baltimore and Annapolis Railway (WB&A), a modern electric rail line connecting Annapolis with both Baltimore and Washington, DC. Schedules were coordinated so that trains from both cities arrived in Annapolis just in time to catch the steamer over to Claiborne. The reverse was true of the return journey from Claiborne to Annapolis.

ESDSC had also aligned its schedule with that of BC&A, at that time operating on its fall/spring/winter routine. This meant there was no morning BC&A steamer to Claiborne, but a BC&A train did depart Claiborne for Ocean City, leaving about 8:30 a.m. The ESDSC voyage to Claiborne took about ninety minutes. Working backward, the steamer *Atlantic* departed Annapolis at 6:30 a.m. in order to arrive thirty minutes before the BC&A train departed Claiborne. WB&A trains would leave Washington at 5:10 a.m. and Baltimore at 5:40 a.m. to connect to the 6:30 a.m. steamer. An analogous coordinated schedule was established for return journeys.[12] When BC&A migrated to its summer peak schedule, typically during the second week of June, ESDSC would adjust accordingly.

Amidst a fanfare of publicity, ESDSC operations began on May 4, 1912. The weather in Annapolis was not auspicious: somewhat warm for that time of year, very humid, and skies filled with rain, at least during the morning.[13] Legendary local captain Charles R. Kerr was at the helm of *Atlantic* as it made its way to Claiborne. Already over sixty years of age, he had spent a lifetime on the water and was highly respected as one of the most senior captains on the Bay. Joining him as captain of *Texas* was John R. Mills, himself about to turn sixty and living in Baltimore. He also had commanded steamboats and steam yachts for decades and was well respected. The new and previously unknown challenger to BC&A had done well to put experienced skippers at the helm of its steamboats.

Operations met with mixed results. The Claiborne-Annapolis connection worked well enough, but things began to fall apart rapidly on the ground route between Claiborne and Bellevue, the connection point to Cambridge served by *Texas*. The unreliable buses employed on the route (this was 1912, after all), combined with primitive road conditions, meant that breakdowns were frequent. As was reported at the time:

> Every thing was lovely for a day. On the second day it was found that the roads were so narrow that trouble occurred whenever a team [of horses] was passed. On the third day it rained. The big machines went into the ditch. There they remained. The $26,000 worth of fine automobiles are now in storage and the force of mechanicians [sic] and chauffeurs have sought other fields.[14]

By May 11, after just one week, the feeder connection via bus from Claiborne to Bellevue was abandoned.[15] Instead, *Texas* was used to provide direct service between Cambridge and Annapolis bypassing the connection to Bellevue and Claiborne.[16] So now ESDSC operated two steamboat lines to Annapolis, one from Claiborne and one from Cambridge.

Overall, the new service was widely praised, especially the rapid reduction in typical travel time from Annapolis to Cambridge, from twelve hours to under five on the swift steam yacht *Texas*. However, the primary ESDSC service remained oriented around Claiborne.

ESDSC continued its operations using *Texas* (Cambridge) and *Atlantic* (Claiborne) for seven months, until 8:00 p.m. on December 7, 1912, when tragedy struck. *Atlantic*'s steam engine failed, resulting in a complete loss of propulsion, as well as electrical power and heat. This all transpired during a dark winter night. The steamer ended up drifting off Bloody Point overnight and into the following morning, with passengers freezing in the wintry weather, in a steamer without working boilers. Fog surrounded the darkened steamer as it wallowed and drifted in the blackness, risking collision with another vessel or running aground. After a tense night, salvation emerged the following morning when the steamer *Virginia*, which had encountered the disabled *Atlantic* and come to its rescue, took on board the passengers from *Atlantic*.[17] *Atlantic* was immediately taken out of service, never to fully return.[18]

The absence of *Atlantic* required a reshuffling of the fleet. *Texas* was shifted to the Claiborne-Annapolis route and would continue on that route until the company folded in 1916. To backfill on the Cambridge-Annapolis route, ESDSC chartered the large steamer *City of Milford*.[19] This was a relatively new boat, built in Milford, Delaware, in 1906 by Abbott Shipbuilding. It was a third larger than *Atlantic*. Up to that point, *City of Milford* had been operated by the Maryland Steamboat Company, connecting Baltimore to Onancock, Virginia, so its captain and crew were familiar with the Chesapeake. Service started in mid-December and was to persist throughout 1913. The new steamer worked so well under charter that it was acquired by ESDSC President Andrew McIntosh in April 1913.[20]

Meanwhile, ESDSC thought about expansion by creating additional feeder routes and by adding freight service. In January 1913, the small gasoline-powered boat *A.J. McIntosh* initiated a new service for freight between Cambridge and outlying locations around the Choptank River region, including Tilghman's, Oxford, and Secretary.[21] Later, in September 1913, McIntosh acquired the ancient paddlewheel steamer *Gen'l J.A. Dumont*, originally constructed in 1862 as the *James F. Freeborn* by the Brooklyn-based shipbuilder Lawrence and Foulks.[22] Plans for this latest addition to the fleet seemed unclear. The old steamer, perhaps in ill repair, seems to have languished in Annapolis waiting for assignment.[23]

Confrontation with BC&A

Not surprisingly, BC&A, operating its own steamboat and railroad operations within spitting distance of the new ESDSC wharf, was not thrilled at competition from this ambitious upstart with deep pockets. The friction that had emerged during the initial pier construction in 1911 continued after operations had begun. By July 1912, ESDSC was complaining stridently in the media about BC&A's predatory behavior.

The competitive threat from ESDSC to BC&A was real, and General Manager Willard Thomson knew it. ESDSC offered faster service than BC&A. It took less time to travel from Baltimore to Claiborne on the ESDSC steamer from Annapolis, *including* the connecting train from Baltimore to Annapolis, than it did to take the BC&A steamer from Baltimore to Claiborne. The additional one-hour train ride using ESDSC was more than offset by the much faster trip from Annapolis: one and a half hours, versus three and one-half hours from Baltimore. Thus, Baltimore passengers for Claiborne would save an hour by taking ESDSC steamers instead of the BC&A steamer. Moreover, unlike BC&A, ESDSC offered a connection to the morning BC&A train during the autumn/winter/spring period.

ESDSC also beat BC&A on price. Passengers using ESDSC from Baltimore paid a total of $1.15 to take the Washington, Baltimore and Annapolis Railway service from Baltimore to Annapolis and then the ESDSC steamer to Claiborne. Passengers on BC&A paid $1.32 for their one-way ticket from Baltimore to Claiborne, 15 percent more than the ESDSC fare.[24]

Unable to compete on price or speed, BC&A tried to undermine the market advantage of ESDSC through its traditional predatory behavior. It was determined to drive this latest competitor out of business the same way it had done to other upstarts for the previous fifteen years. It employed a variety of imaginative methods.

One way BC&A made life complicated for ESDSC passengers was by refusing to sell them tickets in advance on its rail service from Claiborne to Ocean City, even for passengers originating in Baltimore. Thus, a passenger going to Ocean City could buy in Baltimore a through ticket for the BC&A train if they were taking the BC&A steamer, but not buy a BC&A train ticket if they were taking an ESDSC steamer. BC&A instead required ESDSC arriving passengers in Claiborne to purchase separate tickets at the Claiborne ticket office and to recheck baggage in Claiborne, complicating journeys and adding time.

BC&A also employed the classic monopoly strategy of bundling its services, reducing prices on the services on which it competed and increasing prices for services where it did not. It offered discounted fares on the rail line for passengers of BC&A steamers, discounts not available to ESDSC passengers.[25] The end result was that connecting ESDSC passengers paid three cents per mile to ride the BC&A train to Ocean City whereas BC&A's own connecting passengers were charged only one and a quarter cents per mile.[26]

Sometimes the resistance from BC&A bordered on peevish. ESDSC endeavored to build a covered walkway between the ESDSC and BC&A wharves to allow for convenient connections in inclement weather. BC&A forbid this since some of the walkway would be on its property. They wanted ESDSC travelers to be subject to the hazards of unpredictable weather, even while their own passengers could embark aboard BC&A trains in a comfortable, covered terminal.

A legendary approach employed by BC&A to advantage its own passengers over those of ESDSC involved whether the BC&A train would wait for a late-arriving steamer. The BC&A train would inevitably hold its departure for a behind-schedule BC&A steamer, even if the delay for the train stretched into an hour or more. In contrast, there were several examples of the BC&A train blowing its whistle and heading out even as a connecting ESDSC steamer was only minutes away from docking. Complaints reached an elevated level in November 1912 when connecting ESDSC passengers, who had already landed and were starting to run from the ESDSC wharf to the BC&A terminal, watched in anger as the train conductor, despite seeing the frantic efforts of the connecting passengers, and perhaps wearing a smile, ordered the train to depart without them even though they were only seconds away from boarding.[27]

The dirty tricks continued. BC&A tried to inconvenience ESDSC passengers further by changing its schedule—without advance notice to ESDSC. It had maintained the same schedule for a decade or longer: a single 4:30 p.m. steamer from Baltimore to Claiborne from mid-September to early June, and two steamers (6:30 a.m. and 2:30 p.m.) during the summer months. Train departures were coordinated with steamer arrivals. ESDSC adjusted its own schedule in mid-September, presuming the 5:55 p.m. train from Claiborne would return to the expected 7:25 p.m. departure. Its steamer would arrive around 7:00 p.m. However, in 1914, the ESDSC 7:00 p.m. steamer arrived on time only to find that the train had already left, on the revised schedule, at 5:55 p.m.[28] The passengers were stranded in Claiborne for the night or forced to return to Annapolis. BC&A decided to keep its earlier departure throughout the winter months, and kept that a secret from ESDSC. The same thing happened again in January 1916, when the morning BC&A train departure from Claiborne was suddenly advanced from 9:55 a.m. to 8:15 a.m. Passengers on the ESDSC steamer arriving on schedule at 9:00 a.m. missed the train. BC&A did not publish the details of the schedule change in advance and suggested that passengers visit the BC&A ticket office in Baltimore to obtain the new schedule.

ESDSC complained loudly and publicly. BC&A's responses to these complaints were hardly encouraging and bordered on being snippy. Thomson, now in his twenty-second year as general manager of the rail line, responded dismissively to complaints in a letter to McIntosh, denigrating one of his steamers as "your little boat" and suggesting McIntosh was "perhaps ignorant of the methods employed by your captain."[29]

That did it. One wonders if McIntosh, imbued with the spirit of Baltimorean Edgar Allan Poe, saw himself as Montresor and Thomson as Fortunato: "The thousand injuries of Fortunato I had borne as I best could, but when he ventured upon insult I vowed revenge."[30] ESDSC raised the stakes and formally filed charges against BC&A in July 1913 with the Interstate Commerce Commission (ICC), the federal agency authorized to regulate railroads beginning in 1887 and steamboat lines beginning in 1906. ESDSC petitioned the ICC to intercede on its four demands:

- ESDSC insisted that BC&A hold trains for a late-arriving ESDSC steamer, to the same extent it does for a late arriving BC&A steamer.
- ESDSC wanted BC&A to permit a covered walkway between their wharf and the BC&A rail jetty, so as to permit more convenient connections.
- ESDSC demanded advance notice of planned changes in BC&A train schedules so it could alter its own schedule accordingly.
- ESDSC asked for a fair rate structure. They wanted the costs to ride the BC&A train to be the same, regardless of which steamer line passengers had used to get to Claiborne.

The ICC initiated an investigation, together with formal hearings at which McIntosh himself represented ESDSC. Perhaps fearing an adverse outcome, or simply employing a delaying tactic, BC&A decided to preempt any ICC action by agreeing to enter into direct negotiations with ESDSC. In the end, BC&A, at least on paper, committed to meeting all of the latter's demands. The local newspapers read this as a BC&A capitulation in the face of a potential adverse ICC ruling: "every demand Mr. McIntosh made on the part of his company was accepted by the Baltimore, Chesapeake and Atlantic Railway Company."[31] Specifically, however, BC&A agreed only to the following:

- When requested by the ESDSC Claiborne manager, BC&A trains would wait for a late ESDSC steamer up to ten minutes, but would do so only once per month.
- BC&A would allow ESDSC to build its covered walkway for a "nominal" monthly rent. (In the end, however, BC&A's version of "nominal" was ten times as costly as ESDSC's interpretation.[32])
- BC&A would provide notice of schedule changes for trains departing Claiborne.
- BC&A committed to working out an equitable arrangement on fares with ESDSC, with details to be negotiated.

The latter concession did not hold, and BC&A adamantly refused to simplify its rate structure to accommodate ESDSC's demands. The strategy of delay had worked, and the fact that the dispute was centered only around fares put the matter within the Maryland Public Service Commission (PSC) as opposed to the ICC. This appears to have been a clever tactic by BC&A, which probably exercised more influence over the Maryland authorities—given its criticality to the Maryland economy—than it did to the federal authorities.

As a result, ESDSC responded in late 1913 with a new formal complaint to the PSC, the state authority responsible for regulating public utilities, including railroads and steamboat companies.[33] However, after review, the PSC summarily dismissed ESDSC's complaint, and BC&A evaded any need to alter its rate structure. The PSC did not feel BC&A should be forced to facilitate the operation of a competitor whose primary business objective was to exploit a rail line and terminal (in Claiborne) that BC&A, alone, had borne the cost of constructing and maintaining. The PCC concluded that the competitor sought, unfairly, rights to use those facilities on an equal basis without investing in them, and that:

> . . . if it gets it the Defendant [BC&A] will be deprived of the revenue it now derives from the water division of its line, because it has not been shown, and there is no reason to suppose, that a rival line for a part of the trip will increase the traffic on the rail division to the point where the increase in revenue thereon will compensate for the loss of the water division.[34]

Just around the time that this unfavorable ruling was revealed, McIntosh resigned as president of ESDSC.[35] Willard Thomson had won another victory. McIntosh was replaced as head of ESDSC by co-investor and earlier Vice President Bernard A. Sinn.[36]

Perhaps with confidence ratcheted up by this favorable PSC ruling, BC&A intensified the pressure. For two decades, its Claiborne route had consisted of a single daily trip, except during peak summer season when two trips would be made.[37] In September 1913, it added a second daily trip to Claiborne, the first time this was done for months outside the peak summer season. One might question the business logic of adding more capacity during the slow winter period given that, with the additional capacity already offered by ESDSC, the second BC&A departure would not be profitable. The additional capacity appears to have been designed less to make money for BC&A than to eat into ESDSC's marketplace. Indeed, the additional trips ended immediately after ESDSC went out of business in 1916.[38] But it did cost BC&A. An uninterrupted string of a dozen profitable years turned into losses from 1913 to 1915, the only full years in which ESDSC operated.

BC&A also decided in 1914 to reinvigorate its legal action, especially after ESDSC acquired the Claiborne Wharf and Warehouse Company in 1913. BC&A filed another complaint with the Circuit Court of Talbot County on July 7, 1914, politely but firmly reminding the court that ESDSC, as new owner of Claiborne Wharf and Warehouse, was subject to the same injunction and had continued to ignore the court's ruling. The matter remained unresolved.

Not all of the challenges faced by the new steamboat line arose from BC&A's maneuvering. Some of the difficulties encountered by

ESDSC were self-inflicted, especially as 1914 drifted into 1915 under the new president, Sinn. Unlike his predecessor, McIntosh, Sinn was not particularly familiar with boat operations, and performance began to struggle. The primary service from Cambridge to Annapolis (via *City of Milford*) and Claiborne to Annapolis (via *Texas*) worked well enough through 1914, albeit with periodic but expected halts in service due to equipment failures or maintenance needs.

However, the ancillary feeder operations struggled mightily. ESDSC seemed to be a magnet for boat calamities in Annapolis. The gasoline power boat *A.J. McIntosh* caught fire and exploded in Annapolis on October 2, 1914. A few months later, on December 22, the sidewheel steamer *Gen'l J.A. Dumont* caught fire and burned on the Severn River. Another small steamer, *Oak Island*, may also have been acquired by ESDSC. In any case it would not have been in service for long: *Oak Island* foundered at the pier in Annapolis on June 1, 1915.[39]

One senses that the operation was starting to fall apart. The Cambridge service using *City of Milford* appears to have ended in December 1914. Perhaps to raise funds and/or repay initial investors, that company-owned steamboat had already been sold in autumn 1914 to John W. R. Crawford, one of ESDSC's initial investors. It had been leased for its last few months of service until a subsequent sale could be arranged.

Then, in January 1915, ESDSC acquired the small steamer *York River*, built as *Corsair* in 1888 by Joseph Provencher in East Providence, Rhode Island. This old steamer, far smaller and older than *City of Milford*, was put into operation on a freight route from Baltimore to Cambridge. However, just a month or two after starting operation, *York River* rammed a schooner off Baltimore and had to be sent to the repair yard.[40] The US District Court later ruled that *York River* was at fault in the collision, creating additional financial liabilities on a struggling ESDSC.[41]

Texas itself suffered a broken rudder on May 6, 1915, and was left adrift in the Bay until the crew could make repairs. The lack of redundant steamer capacity became clear in September 1915 when *Texas* was again taken out of service for scheduled repairs. *York*

River was put on the Claiborne route in place of *Texas*. However, *York River* promptly became disabled, and its passengers had to be rescued by the BC&A steamer *Cambridge* on September 22, 1915. Given the lack of options, ESDSC management put the power houseboat *Mermaid* in operation on the Claiborne-Annapolis route, at least until *Texas* could return to service.[42] Up to that point, *Mermaid* had served as a floating office for ESDSC in Claiborne and as a courier vessel departing at 2:00 a.m. from Baltimore to bring newspapers to Claiborne for distribution on the Eastern Shore.

The numbers tell the story. Freight and passenger revenue earned by ESDSC in fiscal year 2015 (ending June 30 of that year) cratered to only half the level of the previous fiscal year.[43] The termination of *City of Milford* on the Cambridge route was painful. Compounding this was the loss of three boats—*A. J. McIntosh*, *Gen'l J.A. Dumont,* and *Oak Island*—in the 1915 fiscal year.

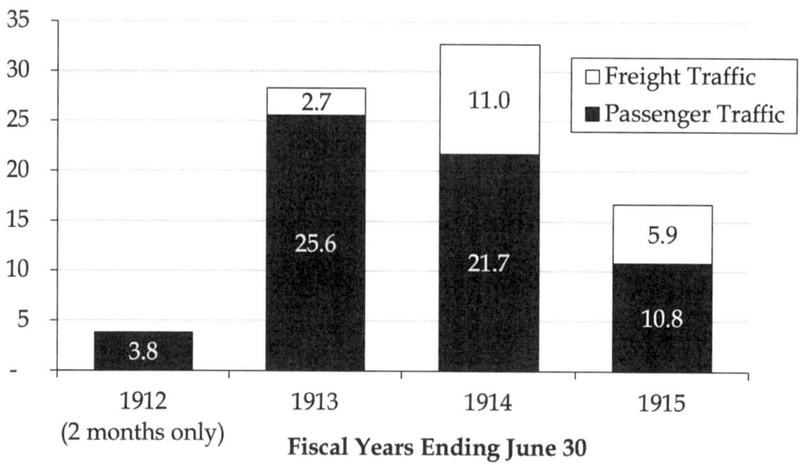

Worse, the company was hemorrhaging cash. Since starting operations in 1912, the company had never earned a profit. Income from all sources barely reached half of the annual operating expenses. By June 30, 1915, total annual deficits rose to almost $200,000, and the available capital stock and funded debt was overwhelmed by the deficits. ESDSC was no longer paying its bills. Bankruptcy loomed. It was time for ESDSC's investors to go big or go home.

They decided to go big.

The only viable scenario was to broaden the line's reach by acquiring a broader set of steamboat lines in the Bay, improving its ability to compete with BC&A by taking over some of BC&A's monopoly routes. This was not far-fetched. ESDSC owners hoped to take advantage of changes in regulatory policy following, of all things, the building of the Panama Canal. A brief digression is warranted.

The Panama Canal Act

In 1912, Americans looked with great interest to the opening of the Panama Canal, then in the final stages of construction. It was expected that the canal would lead to a boom in cargo shipping from coast to coast, and, in doing so, create a long-sought competitor to the transcontinental railways that at the time dominated transportation. Some estimates were that two-thirds (or more) of freight moved coast-to-coast by rail might ultimately shift to steam vessels using the canal.[44] However, there was a legitimate concern that the mighty railways might seek to dominate that coastal trade, using their own fleets of ships with discounted rates to drive out independent competitors. The railroads would then jack up steamer rates once the competition was vanquished. It is a pattern that had been seen often, not least with BC&A's concurrent efforts to crush ESDSC. Congress decided early on that ships owned by railway companies would not be able to use the canal, thus forcing railways out of the coast-to-coast seaborne trade and protecting the new, independent shipping companies.

This debate took place during one of the most heated elections in United States history, and one of the few where antitrust platforms played a central role in the political debate. Incumbent Republican President William H. Taft, Democratic challenger Woodrow Wilson, and Progressive candidate Theodore Roosevelt all staked out positions on the issue of breaking up monopolistic trusts, including those operating major railway and shipping companies.

These two trends converged in the Panama Canal Act of 1912, which specified how the canal would work, how tolls would be priced, and so forth. Section 11 of the act amended the 1887 Interstate Commerce Act to specify that railroads could not own or control steamship companies operating in coastal trade that passed through the Panama Canal. However, before final passage, the act was modified to expand the ownership restriction such that, after July 1, 1914, it would be unlawful . . .

> for any railroad . . . to own, lease, operate, control, or have any interest whatsoever . . . in any common carrier by water operated through the Panama Canal *or elsewhere* with which said railroad or other carrier aforesaid does or may compete for traffic or any vessel carrying freight or passengers upon said water route or elsewhere with which said railroad or other carrier aforesaid does or may compete for traffic. . . .[45] [Emphasis added.]

There was a potential exemption. The act also gave the ICC the authority to waive this provision should a joint ownership of railroads and steamer lines be seen as conducive to competition. Accordingly, the Pennsylvania Railroad applied to be exempted from the need to split its steamer and railroad businesses. This appeal failed. In 1915, the ICC ruled that the railroad must divest all of its steamboat operations in the Chesapeake Bay, with the exception of the BC&A steamers to Claiborne and the MD&V steamers to Love Point. These two specific operations were seen as extensions of the railroad lines rather than alternative transport modes competing with railroads.[46] Pennsylvania Railroad would still have to divest all other steamer operations in the Chesapeake, which at the time were quite considerable.

ESDSC saw an opportunity arising from this forced sale. They hoped to take over these other steamboat lines, and ESDSC financier John W. R. Crawford visited the Pennsylvania Railroad headquarters to make an offer to buy them.[47] In the end his offer was deemed inadequate, and the opportunity was lost.[48] This left ESDSC with its own troubled steamboat routes and the same operational and competitive challenges as before.[49] ESDSC was without any more cards to play. (In the end, upon the start of World War I, the impetus to disrupt freight operations dissipated, and BC&A did not have to divest its lines.)

Within a few weeks of that aggressive offer being turned down, ESDSC surprised everyone by announcing it was terminating all of its steamer services and winding down its operations. It had given up. The last trip was made on April 30, 1916. The attorney for ESDSC, Harry E. Karr, summarized for public consumption that "the backers do not see the use of continuing a losing game."[50] ESDSC surrendered to BC&A the same day the Irish rebels behind the Easter Uprising surrendered to British authorities. But in the same way that the Irish rebellion was not over and done with in 1916, the ashes of ESDSC would soon arise to once again challenge BC&A.

In the end, BC&A had managed to squash the upstart, aided and abetted by ESDSC's own operational failures. The only thing remaining was to sell off the remaining assets in an attempt to allow debt holders to recover some of their losses. One of the original investors, John W. R. Crawford, was also a debtor, holding some $4,200 in promissory notes. He sued ESDSC to force liquidation and sale of the assets. First to go were the three remaining boats in the company: *Texas*, *York River*, and *Mermaid*. All three were seized, put up for public auction by the US Marshals, and sold off in November 1916.[51] (Captain John R. Mills of the steam yacht *Texas* died that same month from typhoid fever.) The Claiborne wharf and adjacent property was acquired by Harry E. Karr, who, as we shall soon see, was able to unload that property within two years.[52]

The Eastern Shore Development Steamship Company was no more. Sinn went back to his banking activities in New York. Crawford focused again on his oil interests, being elected president of Union

Oil in 1920. McIntosh reverted to his yachting pursuits, elected commodore of the Atlantic Yacht Club on Long Island in 1924, a position he held for only a fleeting time before his death in 1928.[53]

While the experience of ESDSC was both brief and terminal, its legacy would persist in three important ways. First, it had built a new wharf in Claiborne, now idle and just begging for someone to put it to good use. Second, the experience of ESDSC had revealed that a steamboat service from Annapolis to Claiborne could generate passenger traffic, especially given that its service would be cheaper and faster for Baltimore passengers than a steamer direct from Baltimore. Third, it made apparent that none of this would work unless the competing steamboat line could operate without dependence on BC&A's monopoly rail system. Only in this way could an operator be immune to BC&A's inevitable predatory practices.

The last item would require a major technical revolution. And one was just getting started, thanks to Henry Ford.

Notes

1. Business must not have been successful because A. J. McIntosh was sued for non-payment of debt. See "Judgment Against A. J. McIntosh," *New York Times*, April 21, 1897. He ended up declaring bankruptcy in an effort to free himself from $32,000 in debts. See "Andrew J. McIntosh Bankruptcy," *New York Times*, February 5, 1903. A court accepted his bankruptcy and his debts were erased. See "Yacht Broker Freed from Bankruptcy," *Sun* (New York, NY), October 24, 1903.
2. "The D., L. & W.'s Big Purchase," *Brooklyn Daily Eagle*, April 3, 1906.
3. McIntosh had borrowed about $4,500 (in current dollars the equivalent of $150,000) from his father, a successful manager with Scribner & Sons then residing in Philadelphia. His father died in 1905, but the father's will notably snubs son Andrew, granting him only $100 while leaving the rest of his entire estate of $59,000 (valued today at almost $2 million) to his siblings instead. Thus, the sale of the yacht basin property was probably the source of cash for his investments.
4. *Annual Report of the Bureau of Statistics and Information for Maryland*, 1910 (Kohn & Pollock, 1911), 346.
5. "Claiborne Wharf Contest," *Evening Sun* (Baltimore, MD), August 3, 1911.
6. "Bill of Complaint" in Baltimore, Chesapeake and Atlantic Railway Company v. The Claiborne Wharf and Warehouse Company, case no. 853 (filed August 4, 1911, Circuit Court of Talbot County), 1–2. Maryland State Archives, Equity Papers, MSA T-1628-59.
7. "Injunction" in Baltimore, Chesapeake and Atlantic Railway Company v. The Claiborne Wharf and Warehouse Company, case no. 853 (filed August 11, 1911, Circuit Court of Talbot County), n.p. Maryland State Archives, Equity Papers, MSA T-1628-59.
8. "Answer of Defendant" in Baltimore, Chesapeake and Atlantic Railway Company v. The Claiborne Wharf and Warehouse Company, case no. 853 (filed September 9, 1911, Circuit Court of Talbot County), 1–3. Maryland State Archives, Equity Papers, MSA T-1628-59.
9. The blueprint was submitted as an attachment to the court case records. As no actual photograph of the ESDSC pier has emerged, this is one of only two depictions of how that wharf looked and what structures were associated with it. The other is the plan for modification to the pier submitted in March 1919 by the Claiborne Annapolis Ferry Inc.
10. "New Bay Line Is Ready," *Sun* (Baltimore, MD), May 2, 1912.
11. The son wore a prosthetic limb because his own leg had to be amputated after gangrene set in, a result, it is said, of his mother refusing to pay a doctor for proper treatment. See Wyn Derbyshire, *Hetty Green, the First Lady of Wall Street* (Spiramus Press Ltd., 2019), 58.

12. For the first few days, the trains heading to Claiborne left ten minutes later, but that probably did not leave enough of a margin, so the departure time was moved earlier. In the evening, trains left Washington at 4:05 p.m. and Baltimore at 4:35 p.m., connecting to a 5:35 p.m. steamer, which put passengers in Claiborne thirty minutes before the scheduled 7:35 p.m. BC&A train to Ocean City. The slower BC&A steamer from Baltimore, having departed at 4:10 p.m., would arrive just in time for the 7:35 p.m. train.
13. "Summary of the News," *Sun* (Baltimore, MD), May 13, 1912.
14. "New Steamer Line Great Addition to City," *Washington Times*, May 26, 1912.
15. "Order No. 720, Case No. 363," in *Report of the Public Service Commission of Maryland for the Year 1912* (Sun Book and Job Printing Office, 1913), 138.
16. "Change in Eastern Shore Trips," *Sun* (Baltimore, MD), May 16, 1912.
17. "Twenty-Eight Rescued from Helpless Ship," *Washington Times*, December 8, 1912.
18. The steamer went into repair over the next few months and was eventually sold to Booz Brothers Inc. shipbuilding company in Baltimore in September 1913.
19. "Port Paragraphs," *Sun* (Baltimore, MD), January 12, 1913.
20. "Changes in Vessel Owners," *Sun* (Baltimore, MD), April 19, 1913.
21. "Extends Its Line," *Cambridge Daily Banner*, January 9, 1913. This article does not identify the boat by name. The name is identified in "Brief Local News," *Cambridge Daily Banner*, January 22, 1913. This apparently lasted only until March of that year, when *A.J. McIntosh* had to be rescued by the US Revenue-Cutter *Apache* after having run aground off Oxford. See *Annual Report of the United States Revenue-Cutter Service for the Fiscal Year Ended June 30, 1913* (Government Printing Office, 1913), 24. The feeder line built around *A.J. McIntosh* was shifted to the Miles and Wye Rivers, connecting directly with Claiborne. See "In Maryland and the Virginias," *Sun* (Baltimore, MD), July 26, 1912.
22. The ship later became the US Navy vessel *Nansemond* and then the US Revenue Cutter Service *W.H. Crawford*. It became *Gen'l J.A. Dumont* in 1900. The name is variously written as *General James A. Dumont*, or *Gen. James A. Dumont*. Here we will use the name *Gen'l J.A. Dumont* since that is what was written on the paddlewheel housing and how the name was recorded in the various editions of *Merchant Vessels of the United States*.
23. "The Local Department," *Denton Journal*, September 6, 1913.
24. "Case No. 616," in *Report of the Public Service Commission of Maryland for the Year 1913* (Kohn & Pollock, 1914), 459–64.
25. "Friction Over New Eastern Shore Line," *Evening Sun* (Baltimore, MD), July 6, 1912.
26. "Calls B., C. and A. Unfair," *Sun* (Baltimore, MD), July 30, 1913.

27. "BC&A Train Will Not Wait," *Sun* (Baltimore, MD), November 16, 1912. This story is typically associated with the later Claiborne-Annapolis Ferry Company. However, it was ESDSC that was subjected to this action, not the Claiborne-Annapolis Ferry Company.
28. A 2:30 p.m. departure from Baltimore was common in the summer schedule but had not been used previously in the winter/spring/fall schedule. Starting in 1916, once ESDSC has ceased operations, the fall/winter/spring schedule was shifted back to a Baltimore departure at 4:00 p.m.
29. "Calls B., C. and A. Unfair," *Sun* (Baltimore, MD), July 30, 1913.
30. The opening line of *A Cask of Amontillado* by Edgar Allan Poe, first published in 1846.
31. "B., C. And A. Makes Terms," *Sun* (Baltimore, MD), July 31, 1913.
32. "Answer of Defendant" in Baltimore, Chesapeake and Atlantic Railway Company v. The Claiborne Wharf and Warehouse Company, Case No. 853 (filed September 30, 1911, Circuit Court of Talbot County), 2. Maryland State Archives, Equity Papers, MSA T-1628-59.
33. "Case no. 616," in *Report of the Public Service Commission of Maryland for the Year 1913* (Kohn & Pollock, 1914), 459–64.
34. "Order No. 1504, Case No. 616," in *Report of the Public Service Commission of Maryland for the Year 1913* (Kohn & Pollock, 1914), 464.
35. "President McIntosh Resigns," *Sun* (Baltimore, MD), November 23, 1913.
36. McIntosh went on to try to form a new steamboat company operating between Annapolis and points on the Patuxent River. The new company, Eastern and Western Steamship Company, appears to have never entered operations. See "New Ship Line for Annapolis," *Sun* (Baltimore, MD), January 4, 1914.
37. Outside of summer, there was one trip per day, departing Baltimore at 4:10 p.m. (or 4:30 p.m. before 1898). Starting in late 1913, a second 6:15 a.m. or 6:30 a.m. trip was added. The afternoon trip was shifted from 4:10 p.m. to 2:30 p.m. in late 1914.
38. The schedule is revealed in the numerous advertisements issued by BC&A in *The Sun* (Baltimore, MD) and other newspapers.
39. US Department of Commerce, *Merchant Vessels of the United States for the Year ending June 30, 1915* (Government Printing Office, 1917). The ownership status of *Oak Island* is unclear. Media reports in January 1914 suggest it was going to be used by A. J. McIntosh as part of his new company. However, reports in summer 1915 reference new crew members and captain for *Oak Island* as part of ESDSC. The vessel was put up for auction shortly before that point. A reasonable scenario is that McIntosh had acquired the vessel, intending to put it into service, but had failed to do so, leading ESDSC to acquire the vessel in an attempt to duplicate that operation. Then it sank.
40. "Steamer in Crash," *Evening Sun* (Baltimore, MD), March 6, 1915.

41. "Richmond Gets Decision," *Sun* (Baltimore, MD), May 4, 1915.
42. "Bay Steamer Disabled," *Sun* (Baltimore, MD), September 23, 1915.
43. As a regulated utility, ESDSC was required to file annual financial information with the Maryland Public Service Commission. These data are included in the PSC annual reports.
44. Russell L. Dunn, "Effect of Panama Canal on Sea Traffic," *Congressional Record—Senate*, April 1, 1914, 6099.
45. Joseph V. Fuller and Tyler Dennett, eds., *Papers Relating to the Foreign Relations of the United States, With the Annual Message of the President Transmitted to Congress December 3, 1912,* (US Government Printing Office, 1919), 473. See also US Department of State, Office of the Historian, Document 661, history.state.gov/historicaldocuments/frus1912/pg_473
46. For example, the Maryland Public Service Commission, which regulated utilities and transport companies, included the Love Point and Claiborne ferries within the railroad category, not within the separate water transport category (where ESDSC and other ferry companies were grouped).
47. "Pennsy Awaits offer for Bay Boat Lines," *Sun* (Baltimore, MD), March 8, 1916.
48. "Morse After Bay Boats," *Sun* (Baltimore, MD), March 24, 1916.
49. In the end, the ICC deferred the requirement that PRR divest its ferry lines after the politicians and merchants of Baltimore expressed concerns about being cut off from service altogether. The steamboat lines at that time were not making money, and it was proving difficult for PRR to unload them. By 1923, BC&A was entering into bankruptcy, and the ferry lines were split off anyway, apart from the one remaining line connected to a rail network (Love Point).
50. "To Cut Out Boat Line," *Sun* (Baltimore, MD), April 30, 1916.
51. "Yacht Mermaid, Which Ran to Cambridge, Sold," *Cambridge Daily Banner*, November 14, 1916. This article contains several factual errors. It confuses *Mermaid* with *Texas* as the steamer owned by Hetty Green (actually owned by her son) that made the trips to Cambridge.
52. A substantial debt holder was the Continental Trust Company, which held a mortgage from ESDSC for $77,250, established back in 1912 to fund the cost of constructing the wooden wharf in Claiborne. The interests of Continental Trust and Crawford were merged by the courts in May 1917 and the remaining property of ESDSC put up for auction in June 1917.
53. McIntosh did play a minor role in the future of Claiborne. In 1912, McIntosh had acquired a number of adjacent lots in Claiborne, including the large "hotel lot." In 1919, he sold most of them to the Maryland Tuberculosis Association. These lots formed part of the property that became known as Miracle House. McIntosh also donated an empty building to the "Kiddies Club of Claiborne," a local charity.

VII

Harrington's Quest

The rapid collapse of the Eastern Shore Development Steamship Company (ESDSC) might have discouraged others from contemplating a similar venture, but it did not. Even before that line had failed, plans were being prepared for another cross-bay ferry between Annapolis and Claiborne. This time the primary promoter was not a yacht broker from Brooklyn, but instead the just-elected governor of Maryland and a lifetime resident of the Eastern Shore.

In some ways, the experience of ESDSC helped inform the new venture. It both demonstrated the superiority of an Annapolis-based route across the Chesapeake as well as the futility of trying to be both competitor to and dependent upon the Baltimore, Chesapeake and Atlantic Railway (BC&A).

Perhaps ESDSC had just missed an opportunity. At the same time when their effort to bring passengers from Annapolis to the BC&A railroad terminal was unraveling, a major revolution in ground transport was underway. We were drifting away from the era of steam locomotion and entering the automobile age. Motor vehicles, powered by internal-combustion engines, were replacing steam-powered locomotives in both passenger and freight transport.

Henry Ford's Model T automobile had entered the market in

1908, and its mass production and relative affordability was enabled by Ford's innovations in assembly-line operations. By 1916, the year ESDSC entered liquidation, there were already 3.6 million registered motor vehicles in the United States. Within three years, the number would more than double to 7.6 million. By 1924 it would double again to 17.6 million, with *another* nine million added by 1930.[1]

Maryland shared in this expansion. By 1916, there were more than 44,000 motor vehicles registered in the state, and that number would rise to more than 324,000 by 1930.[2] Maryland's population was 1.6 million in 1930, which meant there was in 1930 one motor vehicle for every five residents, about the same ratio as for the nation as a whole.

The widespread introduction of automobiles had many implications, but the salient one for this moment in Chesapeake history was that it freed merchants and travelers from dependence on monopolistic railroad companies such as BC&A and its Maryland, Virginia and Delaware Railway (MD&V) subsidiary. Once the road network was improved, it would be possible to sideline railroads entirely from the operating model of the new ferry. BC&A could no longer crush the new entrant—*if* the ferry could move vehicles as well as passengers. The railroads had been defanged.

This trend likely influenced the decision taken in 1916 by newly elected Maryland Governor Emerson C. Harrington to push for a new Annapolis-based ferry, one that would carry passengers *and* their automobiles across the Chesapeake Bay. Harrington made this one of his top priorities after he was sworn in that January. In the end, Claiborne would be, once again, the beneficiary of this decision, though that would likely not have been the case had ESDSC not created the second wharf in that location. Once again, thirty years after Claiborne had been selected in a flawed business plan, a second failed business venture had set the starting conditions that led to Claiborne's continued dominance in cross-bay ferry traffic.

Maryland Governor Emerson C. Harrington led the creation of Claiborne-Annapolis Ferry Inc. Unknown photographer, 1911. Maryland State Archives, Comptrollers of Maryland Photographic Collection, MSA SC 5161-1-22

Emerson C. Harrington

The new governor was a creature of the Chesapeake, born in Tobacco Stick on the Little Choptank River, near Cambridge in Dorchester County. (Tobacco Stick, later to become famous as a place where abolitionist Harriet Tubman had been enslaved, changed its name to Madison in the late 1800s.) Harrington was schooled in Annapolis at the prestigious St. John's College, completing his master of arts degree in 1886, the same year that Joseph B. Seth launched his ill-fated venture to link Bay Ridge to Claiborne by rail-transfer ferry. Harrington started his professional career as an assistant professor at St. John's College, teaching Latin and mathematics, before returning to the Eastern Shore to teach at a private academy in Cambridge. He soon switched vocations, studying law and being admitted to the bar in 1898 and starting his own Cambridge-based law practice.

The next year, he ventured for the first time into elected office, winning the position of state's attorney for Dorchester County. By all accounts he was an aggressive prosecutor—particularly when it came to laws on oyster harvesting and alcohol—and this quite possibly led to his defeat for re-election in 1903.[3] Nonetheless, Harrington had built a position of support within the Dorchester Democratic Party and used this to advance to the state capital in Annapolis, first as insurance commissioner (1910) and then as the elected comptroller of Maryland in 1911. His nomination for that post by the Democratic Party referred to him as "a gentleman and lawyer of high personal and professional character . . . possessed of ability and experience in public affairs."[4] Others viewed him more critically: " . . . when [Harrington] does not want to make up his mind he can sit longer and misunderstand oftener and ask more irrelevant questions than any man in the civilized world."[5]

Four years later, Harrington ran on the Democratic ticket for governor and eked out a narrow victory. The newly elected governor assumed office at a time of heated debate in the United States on a number of contentious issues, including prohibition, woman suffrage, race relations at a time of Jim Crow, and antitrust policies. Locally, there were efforts in Baltimore to annex adjacent regional communities, and this was the subject of heated debate.[6]

Harrington took a clear position on the first issue of prohibition, echoing his strong stance as Dorchester County prosecutor a decade earlier:

> It is my opinion, and it has been my experience, that crime is greatly lessened in all sections where Prohibition prevails and in proportion as the temperance or local option of Prohibition laws are enforced. Not only is crime lessened, but there are fewer court trials and in my opinion greater prosperity. There is everything in favor of Prohibition and very little against it that I know of.[7]

When it came to the issue of women's suffrage, Harrington eventually punted and left to his successor the decision on whether to put to the Maryland legislature the proposed Constitutional amendment granting women the right to vote.[8]

He was less ambivalent on the issue of race relations, at least the "equal" part, if still accommodating the "separate" part. A speech given by Governor Harrington in 1918 celebrating Morgan College (an historically Black college, now the Morgan State University) is summarized as follows:

> The Hon. Emerson C. Harrington, governor of Maryland, recently spoke in Baltimore encouraging words on Negro education.... Governor Harrington declared that the progress of the Negro during the past fifty-off years of his freedom justifies the provision which has been made for his education and the efforts that have been put forth by his friends ... and that the thinking white people everywhere wish to have the Negro own his home, live under sanitary and moral conditions, cut down his death rate, and secure more enlightenment.[9]

But with respect to the separation of races, Harrington was seen, at least in the Black community, as someone opposed to ongoing efforts to relax Jim Crow. In 1931, his perceived role as leader of the efforts to sustain these inequitable laws even led to calls in the Black community to support a new bay bridge, a structure that would punish Harrington by undermining his business interests. As was reported at the time in the leading Baltimore newspaper for the Black community:

> ... The opposition to the jim crow law repeal was led by ex-Governor Emmerson Harrington, president of the [company] operating a ferry from Annapolis to Claiborne.... The best way to kill Harrington and his gang is to support the proposals for a Chesapeake Bay bridge, which will eliminate the need for a ferry and bring civilization closer to the shore.[10]

The final issue, when it came to dealing with powerful business and corporate power, is the one most relevant to the history here.

On this, Harrington's views were clear and quite progressive and mirror the views held a century later by modern progressive politicians. As he explained in his comments to the 1918 National Governors' Conference, addressing the rise of Bolshevism in Russia:

> . . . the surest way to avoid socialization of such a character, or anarchy, is for us to have such form of government with such legislation that gives equal and just privileges and equal and just opportunities to every citizen of our country. Public corporations and big business must now understand that they can only exist when they recognize that their existence is permitted for service and not for self and they are the servants and not the masters.[11]

This quite possibly informed one of the first acts proposed by newly elected Governor Harrington: to challenge the entrenched BC&A monopoly on cross-bay transportation. However, as we shall see later, his views would change once *he* became a primary owner of BC&A's replacement company, when Harrington would go to great lengths to protect *his* monopoly from new entrants.

Plans for a New Ferry

In February 1916, with Harrington's blessing, Maryland State Senator William Oscar Collier of Talbot County introduced legislation to establish a new car-ferry operation between Annapolis and Claiborne and simultaneously to improve the surface roads between Claiborne and Easton. The legislation allocated $300,000 for these purposes, to be split evenly between acquisition of a suitable ferry and improvement of the road system.

Collier's legislation was supported by a report prepared by a committee formed to study the issue, led by the ever-present Joseph B. Seth.[12] Though the route would originate from Annapolis, the ferry was positioned as a way to boost trade with Baltimore, which also served the political interests of Governor Harrington. And once again, there was the motive to protect Baltimore from its competitor to the north, Philadelphia. Seth seems to have repurposed the same rationale he had developed in 1886 during the creation of the Baltimore and Eastern Shore Railroad Company, writing thirty years later:

> . . . it will be the means of bringing Baltimore and the lower part of the Eastern Shore into closer relations and that it will bring back to the city much of the trade that is now going to Philadelphia because of the superior transportation facilities between the peninsula counties and the Pennsylvania metropolis.[13]

Protecting Eastern Shore trade against intrusion from Philadelphia was not Seth's only lifetime obsession. A long-time supporter of the Confederacy, he was also busy that year promoting the Lost Cause by erecting a statue to honor Confederate soldiers. The monument, placed on the green in front of the Talbot County Courthouse located in Easton, was dedicated on June 16, 1916. In March 2022, amidst much acrimony, it was removed, leaving behind only a statue of Frederick Douglass, a person characterized by Seth in his autobiography as "practically unknown."

The ferry legislation proceeded easily through both the Maryland Senate and the Maryland House of Delegates. However, a last-minute amendment reduced the funding allocation from $300,000 to $50,000.[14] This would lead one observer years later to characterize the passed legislation as a "joke" since that amount was not nearly enough for the purchase of a suitable ferry and to support the other start-up costs.[15] So, Harrington had his ferry scheme, but without enough money to actually buy a ferry. It was left up to the State Roads Commission to approve any specific plan, and that commission engaged engineer Frank W. Seth of Easton (nephew of Joseph B. Seth) to validate the plans.[16]

The amendment that reduced funding from $300,000 to $50,000 had long-lasting implications and might well have crippled the effort altogether were it not for Harrington's determination and inventiveness. It became difficult for the state to secure *any* suitable ferry at that reduced budget. As months passed, frustration began to grow on the Eastern Shore—Harrington's promise to his Eastern Shore neighbors, friends, and constituents remained unfilled.[17] But the lack of progress was not due to a lack of effort. The first solution put forward was to acquire *Castleton*, a sidewheel steamboat built in 1888 as *Erastus Wiman* and serving as a Staten Island Ferry until being withdrawn from service in 1905.[18] Discussions were reportedly underway in November 1916, but by July 1917 no transaction had yet taken place.[19]

All planning was interrupted that same month when the US War Department, ramping up for the country's entry into World War I, announced plans to acquire the entirety of Kent Island for purposes of creating an artillery proving ground, replacing the one in Sandy Hook, New Jersey. The resulting testing grounds, laboratories, and other facilities would create a major economic boom on this quiet part of the Eastern Shore. This prospect led to the tabling of plans for the Claiborne-Annapolis ferry, and to consideration of an alternative that would link Baltimore or Annapolis directly with Kent Island by car and passenger ferry, perhaps using the existing ferry terminal at Love Point or a new one built on Kent Island's western shore opposite Annapolis. The fact that the federal government—not the state—would subsidize the operation of such a ferry had additional appeal to frugal Maryland politicians.[20]

By September 1917, the War Department plans for Kent Island were abandoned when both the US Senate and the House of Representatives voted it down following ardent opposition from Kent Island residents.[21] The Claiborne-Annapolis option was back on the table. However, the delays had been costly, at least when it came to acquiring *Castleton*. Before the Marylanders could execute any deal, *Castleton* was taken out from under their noses by the Chesapeake Ferry Corporation of Virginia, for use out of Norfolk.[22]

It was back to the drawing board. The advent of World War I had pushed up prices for steamers of all kinds across the globe, and the $50,000 budget cap—the "joke"—available to Governor Harrington proved woefully inadequate. Pressure on Harrington continued. In March 1918, the Maryland legislature debated a bill introduced by

Maryland State Senator Orlando Harrison of Worcester County to force the State Roads Commission to complete the line and open it for service no later than July 1 of that year. Harrington was being driven to make good his promise, just as the opportunities to acquire a suitable used ferry steamboat with his budget were vanishing.[23]

The clock was ticking. The year 1919 would be the last full year in Harrington's term as governor, and he still could not point to development of a Claiborne-Annapolis ferry route, as promised in the first month of his administration three years earlier. His credibility was on the line. The inability of the state to acquire a suitable ferry forced Harrington to consider a novel approach. Perhaps the state might not actually own or operate a ferry but would instead contract with a private company to do so, providing a generous annual subsidy for the operating costs of the ferry instead.[24]

Initial efforts at this backup plan seemed unpromising. Harrington had been unable to get investors in Maryland to back such a new company, especially given the risks involved. However, once Harrington broadened his search to New York he found success. In February 1919, he announced boldly that negotiations with potential operators were almost concluded, that a ferry had been secured, and that service would start April 1. With only eight months left in his four-year term, it appeared, finally, that Harrington would get his ferry.[25] And in a pattern typical of this history, the funding arose only because of decisions made out of the region. Claiborne's fate was once again in the hands of New York-based entrepreneurs, as it had been in 1894 and 1912.

A Novel Strategy

The details of how this came about were generally lost to history until the examination of internal corporate documents for the new ferry line, squirreled away in the Maryland State Archives (and possibly untouched since 1941). The new strategy for the ferry operation was conceived by Charles W. Harrison, an entrepreneur born in Elizabeth City, North Carolina. Achieving financial success during World War I, Harrison was, in 1917, to "return a millionaire to the town [of Elizabeth City, where] he had left a travelling salesman."[26] Harrison, who often used the title "captain" but who in reality had far more experience in raising and dowsing companies than sails, approached Harrington and offered to set up the new ferry company if he could be given a three-year contract, with a $1,500 per month subsidy. Though based at the time in New York, Harrison was well known around the Chesapeake Bay, having operated a number of shipping companies in the area.

It was a clever approach. It would allow Harrington to declare victory, even if his $50,000 budget would not quite last all three years. Once the ferry was operating, Harrington logically assumed the Maryland government would be forced to cough up additional funds to keep it going. Without many options left, and his term as governor running down, Harrington agreed, and Harrison went off to organize financing.

Harrison needed deep pockets for this new venture. While he had made a small fortune in barges and towing during the First World War, he had also "lived on a scale according to his income" and was approaching financial distress.[27] By the end of 1919, he would be essentially bankrupt, with the local sheriff coming to seize his high-end furniture from his residence in New York City.[28] The new ferry line would not only bail out Harrington, but it would also accomplish the same for Harrison.

Harrison lined up two New York-based investors to join him in the new venture. Hampden D. Mepham, originally from St. Louis, was then operating as an investor in transportation ventures out of New York City.[29] Frank A. McNamee was an Albany-based insurance executive and finance chairman of the New York State Democratic Party. Mepham, McNamee, and Harrison were joined by two others with much smaller stakes: Edward L. Smallwood, a New York investor in transportation companies, and John T. Tucker, a Baltimore-based lawyer originally from the Eastern Shore. But in the end, from a finance standpoint, this really became the Mepham-McNamee show. By March 1919, this group of investors had established Claiborne-Annapolis Ferry Incorporated. Mepham was designated as president. Harrison assumed the role of vice president and general manager.[30]

The State Roads Commission was authorized by Harrington that same month to engage Claiborne-Annapolis Ferry Inc. with a three-year contract to operate the long-promised Claiborne-Annapolis ferry line, with an annual subsidy of $18,000 provided by the State of Maryland. Prices were set and approved by the Maryland Public Service Commission at $2 per automobile (including the driver) plus $0.50 for every other passenger.[31] Round trips were discounted at $0.75 for passengers. It is notable that only Mepham and McNamee are referenced in the contract with the State of Maryland—the other investors are not mentioned. This contract had value—it promised an $18,000 annual subsidy from the State of Maryland—and thus became a critical component of the overall financial strategy for the new business.

A ferry was needed for this operation, and once again Harrison was able to help—both the new ferry line and himself. Back in May 1918, before his personal fortune became imperiled, he had joined Harry J. Dike to take over management of (and with an option to buy) the New York and Long Branch Steamboat Company, known locally as the Patten Line. One of the ferries of that company, *Thomas Patten*, would eventually serve on the emerging Claiborne-Annapolis route.[32] Its transfer to the new company would also provide the Patten Line with much-needed cash, since that line had gone into receivership mere weeks after Harrison took over as president.

Another challenge was raising the capital required for the operation. Investors were skittish. Indeed, ferry operations were quite notorious for their level of risk presented to investors. Many had gone bankrupt, including the last two companies to operate from the broader Annapolis area. Founders of the Baltimore and Eastern Shore Railroad had seen their investments vanish in 1894. Likewise, the financiers in the Eastern Shore Development Steamship Company had lost their capital when that company entered liquidation in 1916.

The challenge then for Mepham and McNamee was to finance the company while committing as little of their own capital as possible, following in the tradition of Joseph B. Seth three decades earlier. In this way, if the new company followed the usual pattern and went belly-up, at least their personal losses would be minimal. However, if by chance the line was successful, they stood to prosper from the profits. They were also facilitated in this approach by Governor Harrington and some of his important friends, assistance that would be amply rewarded in the years to come.

Mepham and McNamee formally registered the new ferry company with share capital of $300,000, which was a lot for the time (about $7 million in 2024 dollars), but which was for the most part based on speculative valuations of intangible assets. That capital consisted of the following elements, which hint at clever financial maneuvering:

- $100,000 from the assignment of the Maryland contracts to the new company, based on a purely subjective assessment of the value of that subsidy. The equity associated with this investment went solely to Mepham and McNamee, since they were the only ones listed in the contract.
- $15,000 from an indemnity bond, required by the State of Maryland to ensure the company would operate the ferry for at least twelve months.
- $177,500 for all rights and title to the ferry *Thomas Patten* based on a gross valuation of $250,000 less the $72,500 that had to be paid for the ferry. This was the ferry intended for use on the Chesapeake Bay. It had been secured by Mepham and McNamee, so here all of the equity associated with this went to those two investors.
- Finally, a cash contribution of $7,500 from Mepham and McNamee.

In reality then, most of the value associated with the new company was ephemeral, with only $7,500 (about $150,000 in 2024 dollars) in actual cash contributed by the investors. The only physical asset was the ferry itself, with a speculative gross valuation of $250,000—far in excess of what was most likely paid or what it was worth, especially now that the price surge from World War I had wound down. For example, *Majestic*—a ferry of similar vintage, size, and capability—would be put into service by the new company in 1922 for only $52,200, including refit costs.

Mepham and McNamee then turned this valuation—aggressive as it might be—into collateral for the issue of $100,000 in ten-year bonds with annual interest of 6 percent, secured by a deed of assets to the Union Trust Company of Baltimore. Much of this sum was used right away to pay off the $72,000 actually incurred in the acquisition of *Thomas Patten*, thus relieving Mepham and McNamee of any personal obligations for this acquisition.[33]

Why would Union Trust Company back the bonds of this new company, with zero track record and with minimal financial exposure by the principals? Their specific c alculations remain a mystery. However, Mepham and McNamee for certain had found a friendly face at Union Trust Company, in the form of that bank's returning president. This was none other than John M. Dennis, the partner and confident of Governor Harrington who had "retired" (at age fifty-two) from his post as Maryland's treasurer in 1918 to reassume this corporate role.[34]

Thus was born Claiborne-Annapolis Ferry Inc., valued at $400,000. The shares in the new company were allocated as follows:[35]

Frank A. McNamee	23
Hampden D. Mepham	24
Hampden D. Mepham and Frank A. McNamee, jointly owned	59,950
Edward L. Smallwood	1
John T. Tucker	1
Unidentified (most likely Charles W. Harrison)	1
Total Shares	60,000

Harrington was aided by John M. Dennis (above), at that time head of a major Maryland bank. Painting by DeNyse Perrine, 1927. Maryland State Archives, Maryland State Art Collection, MSA SC 1545-1164

In summary, the process was a financial coup by Mepham and McNamee. They ended up owning 99.99 percent of a company valued at $400,000 for a total cash outlay of $7,500. The entity most at risk—holding the bag as it were—was Union Trust Company of Baltimore.

Once the company had been established, there was no longer a need for Edward L. Smallwood, who had deep financial pockets and was well respected in New York, to be identified as an investor. He had not even attended any of the company's board or shareholder meetings. Almost immediately upon the company's founding, Smallwood dropped off the board and out of the company. There was now a vacancy on the board, which would not be filled until early 1920.

Establishing the New Ferry Line

The ferry chosen by the emerging company for the new operation was *Thomas Patten*. This 202-foot-long steamer had been built in 1901 by T.S. Marvel & Company in New York and was a classic coal-fired, steam-powered, sidewheel passenger steamer, operating around the New York region for many years. For use in Maryland, it would be reconfigured to carry thirty-five automobiles and would be able to cross the Bay from Annapolis to Claiborne in one hour and fifteen minutes. Since the ferry had not originally been designed to accommodate automobiles, some modifications would be required. The upgraded ferry would be christened *Gov. Emerson C. Harrington*, after the then-serving governor and driving force behind the new ferry company.

Work would need to proceed in both Annapolis and Claiborne to accommodate the new ferry. Fortunately for the ferry company, these costs were borne by the State of Maryland.[36] For Claiborne, the plan was to upgrade the original pier, completed in 1912 for the Eastern Shore Development Steamship Company, right next door to the BC&A rail and ferry terminal. The pier would have to be lengthened to accommodate the larger ferries and strengthened to manage the automobile traffic. The State of Maryland proceeded to acquire that pier and the adjacent land from Harry E. Karr, who had picked it up just a few years earlier at the auction of assets from the defunct ESDSC.

For a time, there was concern that the start-up might be derailed by an incident on the water. On March 12, company President Mepham, General Manager Harrison, and State Roads Commission Engineer William Perot left Annapolis for Claiborne to inspect the latter's facilities for the new ferry line. They departed Claiborne for the return journey to Annapolis at 8:00 p.m. in a "stiff gale"—and then nothing was heard from the group through the rest of the night. They were feared lost, and panicked phone calls were made in an attempt to learn what had happened. An intensive search of the waters between Claiborne and Annapolis was undertaken. At 12:45 p.m. the following day, the boat, its engine having failed, was located and those aboard brought to safety after having spent the night on the Chesapeake Bay.[37] (A photograph taken by a Claiborne resident appears to depict the three gentlemen standing on the pier during the renovation. That image might have been the last ever for them, had the trip back resulted in their fatalities.)

Captain Harrison in the end departed Claiborne-Annapolis Ferry Inc. just before operations got underway, although he will reemerge in the story a bit later.[38] Harrison had misgivings about the Claiborne-Annapolis route altogether and preferred a more direct Baltimore-to-Love Point connection instead. This initiated a debate that would continue for the next two decades, ultimately leading to the end of Claiborne's role as a transit hub. In this instance, however, he had been overruled by Governor Harrington.[39] Still, Harrison had been a critical partner to Harrington in the whole venture and was credited by Harrington with linking him up with the New York investors in the first place.[40] As one journalist reported at the time:

> Capt. C. W. Harrison, one of the practical steamboat men of the East, realized the possibilities and laid his plan before Governor Emerson C. Harrington. Both entered enthusiastically into the work and the Claiborne-Annapolis ferry resulted. Capt. Harrison always believed that the Love Point route would provide the only practical one, but he was over-ruled, and after the ferry had been successfully placed into operation, he turned his time and attention to the duties of operating the Baltimore and Southern Navigation Company's line of steamers. [41]

The new general manager for Claiborne-Annapolis Ferry Inc. was Thomas C. B. Howard, well known for his earlier role as commander of Maryland's "Oyster Navy" and more recently as a captain of BC&A steamers operating between Baltimore and Claiborne.

In the end, the April 1 target date for the start of operations could not be met. There was still work being undertaken to ready the upgraded Claiborne pier and adjacent roads. Nor was the ferry itself ready. The renamed *Gov. Emerson C. Harrington* ran aground twice in the Shrewsbury River in New Jersey while on its way south—it would take several weeks to free the ship.[42] Once freed, it was again delayed by fog off the coast of New Jersey. Upon arriving in the Chesapeake, the ferry required additional time for repairs and upgrades. (One is reminded of the hopes that surrounded the anticipated arrival of the rail-transfer ferry *Groton* in 1890, only to see that steamer burn and sink on the way down from Connecticut.)

Finally, on June 19, 1919, six months before the end of Harrington's term as governor, the inaugural run of the new Claiborne-Annapolis Ferry operation took place. It was an exceptionally pleasant mid-June day on the Chesapeake, with plenty of sunshine, temperatures in the high 70s, and gentle breezes.[43] The heat and humidity for which the Chesapeake summers are legendary had yet to make their presence known. The assembled guests could not have asked for a nicer day to celebrate the opening of the ferry.

There were two such commemorations that day. The first event took place in Annapolis, to which *Gov. Emerson C. Harrington* arrived with six hundred invited guests from the Eastern Shore, having departed earlier that morning from Claiborne. Governor Harrington addressed the crowd in Annapolis, emphasizing the need to bring competition to railroad-controlled steamer lines and to ensure stronger commercial links between Baltimore and the Eastern Shore. From there the ferry returned to Claiborne, where the celebrations continued. Almost fifteen hundred passengers were aboard that return trip to Claiborne. One of them was Joseph B. Seth, who also addressed the crowd upon arrival in Claiborne, almost exactly twenty-nine years after celebrating the opening of the first major ferry line to Claiborne's shoreline along Eastern Bay.[44] This first venture then had not lasted a year. Perhaps this newest venture would see more success.

Governor Harrington's support for the company had been complete. He had pushed for the ferry when first inaugurated into office in 1916. When state operation proved impossible, he looked far and wide for potential investors willing to finance the new operation. He pressed the State Roads Commission to issue a contract to those new investors. The risks to those investors were made manageable by the friendly support of Union Trust Company, headed by his colleague and friend John M. Dennis. Moreover, Harrington's relationship with the ferry was about to become far more intimate.

On January 14, 1920, Emerson C. Harrington formally turned over the Maryland governorship to the newly elected Albert C. Ritchie, his long-time political ally. (This is the same Albert C. Ritchie who had earlier defended a BC&A captain in Virginia against charges that the captain inadequately enforced segregation.) Exactly eight days later, filling the position that had been conveniently left vacant by Edward L. Smallwood's departure nine months earlier, and without publicity, Harrington was elected a director of Claiborne-Annapolis Ferry Inc. Thus began a two-decade career with the company whose birth he helped engineer from the governor's office.

The Ferry Line Expands

There were other changes—former politicians were taking over. At the next board meeting, on February 18, Baltimore lawyer John T. Tucker resigned from the board and was replaced by James F. Strange, who had just left office as the mayor of Annapolis. Frank A. McNamee resigned as treasurer of the company and was replaced by George H. Dawson Jr., a lawyer from Cambridge, Maryland, who was connected via family ties to Harrington.[45] Finally, Harrington himself was elected vice president of the company, just five weeks after leaving his position as governor.[46] Again, there was little publicity about Harrington's increasing engagement with the ferry company. He was now both an officer and a director of Claiborne-Annapolis Ferry Inc.

Operations continued through the course of these management changes, and the ferry proved increasingly popular. However, it was clear from the onset that operating the line with only one steamer was impractical since the vessel would need to be taken out of service on a regular basis for overhaul. Plus, it would be advantageous to have additional ferry capacity for peak periods or in case of an unscheduled downtime due to mechanical failure. The contract with the State of Maryland obligated the company to run three round trips per day in the peak season (summer) and two round trips per day otherwise.[47] Moreover, state officials encouraged the company to add an additional early morning trip (departing at 4:00 a.m.) to bring the mail and newspapers from Baltimore to the Eastern Shore.[48]

The ferry line managers looked around for an additional ferry but ran into challenges. The steamer *Cape May* of Philadelphia was ruled out because it drew eleven feet and that would require extensive dredging in Claiborne.[49] The ferry *Stony Creek* was examined but seen as too small.[50] *Oyster Bay* at Greenwich, Connecticut, was investigated in detail, but it was taken over by another operation before it could be acquired.[51] *Carmania* at Staten Island was evaluated, but an estimate of $75,000 to bring it into operation ruled it out of consideration.[52] This left one boat, the aging *Gen. Lincoln*.[53] It could be put into service at an acquisition cost of $7,500 and necessary repairs of $10,000 for a total of only $17,500. Mepham characterized this ferry as similar to the *Gov. Emerson C. Harrington*, which is notable in that he had valued the *Harrington* at $250,000—fourteen times as much—for purposes of establishing the capital of the company.[54]

Eventually they settled on *Gen. Lincoln*, an old steamer built in 1878 as *Nahant* by G. Pierce in Chelsea, Massachusetts. The 160-foot sidewheel steamboat arrived in the Chesapeake on July 4, 1920, and began service a few weeks later, allowing *Gov. Emerson C. Harrington* to enter a shipyard for much-needed overhaul.

Already two decades older than *Gov. Emerson C. Harrington*, *Gen. Lincoln* proved problematic in service. It could only carry ten to fifteen automobiles, less than half of the capacity of *Gov. Emerson C. Harrington*. Because of this, *Gen. Lincoln* was removed for service on August 7 once *Gov. Emerson C. Harrington* returned from its overhaul, and itself was taken into a shipyard for maintenance and repair. Returning to service, it then ran aground on March 9, 1921, off Tolly Point near Annapolis, stranding passengers, including former Governor Harrington and his wife, until they could be taken off by motorboats and a subchaser dispatched from the US Naval Academy.[55] By July 1921 the company decided to sell the ferry as soon as possible and to otherwise deploy it only when absolutely needed to meet peak demand or replace *Gov. Emerson C. Harrington* when the latter entered overhaul.[56]

Such a need emerged over the Independence Day holiday period in 1922, when the volume of traffic was greater than *Gov. Emerson C. Harrington* alone could support. *Gen. Lincoln* suffered a catastrophic failure on July 1, 1922, when the steamer's two paddlewheel boxes collapsed and broke off in a sudden squall off Bloody Point at the southern tip of Kent Island. The aft bulkhead failed, and water started filling the vessel. Contemporary reports point to panic amongst the crew and passengers, with the crew accused of making their own escape while abandoning the passengers. Upon hearing distress blasts from the steamer's whistle, the nearby steamer *Lancaster* lowered boats and began rescuing passengers. *Gov. Emerson C. Harrington*, which had departed Claiborne just after *Gen. Lincoln*, arrived on the scene and took *Gen. Lincoln* under tow to Annapolis, arriving late that night.[57]

Financial Challenges and Harrington Takes Over

Despite the appeal of the new service, by July 1921, Claiborne-Annapolis Ferry Inc. was in financial distress. The inadequacy of *Gen. Lincoln* would force the company either to acquire another ferry or to fund expensive upgrades. Money was tight. The original investors, Mepham and McNamee, had already advanced the company $25,000 back in February 1920 and had to commit another $5,000 in working capital in July 1921.[58]

These advances, in addition to the original investments and other claims, created liabilities totaling $71,358 owed to the New York investors. The board met on July 8, 1921—a meeting at which Harrington presided and Mepham and McNamee were absent. At that meeting, Harrington informed the other board members that this claim "if pressed, would bankrupt the Company."[59]

It turned out that Harrington had already preempted this issue and, in doing so, engineered a financial transaction that would end up with him running the company and with Mepham and McNamee out of it. The day before, on July 7, 1921, Harrington and McNamee (representing both himself and Mepham, who was in Brazil at the time) signed a memorandum of agreement that allowed Harrington to purchase from Mepham and McNamee 15,300 shares of stock for the sum of $15,300, payable in installments through that September. Moreover, the agreement also transferred all claims against the ferry company to Harrington. At this point, McNamee exited the company.[60]

The transition was codified in September 1921 when the board of directors unanimously elected Emerson C. Harrington as president of Claiborne-Annapolis Ferry Inc. Orlando Harrison, then a Maryland state senator from the Eastern Shore and a longtime supporter of the ferry effort, was elected vice president. At this same meeting Hampden D. Mepham also resigned from the board, "having parted with all his interest in the company."[61] The takeover was complete: all of the original New York investors were out, and the company was now under the control of Harrington and his Maryland colleagues, most of whom were retired politicians. It was a reversal of the financial engineering of the original Baltimore and Eastern Shore Railroad Company in 1894, one that had resulted in New York-based investors displacing investors hailing from Maryland's Eastern Shore. This time the Marylanders ended up in charge.

Harrington's emerging role in the company was not without controversy, especially since he took over merely eighteen months after leaving office. His earlier roles as director and vice president had been achieved without publicity, but his new role as president could not be hidden. In a preemptive strike against potential controversy, just before he took control, Harrington published an open letter to the stockholders of the company, defending his role in Claiborne-Annapolis Ferry Inc. and laying out his vision. The arguments he made are, to be generous, curious.

Harrington first claimed he had no conflict of interest when, as governor, he supported the creation of the company:

> I would like to explain that I was not personally concerned whatsoever from a financial standpoint in the starting of the Ferry. . . . The State had nothing to do with the organization and financing of the Company whatsoever. . . . We had nothing whatever to do with the financing of this Company. These New York parties [Mepham et al.] organized the Company and we made the contract with them.[62]

This argument is a bit specious. That contract from the State of Maryland issued under Governor Harrington constituted one-third of the stated equity in the new company. Without it, the company would not have been able to establish its capital base and most likely would not have been able to borrow the $100,000 to get started. Moreover, John M. Dennis, the close former colleague of Harrington, was president of Union Trust Company, the bank that guaranteed the $100,000 in bonds to buy *Gov. Emerson C. Harrington* and to fund working capital.

Second, Harrington defended his decision to participate in the company as a director, conveniently leaving out that he had also been elected as an officer of the company just five weeks after leaving office:

> After my term for Governor ended, I wanted to see the Annapolis Ferry better run and then I consented to act as one of its directors on certain conditions; that the control and management should be at this end. . . . My interest in this Ferry is to see it run. I have not a dollar of any kind in it, nor have I ever received a dollar from it. I do not want to make a dollar on this Ferry, but I do want to see it put in proper shape.[63]

Again, his argument falls flat. Harrington was not a passive participant. He was elected the vice president of the company in February 1920—the second highest position in the company—and was actively involved in the operational decisions of the company, as the minutes of the meetings of the company's board of directors clearly indicate. (These minutes became publicly available only upon the sale of the company to the State of Maryland in 1941.) Starting in November 1920, Harrington presided at the board of directors' meetings, effectively operating as chief executive and chairman in the absence of Mepham or McNamee.[64]

Third and finally, Harrington outlined his personal aspirations with respect to the company:

> Now, what I propose is to obtain an option upon as much stock as I can and then sell it to the people of Baltimore or the Eastern Shore who are interested in this Ferry and want to see it run. All of the money received above the purchase price will be turned into the Treasury of the Company for putting it into shape and guaranteeing its continuance and not one dollar will be otherwise spent. . . . My interest is alone in the successful running of the Ferry, and is now very popular with us, and not from a personal financial standpoint of any kind.

The disclaiming of a financial interest is, at best, misleading. In 1920, after joining the company as a director and vice president, Harrington owned twenty-five shares, or 0.04 percent of the company. By March 1923, he owned 4,724 shares, or 7.12 percent of the company. By 1927 he owned 19,664 shares, or 32.77 percent of the company.[65] The eventual sale of the company in 1941 would generate considerable wealth for Harrington and his family.

Harrington did have his work cut out for him. By mid-1921, company management was looking to rid itself of *Gen. Lincoln* and demoted it to back-up service. It was taken out of operation completely and laid up after its July 1922 incident.[66] The search had already started for a replacement vessel to serve as backup and complement to *Gov. Emerson C. Harrington*. The company considered buying the steamer *Thomas F. Brennon*, then in New York. The deal fell through when an examination of the ferry suggested its condition was not satisfactory.[67]

Finally, in March 1923, they settled on *Majestic*, a sidewheel steamer of similar vintage and proportions to *Gov. Emerson C. Harrington*.[68] The price was $40,000, or only a fraction of the valuation applied to *Gov. Emerson C. Harrington* in 1919 by Mepham and McNamee.[69] It cost another $12,200 to upgrade the ferry.[70]

Built by Lewis Nixon in Elizabeth, New Jersey, as *Happy Day* in 1903, *Majestic* was two years newer than *Gov. Emerson C. Harrington*, of identical length (202 feet), and only slightly less total volume (717 versus 875 GRT). The purchase of *Majestic* was announced in March 1923, and it began operations almost immediately, filling in the role of substitute ferry during *Gov. Emerson C. Harrington*'s overhauls and operating alongside her as additional capacity during peak periods.[71]

Claiborne Enters Its Golden Age

With operations finally in full swing between Claiborne and Annapolis, passengers now had direct access to both Baltimore and Annapolis by ferry. Connecting passengers could take a train to Ocean City, or, if owners of an automobile, drive there themselves. A bus line started operations to transport those without their own automobiles. The village of Claiborne expanded as an influx of workers on the Claiborne-Annapolis ferry line joined those from BC&A already living there. Later residents would report that virtually every man in the village would be addressed as "captain"—it just made things simpler.

At first, Claiborne-Annapolis Ferry Inc. drew these captains from across the region. The first captain of the Claiborne-Annapolis route, Thomas J. Mann, lived in Norfolk, Virginia. He served as master of *Gov. Emerson C. Harrington* from mid-1919 to early 1920 before returning to his Virginia home. His replacement, Frances M. Luckett, who lived in Baltimore, started on *Gov. Emerson C. Harrington* before shifting to *Gen. Lincoln* in 1921. He died September 1922.

Luckett's replacement as captain of *Gov. Emerson C. Harrington* in 1921 would be the first of an illustrious Claiborne-based family to serve on the Claiborne-Annapolis route. The new captain was Daniel G. Higgins. Higgins had been born near Claiborne in 1895 and worked as a waterman harvesting oysters until serving overseas in World War I. Upon his return in 1918, he took a job as a streetcar conductor in Baltimore. A chance occurrence with someone affiliated with the emerging car-ferry company (perhaps the company attorney John Tucker or John M. Dennis, as both were residing in Baltimore at the time?) led him to return to Claiborne to work with Claiborne-Annapolis Ferry Inc. just as it was starting up—a career that would extend thirty-three years.[72] Daniel Higgins would go on to serve as captain of many steamers on the ferry line.

Daniel was one of three brothers—alongside Gardner and Edward (Ned)—to serve in the early days as masters in the Claiborne-Annapolis Ferry system. Daniel's house was directly across from the village church, an institution that he supported extensively, especially after his young son died. His brother Gardner built a house directly next to the church. Both homes remain today. (Ned, who was still a boy when the line started, would later set up home nearby in Stevensville, on Kent Island.)

Not all early captains on the Claiborne-Annapolis Ferry were from the Higgins family. Besides Mann and Luckett, Thomas M. Woolford served as a senior captain of the line in the early days, starting with *Gen. Lincoln* in 1921 and then transitioning to its replacement, *Majestic*. He had arrived at the ferry line following a stint as a Deputy Commander of Maryland's "Oyster Navy," rising to command the schooner *Bessie Jones* in 1914.[73] Eventually he would be the captain selected to bring into service each of the line's diesel-powered ferries, until his retirement in the early 1940s.

A growing local community in Claiborne emerged to support the new workforce and their families. Claiborne itself emerged as a destination for tourists—until then it was just the transfer point for passengers seeking destinations farther down the line. Up to this point, visitors could be accommodated in a number of bed-and-breakfast establishments such as Maple Hall, Claiborne Hall, and Little Haven-on-the-Bay. Soon after the car ferry began operations, new establishments arose.

The short-lived Motor Inn operated during the summer seasons from 1920 to 1922. Its continued operation into 1923 was possibly upended by the opening of the much larger Bellfonte Hotel close by. Construction of this twenty-two-room hotel on Eastern Bay began in September 1922 and was completed in May of 1923. Owned by Albert J. Wyatt and his wife Mary, it catered to the needs of visitors as well as railroad and ferry workers. In 1926, the Wyatts transferred ownership to Mary's sister, Annie B. Card, who ran the establishment for another twelve years.

One gets the sense that the Bellfonte Hotel may have catered to the broad interests of the local community, which notably included a number of railway workers and sailors. For example, the new owner Annie B. Card, who was originally from Wilmington, Delaware, would be arrested four times (1924, 1925, 1937, and 1942) in that city for "running a disorderly house," contemporary language for a brothel. (One can find no such arrest records for Card in Talbot County.)

Albert and Mary Wyatt also operated the Al-Mar Inn, a restaurant (and rumored center of action for bootlegging during Prohibition) built over the water adjacent to the Claiborne car-ferry wharf. Long-time Talbot County resident Margaret Bryan, who lived with her father B. Frank Sherman in Claiborne, remembers being told by her parents to avoid that store because "it is a rough place."[74]

A second restaurant, Ye Ferry Inn, was created about the same time on the ferry wharf itself. It lasted only from July 1919 to January 1920. This building was then taken over by Robert R. North and his wife Nodie and renamed The Sea Gull Inn. It was an establishment that persisted until 1937 when Robert died while fishing on the Chesapeake. The Sea Gull Inn accommodated the basic needs of travelers waiting for or arriving on the car ferry, offering simple foods and beverages. Accommodations were spartan—wooden benches and tables. Its "restroom" consisted of planks over the water with a hole cut in them.[75]

Merchandise could be obtained at the general store, a business established in the late 1880s and then operated by John W. Bridges until 1921 and Harry P. Yerby afterwards. Claiborne Supply Company continued in operation, run by a partnership of Theodore

T. Jones Jr. and William F. Rowlensen. Recent immigrant Alfred Bergmann, originally from Germany, arrived in Claiborne in 1921 and created Bergmann's Bakery, located right on Claiborne's main avenue. Two gas stations supported the motorists bringing autos on the ferry, one at the general store and one on the entranceway to the ferry wharf itself.

Over time, the growth in the emerging transit hub on Broad Cove, with its community now centered on the railroad and ferry pier, overtook the much smaller and older neighborhood of Old Claiborne, even usurping the latter's name. Moreover, the new Claiborne did not just commandeer the identity of its predecessor. In 1921, the Holy Innocents Chapel was relocated physically from its location in Old Claiborne to a new location on the main road within the larger and newer village of Claiborne.[76]

Why this move? There are several reasons offered in a directory prepared by St. Michael's Parish. One was the increasing "comparative isolation" of the Old Claiborne community following construction of a new state road, which bypassed that neighborhood entirely. Another stated reason was that the original location of the chapel "was located in a section rapidly becoming a colored neighborhood."[77] This latter concern may have reflected rising racial tensions in Talbot County following an incident in which a Black farmer, Isaiah Fountain, was arrested in 1919 for the rape of a local white girl. In a trial that remains a subject of controversy even today, an all-white jury convicted Fountain of the rape. Fountain narrowly escaped lynching by an angry mob assembled outside the Talbot County Courthouse, only to be executed by hanging in the Talbot County jail in 1920.[78]

Holy Innocents Chapel continued to serve the Claiborne community in this new location until the congregation was dissolved in 1926, with the parishioners diverted via car or train for religious services in St. Michaels. At that point, the chapel building in Claiborne was converted into a parish hall for Claiborne's other house of worship, the Claiborne Methodist Episcopal Church.

As with the Holy Innocents Chapel, the Methodist church was

moved to the community's main street—Claiborne Road—in 1921, across the street and a few houses away from the relocated Holy Innocents Chapel.

A final establishment made Claiborne well known in regional circles. For years, campaigns to avoid the spread of tuberculosis during summer school breaks had sought to remove children from infected homes in Baltimore to a location where they could enjoy fresh air and a safe environment. Thus was born what came to be known as Miracle House, a camp for children right off Eastern Bay formed from properties donated by Andrew J. McIntosh, the founder of the Eastern Shore Development Steamship Company, after his company failed in 1916. Operating for several decades, Miracle House earned its name, it is said, from the fact that none of the children occupying that camp ever developed tuberculosis.

Claiborne had evolved from a ferry wharf and transit point into a growing and prosperous small village, now served by two major cross-bay steamer lines and connected by both rail and road to distant locations on the Eastern Shore. Each of the lines had built upon the remnants of failed predecessors who had selected Claiborne as its hub. It was the golden age, but it would last less than two decades. The rise of Claiborne, and its eventual return to a quiet backwater, would all take place in the lifetime of one noted resident: Benjamin Franklin Sherman.

B. Frank Sherman

A sad transition in leadership for Claiborne-Annapolis Ferry Inc. took place in September 1924, when general manager Thomas C. B. Howard died. A former commander of the "Oyster Navy," and a man highly respected in the community, Howard had been with the company since operations had started and had seen the venture through its most difficult early days. His position as general manager was filled formally by board resolution on March 23, 1925. The new general manager was Claiborne-based ticket agent B. Frank Sherman.[79]

More than any other person, Benjamin Franklin Sherman would become strongly associated with the Claiborne-Annapolis

B. Frank Sherman served as general manager of Claiborne-Annapolis Ferry Inc. from 1925 until the end of the ferry line route in 1952. Unknown photographer, n.d. From the B. F. Sherman Family Collection, courtesy of Margaret Bryan

Ferry, across all of its corporate incarnations. He had grown up near Cambridge, going to school until the eighth grade and then working for his father, a miller. The family was of modest means, and Sherman's diet was often supplemented by small game he hunted, including squirrels, rabbits, muskrats ("marsh rabbits"), and nutria. It was said that he was quite fond of the last two.[80]

His youth had been spent in part playing with childhood friend Emerson C. Harrington Jr., son of the Maryland governor and the driving force behind the Claiborne-Annapolis Ferry. Emerson Jr. and Sherman had even served together in combat in the Meuse-Argonne battle in France in 1918, during which Sherman was wounded in a poison gas attack. Sherman was close to the senior Emerson C. Harrington, who treated him almost as another son. It should not be surprising, therefore, that when it was time to find an experienced and trusted person to take over as general manager after Howard's death, the company president looked to Sherman, who was already employed by the company.

While largely self-educated after the eighth grade, Sherman proved a dependable manager, was well-spoken, and communicated effectively as a writer. He also became the leading resident of Claiborne for most of his adult life. He had a passion for fishing and hunting, smoked most of his life, and was known to have a drink now and then. A local bootlegger provided ample supplies of liquor during Prohibition. This "good living" may have contributed to his heart problems later in life.

Sherman, who had been with the company from its first day of operations, would go on to serve as general manager for the next twenty-seven years, until the end of the ferry line's existence in 1952. He would help lead the transition into state ownership in 1941 and would continue afterward as a state employee, continuing to run the ferry system. In many ways it is hard to separate the history of the Claiborne-Annapolis ferry line from the history of B. Frank Sherman.

Notes

1. "State Motor Vehicle Registrations, by Years, 1900–1995," US Department of Transportation, Federal Highway Administration, Office of Highway Information Management.
2. Ibid.
3. Matthew P. Andrews, *Tercentenary History of Maryland* (The S.J. Clarke Publishing Company, 1925), 279.
4. "An Address to the People of Maryland Issued by the Democratic Sate Central Committee of Maryland," *Sun* (Baltimore, MD), November 1, 1911.
5. "While the Governor Walks the Hard Floor," *Sun* (Baltimore, MD), March 19, 1916.
6. Matthew A. Crenson, *Baltimore: A Political History* (Johns Hopkins University Press, 2017), 361–63.
7. Quoted in Ernest Hurst Cherrington, *The Anti-Saloon League Yearbook 1920* (The Anti-Saloon League of America, 1920), 93.
8. Ida Huster Harper, ed., *The History of Woman Suffrage* (National American Woman Suffrage Association, 1922), 257.
9. J. McKeen Cattell, ed., *School and Society: Volume VII* (Science Press, 1918), 29.
10. "Stealing Jim Crow Bill Real Old Stuff," *Afro-American* (Baltimore, MD), April 18, 1931.
11. Emerson C. Harrington, *Proceedings of the Tenth Meeting of the Governors of the State of the Union*, December 16–18, 1918, 13.
12. "For Ferry to the Shore," *Sun* (Baltimore, MD), February 39, 1916.
13. "Inquiry Ordered into Bay Ferry," *Evening Sun* (Baltimore, MD), July 20, 1916.
14. *General Assembly, Senate* (Journal), 1916, MdHR 821259, 2/1/8/16, for Senate Bill No. 344, 1334. Digital image from Maryland State Archives, accessed July 21, 2025.
15. This was State Insurance Commissioner and Talbot County resident W. Mason Shehan, at the opening of the ferry in 1919, as quoted in "'Shores' of Maryland Linked by New Ferry," *Sun* (Baltimore, MD), June 20, 1919.
16. "Inquiry Ordered into Bay Ferry," *Evening Sun* (Baltimore, MD), July 20, 1916.
17. One discarded proposal put forth in November 1916 was to convert two old steamers formerly assigned to Maryland's "Oyster Navy"–*Governor McLane* and *Governor Thomas*–into passenger vessels. They would then tow behind them a barge accommodating the automobiles of those passengers. See "Plans Trans-Bay Ferry," *Sun* (Baltimore, MD), November 16, 1916.

18. "Boat for Claiborne Ferry," *Sun* (Baltimore, MD), November 29, 1916. *Castleton's* official number was 136019. It was built in 1888 by Columbian Iron Works at Sparrows Point, Maryland. The shipyard later became Bethlehem Shipbuilding.
19. "Ferry Still Puzzles," *Evening Sun* (Baltimore, MD), July 10, 1917.
20. "From Annapolis to Kent Island," *Evening Capital* (Annapolis, MD), August 16, 1917.
21. The artillery proving ground was established instead off Aberdeen, Maryland, on the other side of the Chesapeake Bay. It is now a major military facility and an economic engine for Harford and Cecil counties.
22. "Virginia Corporation Acquires the Castleton," *Virginian-Pilot and Norfolk Landmark*, December 2, 1917. It was not long in service in Virginia, for in May 1918 it was completely destroyed by fire in Norfolk.
23. Lack of such options led the governor to consider, briefly, an alternative to the new ferry line: a bridge across the Chesapeake. A committee was formed under States Roads Commissioner Frank H. Zouck (including the familiar Joseph B. Seth) to conduct a feasibility study. In the end, the costs of a new bridge were seen as prohibitive and the concept was abandoned—for the time being. So, it was back to finding a boat for the ferry. See "Zouck Making Survey for Bay Bridge Plan," *Sun* (Baltimore, MD), December 4, 1918.
24. "Getting Ready for the Ferry," *Denton Journal*, February 15, 1919.
25. "Bay Ferry April 1," *Evening Sun* (Baltimore, MD), February 4, 1919.
26. "Riverdale Scheduled for First Trip Next Week," *Daily Advance* (Elizabeth City, NC), November 2, 1917.
27. "Suits Reveal Loss of Harrison Riches," *New York Times*, December 18, 1919.
28. "Seizes Her Furniture," *Sun* (Baltimore, MD), December 18, 1919.
29. There are various spellings of Mr. Mepham's first name. The spelling "Hampden" appears correct based on documents he completed himself, such as his passport application.
30. "Annapolis Ferry at a Premium," *Sun* (Baltimore, MD), April 3, 1919.
31. "State Ferry April 15," *Sun* (Baltimore, MD), March 13, 1919.
32. "Patten Line Changes Hands," *New York Herald*, May 1, 1918. A receiver would be appointed for the line a few weeks later. See "Receiver for Patten Line," *New York Times*, June 8, 1918.
33. Meeting Minutes of the First Directors' Meeting of Claiborne-Annapolis Ferry Inc., March 20, 1919, 29, Maryland State Archives, Maryland Public Service Commission, MSA S245-1, MdHR 19816-1.
34. "John M. Dennis," *Sun* (Baltimore, MD), January 18, 1918. There had been a vote in the Maryland legislature regarding the future state treasurer role and Dennis had lost that vote. This precipitated his retirement.

35. Minutes of the Special Meeting of Stockholders of the Claiborne-Annapolis Ferry Inc., April 14, 1919, 53, Maryland State Archives, Maryland Public Service Commission, MSA S245-1, MdHR 19816-1.
36. Of the $50,000 in funding allocated by the Maryland legislature, $48,000 was used to fund the $16,000 of the three-year annual subsidies of $18,000 per year. (The rest of the subsidy would be funded from the state's annual budget.) Another $2,000 of the initial $50,000 budget was allocated to improve the Claiborne wharf and to build an access road.
37. "Mystery Surrounds Fate of Officials," *Evening Capital* (Annapolis, MD), March 12, 1919; "Governor Excited Due to Balky Boat," *Evening Sun* (Baltimore, MD), March 12, 1919.
38. "Resigns from Ferry Line," *Sun* (Baltimore, MD), May 31, 1919.
39. "Making Next Door Neighbors of the Eastern Shore and Baltimore," *Denton Journal*, October 4, 1919. The new venture began operations in September 1921. By June 1922, it was declared insolvent and a receiver was appointed. The operation was taken over in 1923 by the Baltimore and Eastern Railroad Company. See "Action Soon on M.D.&V. Plan," *Evening Journal* (Wilmington, DE), September 27, 1923.
40. Emerson C. Harrington to company shareholders, in *The Claiborne-Annapolis Ferry Inc.*, March 22, 1921, Maryland State Archives, Maryland Public Service Commission, MSA S245-1, MdHR 19816-1.
41. "Making Next Door Neighbors of the Eastern Shore and Baltimore," *Denton Journal*, October 4, 1919.
42. "To Float Bay Ferry Boat," *Sun* (Baltimore, MD), May 27, 1919.
43. Based on the reported weather in local newspapers.
44. "Shores of Maryland Linked by New Ferry," *Sun* (Baltimore, MD), June 20, 1919.
45. Dawson was the nephew of Thomas W. Simmons, the secretary of state in the Harrington administration. See Dawson's obituary in *News Journal* (Cambridge, MD), April 1, 1933.
46. Meeting Minutes of the Claiborne-Annapolis Ferry Inc. Board of Directors, February 18, 1920, Maryland State Archives, Maryland Public Service Commission, MSA S245-1, MdHR 19816-1.
47. "Contract between the State Roads Commission and Messrs. Mepham and McNamee of New York," Maryland State Archives, Maryland Public Service Commission, MSA S245-8, MdHR 19816-13.
48. Meeting Minutes of the Claiborne-Annapolis Ferry Inc. Board of Directors, August 1, 1919, Maryland State Archives, Maryland Public Service Commission, MSA S245-1, MdHR 19816-1.
49. Official number of *Cape May* was 127566. It was built in 1901 by Harlan & Hollingsworth in Wilmington, Delaware.

50. *Stony Creek* (official number 96684) was built in 1903 as *Huntington* in Noank, Connecticut, by Robert Palmer & Son. Meeting Minutes of the Claiborne-Annapolis Ferry Inc. Board of Directors, August 1, 1919, Maryland State Archives, Maryland Public Service Commission, MSA S245-1, MdHR 19816-1.
51. Official number of *Oyster Bay* was 121007. It was built in 1895 as *Fulton Market* by Robert Palmer & Son in Noank, Connecticut.
52. Official number of *Carmania* was 92729. It was built in 1896 as *Margaret* by Newport News Shipbuilding in Newport News, Virginia.
53. Official number of *Gen. Lincoln* was 130146. The steamer is sometimes referred to as *General Lincoln*. The name of the vessel as it appears in the formal US vessel registers, and as written on the steamer itself, is *Gen. Lincoln*, and that is how it will be named here.
54. Meeting Minutes of the Claiborne-Annapolis Ferry Inc. Board of Directors, May 1, 1920, Maryland State Archives, Maryland Public Service Commission, MSA S245-1, MdHR 19816-1.
55. "Vessel Hits Reef in Mists of River," *Washington Herald*, March 10, 1921.
56. Meeting Minutes of the Claiborne-Annapolis Ferry Inc. Board of Directors, July 8, 1921, Maryland State Archives, Maryland Public Service Commission, MSA S245-1, MdHR 19816-1.
57. "45 Are Rescued from Disabled Ferry Steamer," *Sun* (Baltimore, MD), July 2, 1922.
58. Meeting Minutes of the Claiborne-Annapolis Ferry Inc. Board of Directors, February 18, 1920, and July 8, 2001, Maryland State Archives, Maryland Public Service Commission, MSA S245-1, MdHR 19816-1.
59. Meeting Minutes of the Claiborne-Annapolis Ferry Inc. Board of Directors, July 8, 1921, Maryland State Archives, Maryland Public Service Commission, MSA S245-1, MdHR 19816-1.
60. *Memorandum of Agreement between Frank A. McNamee of Albany, N.Y., and Emerson C. Harrington, Attorney, of Cambridge, Maryland*, July 7, 1921, Maryland State Archives, Maryland Public Service Commission, MSA S245-8, MdHR 19816-13.
61. Meeting Minutes of the Claiborne-Annapolis Ferry Inc. Board of Directors, September 20, 1921, Maryland State Archives, Maryland Public Service Commission, MSA S245-1, MdHR 19816-1.
62. *The Claiborne-Annapolis Ferry*, an open letter to company shareholders, from Emerson C. Harrington, March 22, 1921, Maryland State Archives, Maryland Public Service Commission, MSA S245-1, MdHR 9816-1.
63. A reasonable calculation is that between 1928 and 1941, Harrington and his immediate family realized annual salaries, annual dividend payments, and a

one-time acquisition payout from the Claiborne-Annapolis Ferry Company of about $206,000. In 2024 dollars this would be worth about $9 million.

64. Meeting Minutes of the Claiborne-Annapolis Ferry Inc. Board of Directors, November 17, 1920, and March 28, 1921, Maryland State Archives, Maryland Public Service Commission, MSA S245-1, MdHR 19816-1.
65. Shareholdings are reported in the minutes of the Annual Meeting of Stockholders for March 28, 1921, and March 27, 1923, Maryland State Archives, Maryland Public Service Commission, S245-1, MdHR 19816-1. The shareholdings for 1927 are reported in the Minutes of Extraordinary Meeting of the Shareholders of Claiborne-Annapolis Ferry Inc., September 29, 1927, Maryland State Archives, Maryland Public Service Commission, MSA S245-2, MdHR 19816-2.
66. "Seek Another Boat for Bay Ferry Service," *Evening Capital* (Annapolis, MD), August 28, 1922.
67. Meeting Minutes of the Claiborne-Annapolis Ferry Inc. Board of Directors, August 25, 1922, Maryland State Archives, Maryland Public Service Commission, MSA S245-1, MdHR 19816-1.
68. Meeting Minutes of the Claiborne-Annapolis Ferry Inc. Board of Directors, March 26, 1923, Maryland State Archives, Maryland Public Service Commission, MSA S245-1, MdHR 19816-1; *Majestic* had official number 96688.
69. Memorandum of Agreement for the purchase of *Majestic* between Claiborne-Annapolis Ferry Inc. and Majestic Steamship Line. Maryland State Archives, Maryland Public Service Commission, MSA S245-8, MdHR 19816-13.
70. Meeting Minutes of the Claiborne-Annapolis Ferry Inc. Board of Directors, June 29, 1923, Maryland State Archives, Maryland Public Service Commission, MSA S245-1, MdHR 19816-1.
71. "Buy Another Steamer for Bay Ferry Line," *Evening Capital* (Annapolis, MD), March 27, 1923. The initial news reports suggested the name was going to be changed to one representative of Maryland's history, but this appears not to have been done. The formal transfer of registration did not occur until May. See "News of Baltimore's Port and Shipping Activities," *Sun* (Baltimore, MD), May 5, 1923.
72. Details of Higgins' life are based on interviews with his grandson, Daniel C. Higgins III.
73. Meeting Minutes of Maryland Board of Public Works for August 2, 1914, accessed November 29, 2022, bpw.maryland.gov/MeetingDocsArchives/08%20-%201914%20August%202%20Minutes-Transcript.pdf.
74. Interview with Margaret Bryan on Wednesday, August 31, 2022. The history of this establishment is murky. It most likely was built (or soon taken over) in 1920 by Albert J. Wyatt and his wife Mary E. Wyatt. In 1930 it appears to have been named The Al-Mar Inn, after the owners.

75. The stories about The Sea Gull Inn are from a series of conversations with retired Judge John C. North Jr. Judge North, a prominent figure in Talbot County, is the grandson of Robert North, and he remembers this period from his youth.
76. The probable date of 1921 is supported by a deed transfer of that year from Maple Hall to the Vestry of St. Michael's, the organization to which the Holy Innocents Chapel was subordinated. See *Maple Hall, Inc. to the Vestry of St. Michael's Parish*, recorded October 11, 1921, Talbot County, MD, Circuit Court Land Records, Plat Book 190: 447. The property documented in that deed transfer, lot 101, is where Holy Innocents Chapel can be seen in aerial photographs from the 1930s.
77. H. V. Saunders (Rev.), *Directory: St. Michael's Parish* (St. Michael's Parish, October 1925), 20. This directory includes a summary of the history of the parish, including the circumstances surrounding the 1921 move of Holy Innocents Chapel.
78. See Joseph Koper, *The Isaiah Fountain Case: Outrage and Jim Crow Justice on Maryland's Eastern Shore* (Secant Publishing, 2022), 191, 235.
79. Meeting Minutes of the Claiborne-Annapolis Ferry Inc. Board of Directors, March 23, 1925, Maryland State Archives, Maryland Public Service Commission, MSA S245-1, MdHR 19816-1. His full name was Benjamin Franklin Sherman, but he appears to have never used that full name.
80. Biographical details and other aspects of his history were obtained in discussions with Sherman's daughter, Margaret Bryan, and two of his grandsons, Mark and Chris. They were interviewed on Wednesday, August 31, 2022. Margaret Bryan was ninety-nine years of age at the time and recalled elements of her father's history and service in great detail. She was about thirty-five years old when he died in 1958.

VIII

The Competition Reacts

Governor Harrington, Hampden Mepham, and Frank McNamee were not the only ones to see the potential of an auto-ferry system across the Chesapeake. Soon after Harrington announced his intentions in 1916, other companies and ferry routes began to pop up, all sharing the same business model of carrying passengers and their automobiles and thus escaping the monopoly power of the Baltimore, Chesapeake, and Atlantic Railway Company (BC&A). The common factor among these early competitors is that they based their Western Shore terminals around Baltimore instead of Annapolis and thus sought an Eastern Shore destination closer to Baltimore than Claiborne. Most lasted only a few years. As the competitors failed, Claiborne-Annapolis Ferry Inc. prospered and soon saw itself shift from being a disruptor of monopoly power into protector of its own turf from new entrants. In this, it proved exceptionally capable.

New Car-Ferry Challengers

The success of the Claiborne-Annapolis ferry line spurred mimickers. Ironically, while these new ventures most likely threatened that car-ferry company more than train-centric BC&A, it was BC&A—perhaps just out of habit—that went into action to thwart the new entrants. Claiborne-Annapolis Ferry Inc. could just sit back and watch this happen, in the process absorbing some of the tactics employed by the master monopolist, BC&A. Emerson C. Harrington and his company learned well. These same strategies would prove useful to the firm in future years.

The first threat came from a familiar name. Charles W. Harrison, who had been instrumental in the launch of the Claiborne-Annapolis Ferry, had not given up on his dream of a competing car ferry from Baltimore to Love Point. He had lost that battle with Harrington, but had not abandoned the concept. Upon resigning from Harrington's venture in April 1919, he took a new position that July as head of the Peninsula Ferry Company, proposing to operate a car and passenger ferry service from Baltimore to a new pier to be built adjacent to the Love Point Hotel.[1] It would be one of many such shipping ventures Harrison would attempt to build over the decades, most of which failed quickly. (A few took longer, but all shared the same fate in the end.)

The legalities came first. The Peninsula Ferry Company applied to the Maryland Public Service Commission (PSC) for authorization to carry vehicles and passengers from Baltimore's Inner Harbor to the terminal at Love Point, in this way competing directly with the passenger-only steamers of the Maryland, Delaware and Virginia Railway Company (MD&V) (owned by BC&A), then operating on that same route. It received the authorization in December 1919.[2] From that point things stagnated. Harrison's company struggled to acquire appropriate boats for the route and to raise the funds necessary for their acquisition. It was not until almost two years later, on September 15, 1921, that the Peninsula Ferry Company launched its long-delayed service between Baltimore and Love Point.

From the start, Harrison's aspirations for an advanced ferry operation involved compromises. Instead of two modern diesel-powered, double-ender ferries, the service used the aging, coal-fired sidewheel-steamer *Riverside*.[3] Nor did business materialize as hoped. Predictably, BC&A and its MD&V subsidiary responded to the new entrant by slashing rates on the existing Claiborne and Love Point service, which cut deeply into the revenue of the Peninsula Ferry Company.[4] The lack of modern equipment and its "inefficient schedule" also hampered the company's ability to appeal to regional travelers and merchants.[5]

Harrison, doubling down, attempted to address these challenges and broaden the customer base of his business by including Queenstown as another destination, expanding the routes beyond Love Point. The company also added a new ferry, the 1881-built *Jessamine*, which they renamed *Queenstown*. This was yet another compromise: the steamer had originally been built as a lighthouse tender and was not especially suited for carrying automobiles.[6]

Failure was inevitable and prompt. Ill-financed and unable to compete against the BC&A/MD&V monopoly, the Peninsula Ferry Company was declared insolvent and placed in the hands of a court-appointed receiver in June 1922, after less than a year of operations.[7] But not all hope was lost. Salvation was anticipated in the form of a potential merger with Baltimore and Eastern Shore Ferry Line Inc., another new competitor in the car-ferry business.[8]

This second new ferry venture arose in July 1919 with the objective of carrying vehicles from Baltimore to the Eastern Shore, but on a different route than Harrison's Peninsula Ferry Company, or for that matter, BC&A's route from Baltimore's Inner Harbor to Love Point. In this case the western terminal would be at Bay Shore, at a new pier built directly into the Bay near Sparrows Point. The terminal would be linked by trolley with downtown Baltimore. (Both pier and trolley station remain, now as part of North Point State Park.) Ferries would carry passengers and automobiles a short distance across the Bay to the town of Rock Hall, almost directly opposite on the Eastern Shore.[9] The new operation was financed and led by a who's-who of the Baltimore merchant community, including Charles C. Stieff (owner of a major jewelry company), Felix Angus (owner of the *Baltimore American* newspaper), and T. Rowland Thomas (president of the National Bank of Baltimore).[10]

This new company, led by General Manager Samuel A. Tubman, acquired two elderly ferry boats from New York and brought them to Baltimore for overhaul and upgrades. The boats were of the innovative double-ender design, able to travel in either direction and open at each end for easy loading and unloading of vehicles. *Eastern Shore*, a sidewheel steamer of 831 GRT and 171 feet in length, was constructed in Wilmington, Delaware, in 1885 as *Oregon* and had provided many years of service in New York. Its near-sister *Baltimore*, built in Wilmington as *Maine*, was three years younger and three feet longer.

The company promoted its new service as the fastest and shortest crossing of the Bay, only nine miles in length with the journey taking only one hour and fifteen minutes. Baltimore and Eastern Shore Ferry Line Inc.'s aspirations were quite impressive: there would be sixteen trips per day with each ferry able to carry twenty-eight large trucks and five hundred passengers.[11] It seemed like a very promising venture, and a substantial challenge to the Baltimore-based operations of BC&A.

Although the boats were ready, the piers had to be constructed, and this delayed the start of operations. New roads would be required as well. Baltimore and Eastern Shore Ferry Line Inc. also petitioned Kent County to construct an improved roadway to the new Rock Hall terminal, and this drove further delays. Finally, on August 10, 1921, the ferry line celebrated its new service. It was not an auspicious beginning. The five hundred guests at the celebration in Bay Shore endured pouring rain as they waited for the ferry to arrive to begin that first trip across the Bay. They might as well have gone home. The ferry arrived so late that the first voyage that day was canceled and rescheduled for the following morning.[12] This first day's disappointment was a harbinger.

The new line encountered financial difficulties from the start, exacerbated once again by the aggressive rate cutting taken by BC&A and MD&V on competing lines.[13] (Meanwhile, the fledgling Claiborne-Annapolis Ferry Inc. just sat back, watched, and learned.) Debts held by Baltimore and Eastern Shore Ferry Line Inc. started to accumulate, and unpaid suppliers filed liens against the company's assets. Instead of sixteen trips each day, the schedule in 1921 offered only four per day in most months, increasing to six during the busy summer season.[14]

The future of this new competitor seemed as doubtful as that of the Peninsula Ferry Company, also struggling from the same anti-competitive practices of BC&A. One potential approach to salving the situation would be the takeover by the Baltimore and Eastern Shore Ferry Line Inc. of the equally troubled Peninsula Ferry Company. The latter had labored to operate a parallel route from Baltimore to Love Point and, over the vociferous objections of Baltimore and Eastern Shore Ferry Line Inc. an additional route to Queenstown. However, BC&A was also interested in buying (and then shutting down) the Peninsula Ferry Company in order to remove this bothersome competitor. Baltimore and Eastern Shore Ferry Line Inc. thus contested with BC&A for control of the insolvent Peninsula Ferry Company.

Eventually, the two bidders reached an accommodation: if Baltimore and Eastern Shore Ferry Line Inc. abandoned the Peninsula Ferry Company's Love Point route—leaving BC&A with its traditional monopoly on that route—BC&A would not object to the company taking over the remaining route of the Peninsula Ferry Company between Baltimore and Queenstown. In short, they divided up the market. Baltimore and Eastern Shore Ferry Line Inc. moved forward, shifting the origin of the Queenstown route from central Baltimore and operating routes from Bay Shore to both Queenstown and Rock Hall.[15] By 1924 the newly merged operations were running five trips to Rock Hall daily during the summer months, with an additional daily trip to Queenstown. In the winter, service to Queenstown was eliminated and the line ran only two trips daily to Rock Hall.[16]

The anti-competitive arrangement with BC&A might have insulated the Baltimore and Eastern Shore line from the ravages of BC&A rate cutting, but it had not eliminated all risks. Tragedy struck the line in January 1926. Steamers *Baltimore* and *Eastern Shore* were tied up at a wharf in the town of Gratitude, a short distance from the primary Rock Hall ferry wharf. They had been unable to proceed farther into Rock Hall harbor due to ice conditions and fog. On January 6, a fire broke out inside *Baltimore*, reducing the topsides to cinders within a brief time and threatening to spread to *Eastern Shore*, tied up alongside. Quick action by crewmembers saved *Eastern Shore* from a similar fate, with the crew releasing *Eastern Shore*'s lines and letting it drift away until it grounded itself on a shore nearby.[17] A month later, the wrecked hull of *Baltimore* was sold. Baltimore and Eastern Shore Ferry Line Inc. was now down to a single boat.

The company never recovered. It had struggled to turn a profit each and every year of its operation. In its best years, 1923 and 1924, revenues barely covered basic operating costs and could not come close to covering the additional costs of taxes and interest on the debt. Revenue began to fall after 1923, and by 1926 was at only half of its previous peak, a result of the loss of *Baltimore* that January.

If the company could not flourish as a viable competitor on the cross-Chesapeake routes, and if an anti-competitive deal with BC&A was insufficient to bring prosperity, then there was only one step remaining: a government bailout. The company's best hope was to ask the Maryland legislature to amend a proposed bill on a Chesapeake Bay bridge to include the buyout of Baltimore and Eastern Shore Ferry Line Inc. However, fearing the additional cost of that bailout would sink the bill for the bay bridge, the legislature rejected the proposed amendment.

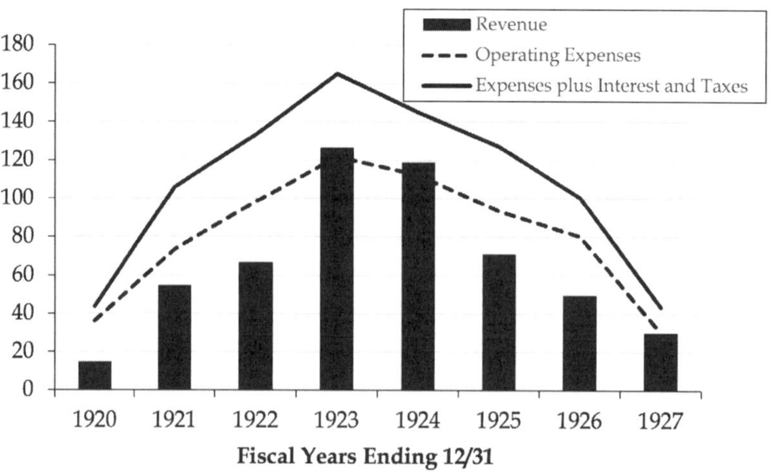

The ferry line was out of cards to play as operating losses continued to mount.[18] The end was near. In August 1927, a receiver was appointed to take over the company, in an effort to protect the interest of debtors.[19] The receiver's job was complicated when in January 1928, just days before a scheduled public auction of the line's assets, *Eastern Shore,* the one remaining steamboat of the line, caught fire and was destroyed at the Bay Shore pier. Arson was suspected, though no one was ever convicted.[20] The auction, suspended after the fire, was finally conducted on April 16, 1929.[21] With the remaining assets sold, Baltimore and Eastern Shore Ferry Line Inc. was no longer.

BC&A Adjusts and Abandons Claiborne

The demise of the two new ferry companies left BC&A as the only real challenger to the new Claiborne-Annapolis Ferry Inc. during the 1920s. As the latter expanded operations, its emerging success and long-term competitive challenge to the old railway company became increasingly clear. Perhaps BC&A's obsession with defeating the Peninsula Ferry Company and the Baltimore and Eastern Shore Ferry Line Inc. sidetracked it from the real threat: the new car-ferry company operating between Annapolis and Claiborne.

The handwriting was on the wall. Claiborne-Annapolis Ferry Inc. cut deeply into the former BC&A monopoly on ferry service to Claiborne and connecting rail service to Ocean City. BC&A was owned by the Pennsylvania Railroad (PRR), and that behemoth had other options. At Love Point, on Kent Island, PRR's other subsidiary, MD&V, remained largely immune from serious competition for its combined passenger steamer and rail operations, especially once the competitive threat from the Peninsula Ferry Company and Baltimore and Eastern Shore Ferry Line Inc. had been crushed.

As far back as July 1919, when the Claiborne-Annapolis route had been operating for only a few weeks, speculation began to arise that BC&A might abandon its Claiborne operation in favor of Love Point. As was reported at the time:

> Those who thoroughly understand the transportation situation pointed out today that it would not be surprising if the Pennsylvania Railroad carried a plan into effect which would eventually result in the elimination of Claiborne as a stopping point for its ferry and divert this traffic, both freight and passenger, over to Love Point on the Maryland, Delaware and Virginia [Railway].[22]

The pressure on BC&A from the new car ferries in Claiborne became apparent in the former's financial results. The happy days between 1900 and 1912 had ended, first driven down by competition from the Eastern Shore Development Steamship Company (ESDSC) from mid-1912 to early 1916. BC&A had begun to recover when ESDSC ceased operations in 1916 but then began to crater once Claiborne-Annapolis Ferry Inc. started operations in mid-1919. BC&A was now hemorrhaging cash.

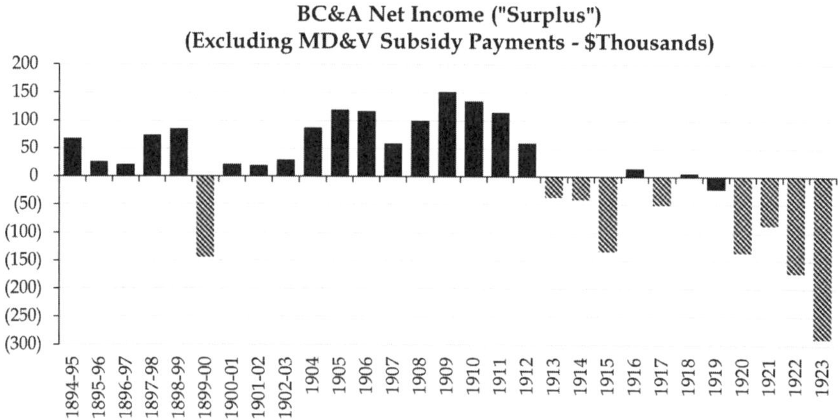

For 1894-1903 data is for fiscal year ending 8/31; reported data for 1904 is average for 12 months over a 16-month reporting period; data 1905-1922 is annual.

The MD&V subsidiary operating from Love Point to Lewes and Rehoboth was in even worse shape, never once having generated a positive surplus for its parent, BC&A. However, the red ink had begun to accumulate even faster after Claiborne-Annapolis Ferry Inc. initiated operations. BC&A had been the guarantor of

MD&V bonds and had already dumped $470,000 into MD&V through 1919. It was unable to continue doing this as BC&A itself fell under pressure from Claiborne-Annapolis Ferry Inc.

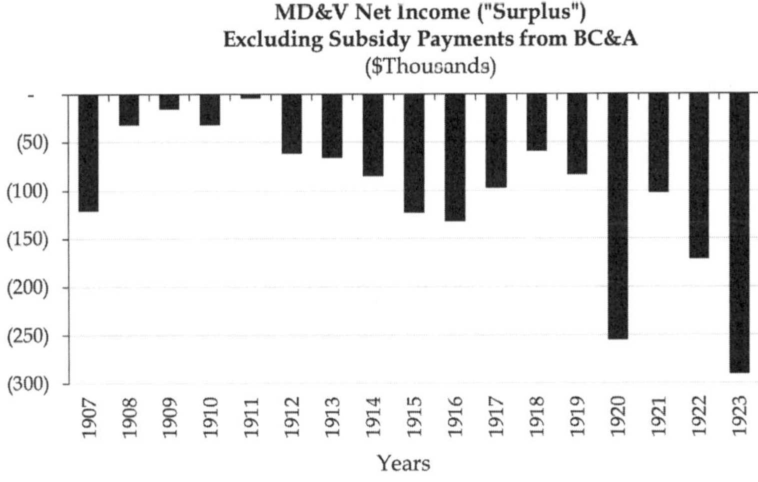

The result was inevitable. In April 1923, MD&V failed to make the interest and principal payments on its bonds and was therefore declared insolvent and handed over to the Girard Trust Company, the guarantor of those bonds.[23] Its assets were put up for auction by Girard the following month.[24] "Parcel 1" consisted of the Love Point-Lewes rail line, all equipment associated with that line, the ferry *Westmoreland*, and the related assets of the Baltimore-Love Point ferry line. This lot was acquired by E.B. Leaf Company of Philadelphia, which announced its intentions to convert all of the properties, including the rail line, into scrap.[25] Parcels 2 and 3, which comprised the remaining ferry operations of MD&V (unrelated to Love Point), were acquired by interests under the control of PRR.

The apparent demise of the Love Point ferry and the rail line to Lewes created panic within the nearby communities on the Eastern Shore, soon to be cut off from easy access to the Western Shore. Backroom negotiations began between PRR and Maryland government officials, including the PSC. A deal eventually emerged. In a bit of financial engineering, at which it seems PRR excelled, a new subsidiary of BC&A was created with the name Baltimore and Eastern Railroad (B&E).[26] B&E would continue to run BC&A's and MD&V's steamer and rail operations. PRR committed to placing a "palatial" steamer on the Baltimore-Love Point route, replacing the old and tired *Westmoreland*.[27]

However, things had to change if B&E had a prayer of becoming cash-positive for its PRR parent. The MD&V bankruptcy and subsequent foreclosure sale in 1923 provided hints of PRR's potential strategies on its routes on the Eastern Shore, leading observers to report:

> It is feared by those well informed on Eastern Shore transportation affairs that the Pennsylvania's step may foreshadow abandonment of the Baltimore, Chesapeake and Atlantic lines from Claiborne to Easton and the railroad ferry from Claiborne to Baltimore.[28]

There was a certain logic to this scenario. The selection of Claiborne as a destination for a ferry from Baltimore was a consequence of the flawed business plan of the Baltimore and Eastern Shore Railroad (B&ES), a plan that had collapsed after only nine months in 1890–1891. When Claiborne was chosen by B&ES in 1886, it was (at least in part) because of its proximity to the rail head at Bay Ridge on the Western Shore, under a scenario where the ferry was moving entire railcars—in effect a rail line across the Chesapeake. Once that plan failed and the decision was made to shift the western terminus to Baltimore, Claiborne remained as the eastern terminus only because the rail line and terminal had already been built and it would be prohibitively expensive for B&ES (then in receivership and hemorrhaging cash) to move the rail line. But over time, geography struck back, and a new terminal at Love Point much closer to Baltimore was created in 1902. A rail line from Love Point to Lewes, Delaware, allowed Love Point arriving passengers another way to reach Atlantic beaches.

Yet the acquisition of MD&V by B&E alone did not address the underlying financial challenges. Moreover, the guiding hand of

BC&A since its creation in 1894, Willard Thomson, was gone, having died in 1917. The new leaders needed a solution that would simultaneously reverse the red ink at B&E's money-losing rail operations and create a way for BC&A to escape the competitive threat of the new Claiborne car ferry. The answer was to solve the two problems simultaneously: to create a new single operation out of the best pieces of both B&E and BC&A, discarding the rest. The key was the rail junction at Queen Anne. Here PRR's Oxford Branch connected its Queen Anne rail station with the PRR station in Easton, and where it crossed paths with B&ES' (formerly MD&V and QARR) east-west line from Love Point to Lewes. By engineering a new connection between the Oxford Branch and the Love Point-Rehoboth line at Queen Anne, PRR could abandon the struggling B&E routes east of Queen Anne and the suffering BC&A routes west of Easton. A new, jagged rail line would instead link Love Point (still a BC&A monopoly) with Ocean City via the Queen Anne and Easton connection. Rather than two parallel operations, there would be a single rail and steamer system from Love Point to Ocean City.

The anticipated decision arrived early in 1924. BC&A announced that it was suspending its scheduled passenger service from Claiborne to Easton and likewise terminating its steamer operations between Baltimore and Claiborne. Love Point would become the Eastern Shore terminal for Baltimore traffic. BC&A expected passengers at Claiborne who wanted to continue by rail to Ocean City to connect between Claiborne and Easton by bus and then take the train to Ocean City, joining passengers already on their way from Love Point (themselves changing stations at Easton).[29] The changes went into effect on May 5, 1924, once the rail system in Queen Anne had been simplified, allowing an easier transit from Love Point to Easton and Ocean City.[30]

These changes had to be approved by the PSC, and there was opposition to some of them, especially to the loss of the Claiborne-Easton rail service. Pressure from the PSC and Eastern Shore politicians led BC&A to back away from fully abandoning the Claiborne-Easton line entirely. Instead, they replaced their scheduled steam-engine passenger service with a small railcar, running

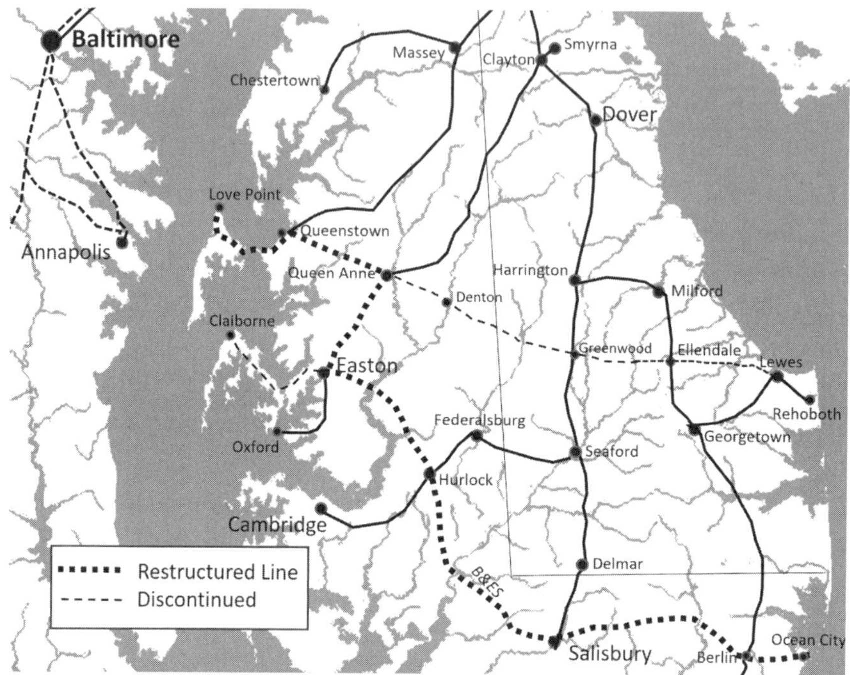

Map 6. The new route structure after 1924 for BC&A and MD&V. The restructured line used the connection between Queen Anne's and Easton to bridge the former BC&A line to Ocean City with the MD&V line from Love Point. The discontinued routes were the lines that BC&A stopped using for passenger service. Note: this is overlayed on a 1928 railroad route map. Source: Base map is from US Geological Survey, detailed and annotated by the author.

on the same rail lines. This railcar, manufactured by the J.G. Brill Company, had a gasoline-powered engine and was thus a far cry from the "Black Cinders and Ashes" of the former steam-powered locomotives.[31] Steam-powered freight-only service from Claiborne to Easton would continue, albeit at a reduced rate of three trains per week rather than two per day.[32]

BC&A redeployed its Claiborne fleet to Love Point, meeting its commitment to resume service from Baltimore. The steamer *Cambridge*, which had served Claiborne for the past twenty-nine years, took over the Baltimore-Love Point route. *Cambridge*'s back-up, *Tred Avon*, was allocated to freight-only service.[33]

The quality of rail service from Claiborne was also to decline slowly over the following decades. BC&A even tried to close down the gasoline railcar service between Claiborne and Easton in 1925, but this did not proceed after the Maryland PSC objected.[34]

These stopgap operational measures, however well-designed, failed to return BC&A to profitability. The rail company was swimming against the tide. People would rather drive their cars to Ocean City than take a train. By November 1927, the PRR decided to cut its losses at its struggling BC&A unit, which included BC&A's B&E subsidiary. PRR announced that all BC&A cross-bay service and rail operations would be abandoned except the steamer to Love Point and the rail line from Love Point to Ocean City (via Queen Anne and Easton). The other properties of BC&A, including those in Claiborne, would be sold under foreclosure.[35] PRR would no longer offset financial losses at these units or guarantee payment of interest on their bonds.

In 1928, BC&A and its far-flung operations were declared insolvent, and all were consolidated into the B&E Railroad, formerly (and confusingly) a BC&A subsidiary. One of the first acts of the new management was to request permission from the Maryland PSC to abandon all passenger service from Claiborne to Easton. Permission was granted.[36] The new owners next asked to remove its freight agents from eight stations along that line, but the PSC approved that action only for Claiborne and Bethlehem.[37] In 1934 the PSC approved the termination of all passenger service between Easton and Ocean City—buses were to be used instead.[38] The decision had been in large part driven by the destruction of the railroad bridge connecting to Ocean City in the calamitous hurricane of 1933. B&E did not have the wherewithal or inclination to replace that bridge.

Freight service out of Claiborne also declined. In 1937 the B&E petitioned the PSC to discontinue and abandon all freight service on the Claiborne-McDaniel line, thereby cutting off Claiborne from all rail service. This was approved, and in November 1938 the process of lifting the rail tracks began, an effort completed by the following April.[39] The rail lines created out of Claiborne in the late 1880s and operational for almost fifty years were no more. The rest of the line east of McDaniel—the location of a large tomato packing plant—saw periodic freight-train operations until the early 1960s, when the line was suspended altogether, with the rails removed over the following decades.

What was left of the old BC&A empire was little more than a steamer from Baltimore to Love Point and a train that connected Love Point through Queen Anne and Easton to Ocean City. Not only had the BC&A monopoly been disrupted by Claiborne-Annapolis Ferry Inc. and its car ferries, the old behemoth that had dominated cross-bay transportation was now just a fading shadow of its former glory. And a new dominant supplier had emerged, led by Emerson C. Harrington, the man who had engineered the demise of the first cross-bay monopolist. In a reversal of roles, it was now Harrington who had the incentive to protect his car-ferry monopoly, and he would prove very skillful in this effort.

Notes

1. "Ferry Company Incorporates," *Sun* (Baltimore, MD), July 26, 1919; "Boat Line in Trouble," *Sun* (Baltimore, MD), December 7, 1919.
2. "Love Point Ferry to Start in Spring," *Denton Journal*, December 13, 1919.
3. "Love Point Ferry," *Denton Journal*, September 24, 1921.
4. "Ferries Fear Pennsy Plans Bay Rate War," *Sun* (Baltimore, MD), October 28, 1921.
5. "Eastern Sho' Folk Ask Good Service," *Wilmington Morning News*, January 10, 1922.
6. "*Jessamine* Renamed *Queenstown*," *Sun* (Baltimore, MD), May 7, 1922.
7. "Says Ferry Co. Is Insolvent," *Sun* (Baltimore, MD), June 24, 1922.
8. "Suggests Transfer of Peninsula Ferry," *Cambridge Daily Banner*, December 9, 1922.
9. "Boat for Ferry Bought," *Sun* (Baltimore, MD), July 23, 1919.
10. "We Are Authorized, as Correspondents, to Offer Baltimore & Eastern Shore Ferry Line, Inc. in the Following Units," *Sun*, August 22, 1920.
11. "New Ferry Across Bay," *Midland Journal* (Rising Sun, MD), August 6, 1920.
12. "First Boat will Sail on New Ferry Today," *Sun* (Baltimore, MD), August 11, 1920.
13. "Ferries Fear Pennsy Plans Bay Rate War," *Sun* (Baltimore, MD), October 28, 1921.
14. "Baltimore and Eastern Shore Ferry Line," *Denton Journal*, April 16, 1921, and May 28, 1921.
15. "More About the Bay Ferries," *Denton Journal*, February 3, 1923.
16. "Notice: Baltimore & Eastern Shore Ferry Line, Inc.," *Sun* (Baltimore, MD), July 4, 1924, and December 31, 1924.
17. "Ferry Burned in Chesapeake," *Evening Journal* (Wilmington, DE), January 7, 1926.
18. "Shore Ferry Shows Big Operating Loss," *Evening Journal* (Wilmington, DE), April 1, 1927.
19. "Ferry Company Receiver Appointed by Consent," *Sun* (Baltimore, MD), July 27, 1927.
20. The company's night watchman was arrested and blamed for the fire but was later acquitted. See "Sale of Ferry Property Postponed Indefinitely," *Sun* (Baltimore, MD), January 13, 1928.
21. "Receiver's Sale of All Property and Assets of the Baltimore-Eastern Shore Ferry Line, Inc.," *Sun* (Baltimore, MD), April 14, 1929.
22. "Pennsy May Shorten Route to Shore," *Evening Sun* (Baltimore, MD), July 25, 1919.
23. "Holds M.D. and V. Has Defaulted," *Wilmington Morning News*, April 5, 1923.

24. "Auction Sales," *Sun* (Baltimore, MD), April 9, 1923.
25. "Railroad Sold at Auction," *Denton Journal*, May 12, 1923.
26. Not to be confused—as it often is—with the earlier Baltimore and Eastern Shore Railroad (B&ES), whose assets were acquired by BC&A in 1895.
27. "Pennsy to Operate New Railroad," *Salisbury Times*, December 31, 1923. Through a series of transactions, *Westmoreland* ended up in the hands of the Marine Sand and Gravel Company for conversion into a barge.
28. "To Take Over Part of MD&V," *Denton Journal*, July 21, 1923.
29. "Connecting the Roads at Queen Anne," *Denton Journal*, February 23, 1924.
30. "To Begin Operation of Ocean City Line," *Sun* (Baltimore, MD), May 3, 1924.
31. John C. Hayman, *Rails Along the Chesapeake: A History of Railroading on the Delmarva Peninsula, 1827–1978* (Marvadel Publishers, 1979), 111–112.
32. "Shorter Route to Baltimore over B.C.&.A.," *Salisbury Times*, May 1, 1924.
33. While BC&A scheduled services from Baltimore to Claiborne ended in 1924, BC&A steamers from Baltimore would still call occasionally in Claiborne for the next five years, operating on excursions or carrying only freight. At other times, the BC&A steamers from Baltimore were diverted from Love Point to Claiborne due to unfavorable weather conditions. For example, in August 1928, *Tred Avon* was operating on a cargo run from Claiborne to Baltimore while *Cambridge*, operating as a passenger steamer, was diverted from Love Point to Claiborne when the railroad line to Love Point was damaged in a storm. See "Terrific Storm Sweeps Three States, Wrecking Crops, Roads and Wires," *Sun* (Baltimore, MD), August 13, 1928. A similar event happened in 1925 when the tracks near Wye Mills were washed out in a storm. See "Eastern Shore Flood Damage Under Repair," *Evening Sun* (Baltimore, MD), August 1, 1925.
34. "B.C.&A. RY May Quit Claiborne," *Salisbury Times*, January 27, 1925.
35. "Bay Boat Lines of B., C. & A. to be Abandoned," *Sun* (Baltimore, MD), November 30, 1927.
36. *Report of the Public Service Commission of Maryland For the Year 1928* (Twentieth Century Printing Co.), Action in Case No. 2819, 225–26.
37. *Report of the Public Service Commission of Maryland For the Year 1929* (Twentieth Century Printing Co.), Action in Case No. 2891, 89–90.
38. "Eastbound Trains to Be Withdrawn," *Easton Star-Democrat*, July 6, 1934.
39. "Railroad Tracks to Be Lifted," *Easton Star-Democrat*, November 18, 1938. See also "Railroad Dismantled," *Easton Star-Democrat*, April 28, 1939.

IX

The Claiborne-Annapolis Ferry Line Expands

While the Baltimore, Chesapeake and Atlantic Railway Company (BC&A) was winding down its Claiborne operations in the 1920s, Claiborne Annapolis Ferry Inc. was doing the opposite, expanding its fleet and restructuring its business for greater financial success. As with BC&A, it was also about to undergo a corporate restructuring.

Operations between Claiborne and Annapolis settled down after 1923 with the employment of *Gov. Emerson C. Harrington* and *Majestic*. There were, however, operational challenges, specifically related to the fact that neither of these ferries had been designed originally to accommodate automobiles. The design of the Claiborne and Annapolis piers required the ferries to dock alongside. Ramps were laid from steamboat deck to pier, and cars would drive up or back down the ramp depending upon the direction of travel. This was laborious and challenging. Occasionally, cars ended up in the water instead. Captain Daniel Higgins himself once drove a car belonging to his brother Ned right off the ramp into the water in Claiborne. Both car and driver emerged and lived to fight another day.[1] Sometimes it was just easier for the crew to lift and manhandle a car through the boat's cargo doors and down to the pier. Turnaround times were slow, which reduced the number of trips each steamer could make per day across the Bay. Backups ensued, and vehicles were often left behind to wait for the next ferry, which might not, and often did not, materialize for many hours. For a company running a ferry operation, as with airlines, it is vital to minimize the turnaround time and maintain schedules. Ferries sitting alongside piers did not generate revenue.

The ferry line was also generating dismal financial returns, losing money each year from 1919 to 1924. By 1926, cumulative profits to date were still negative—even with an $18,000 annual subsidy from the State of Maryland. The company had been unable to pay any dividends during this period.[2] Something had to change.

The Fleet Is Upgraded

In December 1925, ferry management announced plans to acquire a new ferry.[3] This was more than just additional capacity. The new ferry would be powered by modern diesel engines, rather than a coal-fired steam boiler using technology that dated back to the War of 1812. It would also be a "double-ender," a design in which the ferry is identical front and back and able to travel in either direction equally well. This double-ender design would allow rapid loading and unloading of vehicles. Drivers would just motor onto the ferry before departure and then drive off in the same direction upon arrival. The diesel-powered ferry would also be faster, making the trip in just one hour.[4] General Manager B. Frank Sherman traveled to New York in spring 1926 to secure this new ferry at the Staten Island Shipbuilding Company, at a cost of $275,000.[5] He later announced that the new ferry would begin service on July 15, would be able to carry sixty cars and three thousand passengers, and would cut half an hour off the typical trip time from Annapolis to Claiborne.[6]

The ferry he had acquired was *Newburgh*, built by Ward, Stanton & Co. in Newburgh, New York, in 1883. It was actually twenty years older than either *Gov. Emerson C. Harrington* or *Majestic*.

Built as a coal-fired steamer, it was being completely rebuilt as a diesel ferry and double-ender for the Claiborne-Annapolis Ferry. Upon delivery, the ferry was renamed *Gov. Albert C. Ritchie*, after the then-serving governor of Maryland and one of the original supporters of the new ferry line while serving in the Harrington administration.

The new ferry also required the rebuilding of the piers in Claiborne and Annapolis. Unlike *Gov. Emerson C. Harrington* and *Majestic*, which docked alongside the pier and discharged their passengers and vehicles over the side, *Gov. Albert C. Ritchie* would pull directly into a U-shaped opening in the pier, thereby discharging passengers and vehicles directly ahead. The pier in Claiborne would be reconfigured to accommodate either type of ferry, the traditional sidewheel steamers alongside, or the double-ender head-in.

The christening ceremony took place on July 22, 1926, in Annapolis, just in time for the new ferry to finish out the summer season. The first automobile to come aboard carried Governor Ritchie and former Governor Harrington as passengers. After the ceremony, *Gov. Albert C. Ritchie* took its place alongside *Gov. Emerson C. Harrington* and *Majestic* on the Annapolis-Claiborne run.

Majestic Sinks: A Tragedy Narrowly Averted

Majestic did not last long in the fleet. Once *Gov. Albert C. Ritchie* was proven in service, *Majestic* was laid up in Baltimore in autumn 1926 and put on the market. In the spring of 1927, two bidders emerged in what became a heated confrontation. This ultimately involved a near-disaster on Baltimore Harbor, in an incident marred by controversy and exacerbated by racist accusations. Allegations of unsafe operation would emerge, competing with claims of sabotage. It got ugly.

The first person hoping to acquire *Majestic* was the Reverend John E. Smallwood, a Black minister from an inner-city Baltimore congregation of the Church of God. Reverend Smallwood had spent a decade providing social services to the underserved

Black community in Baltimore, especially for indigent persons and prisoners in the Maryland Penitentiary. In 1927, Smallwood created the Ideal Amusement and Excursion Company, intending to employ *Majestic* for excursions to places such as Bodkin Creek, where the Patapsco River meets the Chesapeake Bay.[7] Eventually he hoped to create a Black-oriented amusement park on land off the Chester River on the Eastern Shore.

At a time when much of the South, including Maryland, was still under Jim Crow, Smallwood hoped to create a steamer operation oriented toward the entertainment needs of the Black residents of Baltimore. (About 15 percent of the Baltimore population at the time was Black.) Smallwood's business venture was to collapse in controversy a short while later, but in the meantime, he had started negotiations with Emerson C. Harrington about acquiring *Majestic*.[8]

Also competing for *Majestic* was W. Edward Walton, an entrepreneur from Baltimore who hoped to use the ship on a ferry service between Baltimore and Love Point. Here he would compete with the Baltimore and Eastern Railroad, the company that emerged from BC&A's reorganization in 1924. Walton, who demonstrated later that he was quite comfortable using offensive language in describing Smallwood and his community, managed to step in and reach a deal with Harrington when Smallwood was unable to execute the first payment on the deal he, Smallwood, had negotiated.[9] In reality, neither deal was fully consummated, and the transfer of ownership never took place. So, the events of July 1927 took place with Walton presenting himself as the owner of *Majestic* when, in fact, it was still owned by Claiborne-Annapolis Ferry Inc.

Walton started running excursions on *Majestic*—this was before any official change in ownership—and ran into difficulties from the start. His captain, Frederick A. Travers, put *Majestic* aground off St. Michaels on July 20. He was eventually able to free her, but the grounding and struggle to free the steamer caused some to worry about damage to the hull.[10]

Just four days later, while on a moonlight excursion in Baltimore Harbor, calamity was narrowly averted. The 970 passengers aboard were all Black residents of Baltimore, heading to a planned picnic site at Seven Foot Knoll, just outside Bodkin Creek. In this way, Walton had become a direct competitor to Reverend Smallwood. Just after midnight, while resting in his cabin, Captain Travers was awakened by the boat's oiler, William Bryan, with the news that the boat had sprung a leak and water was fast filling the hold. Travers went himself to look, and upon seeing the deteriorating conditions, immediately ordered full speed and a course change to bring the vessel back to land as quickly as possible.

What happened next depends on which source one consults. The *Afro-American*, a Baltimore newspaper written by and serving the Black community, describes a scene of panic:

> The steamer with 970 passengers and 30 members of the crew, was a scene of terror as women screamed and fainted following the first report that the boat had sprung a leak a short distance this side of Fort Carroll. Panic stricken cries rent the air and a mad rush for lifeboats and life preservers turned the upper decks into a scene of bedlam. Members of the crew were forced to use drastic means in order that women and girls might first be provided with the safety devices. . . . The sudden change in the course caused the crowd to become apprehensive and a cry of "the boat is sinking," caused a wild rush toward the life preservers. Men and women were trampled in the stampede, fists flew and the angry oaths of the men could be heard above the screams of the frightened women.[11]

Captain Travers himself was perhaps less understanding of the panic felt by passengers, even as those passengers feared the boat would not reach safety before it sank:

> You've seen a bunch of crazy cattle: well, that's just the way they acted. . . . Not one acted as if he had any sense. They screamed and hollered and jammed to the rail so that the crew couldn't moor the ship when we got to the dock.[12]

The ship made it to the Clinton wharf of the Pennsylvania Railroad Company (PRR) and was able to dock. The crew forced themselves through the crowd to organize the complete disembarkation of all passengers and crew, after which the steamer slipped beneath the waves, the hull buckling as it did so. Only the smokestack and the top of the pilot house were visible above the murky waters.[13]

Immediately, the cause of the incident became mired in controversy. Two parallel investigations were conducted: a formal one held by the US Steamboat Inspection Service in a courtroom, and an informal one conducted in the pages of the local newspapers. Two competing versions of the incident emerged.

In the first, the white operator of the steamer (Walton) and white captain (Travers) claimed that the ferry had been sabotaged by Reverend Smallwood and his associates, out of frustration that he had been outmaneuvered for the purchase of the ferry by Walton. They contended that (1) Smallwood had warned members of the community not to embark on the excursion because the steamer might sink, (2) someone had opened the seacocks to let water into the hold, and (3) when oiler Bryan tried to investigate the source of the leak he was "interfered with by Negro passengers when he went to the bulkhead."[14]

Smallwood, who was not aboard *Majestic* when it sank, denied all of these accusations and argued the ship was unsafe. John F. Moran, who was affiliated with Smallwood and who was going to serve as chief engineer should Smallwood's purchase proceed, stated in the hearing that *Majestic* was "extremely unsafe" and that the vessel was "worthless." He cited as evidence the poor condition of the walking-beam engine and the coal-fired boiler, the former having been left uncovered during the long winter when the boat, removed from service in 1926, was laid up in Baltimore.[15]

Smallwood also produced a compelling witness in the hearing, Thomas Dennis, a deckhand and one of the few Black crewmen aboard. Dennis reported that *Majestic* had been wedged under a concrete curb of the adjacent pier in Baltimore earlier in the day and that during the thirty minutes it took to release the boat, the wooden deck and hull were strained, and this may have created opportunities for water to enter, especially once the steamer was weighed down with a full load of passengers.[16]

Neither the public debate nor the official hearing reached a firm conclusion during the month of July 1927, pending the conclusion of the planned salvage and inspection of the raised hull. In May 1928, upon the vessel finally being raised, the head of the salvage company reported to *The Sun* newspaper in Baltimore that:

> . . . an examination disclosed that the sinking of the old excursion steamer Majestic near the foot of Clinton street last summer was due to an open port hole. . . . The examination had been made after the boat had been placed in drydock at Sparrows Point. . . . The cause of the sinking was in dispute at the time and remained a mystery until the open port hole was discovered.[17]

One might logically question how a port hole, inevitably placed above the water line in a boat, could cause such a sinking alone. Perhaps the newspaper reporter employed the phrase "port hole" when it should have been a reference to an open seacock. Nonetheless, the article implies that sabotage was the cause.

In the end, the investigation by the US Steamboat Inspection Service failed to resolve these conflicting stories. As the agency reported in 1928, in what can only be seen as a cursory and inconclusive review:

> July 24, 1927. The Str. MAJESTIC, a negro excursion boat, sank in Baltimore Harbor. The matter was investigated on July 25, 26, 27, 28, 1927, and on May 26, 1928, this Board visited the steamer after she had been raised. The testimony shows that this vessel was in good condition when she left Baltimore and this Board was unable to determine the cause of the sinking. Decision rendered on June 6, 1928, dismissing the case.[18]

This summary is notable for two things. First, it concludes that "testimony shows that the vessel was in good condition" when, in fact, there were conflicting accounts of the vessel's condition, including compelling evidence by Smallwood's intended chief engineer, who had inspected the ship before it sailed and called it "extremely unsafe" and "worthless." Also submitted was the testimony of the Black deckhand aboard ship, who raised legitimate indications of damage inflicted on the hull just before the vessel sailed. At a minimum, the report should have acknowledged the conflicting accounts of *Majestic*'s condition.

Second, there is no reference in this official report to an open seacock, or even an open port hole, which might have furthered the case that sabotage was responsible. Given the criminal nature of such sabotage, one would think any evidence of such would have been presented for further legal action. As Sherlock Holmes might have concluded, such absence is itself highly notable and leads one to conclude the investigation was designed merely to put the issue to rest without implicating the *Majestic*'s white owner or crew.

Harrington and Claiborne-Annapolis Ferry Inc. were bystanders in this controversy. The only issue that emerged for them was the demand by the City of Baltimore that the ferry company—still the owners of *Majestic* when it sank—pay to have the wreck removed. The company refused—it legally abandoned the vessel and then argued that under federal salvage laws, it was not obligated to remove the wreck.[19] Perhaps Harrington refused to pay for removal because he did not feel a strong incentive to free up the coal-loading pier of the PRR, which, after all, was its primary competitor on cross-bay ferry and rail transportation across the Eastern Shore. In the end, it escaped any responsibility either for the wreck itself or its removal.[20]

Claiborne-Annapolis Ferry Inc. Is Restructured

While Harrington was seeking to avoid responsibility for the loss of *Majestic*, operations back at Claiborne-Annapolis Ferry Inc. continued to expand, especially after *Gov. Albert C. Ritchie* was put into operation. The owners realized the benefits financially. Net income increased by a factor of ten from 1926 to 1927—bringing cumulative results, for the first time since 1919, into the black—and then doubled again in 1928.

It was then that the company saw a change of ownership structure, one that was engineered in 1927 and which took place in 1928. What was Claiborne-Annapolis Ferry Inc. became, instead, the Claiborne-Annapolis Ferry Company. This was an amiable transition organized by Harrington himself, designed to put the business on a more solid financial footing and, perhaps not incidentally, to strengthen his personal control over operations. In this he was joined by John M. Dennis, the friendly banker at Union Trust Company. Dennis had joined the new Claiborne-Annapolis Ferry Company as the corporation's treasurer in December 1927.[21]

The financial reengineering was advanced on August 8, 1927, and involved a cash payment of $150,000 to the stockholders of record.[22] (Harrington's share would be almost $50,000.) The offer was accepted eleven days later.[23]

The new company was incorporated on August 8, 1927—the same day the offer letter was sent. Sixty thousand shares were issued with a value of $2.50 each, raising the $150,000 in cash required to buy out the old shareholders. When the dust settled, Harrington owned 23,164 shares (38.61 percent of the company), and his son owned another 1,434 shares (2.39 percent).[24] Harrington resumed his role as president, with John M. Dennis at his side as Treasurer and B. Frank Sherman (who owned two thousand shares himself) as general manager and board member. Among the first acts of the new leadership team was to secure $250,000 in bonds, backed once again by the Union Trust Company and John M. Dennis.[25] Why the need for bonds? The company was about to go shopping for a new ferry.

After the restructuring, the recovery from the disappointing performance of the early 1920s was complete. For the first time, in 1928, the new company paid a dividend ($15,000). The restructured company went on to generate strong financial results, and the future looked promising.[26]

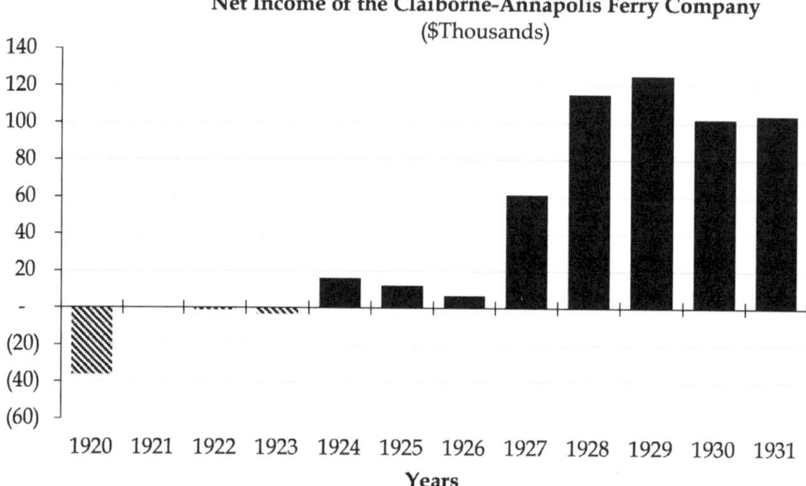

The debt raised by the sale of bonds, supported by the continued positive cash flow, allowed the company to expand the fleet with the first new ferry custom-built for the Claiborne-Annapolis Ferry Company. This modern, diesel-powered double-ender was constructed by Spears Engineers in Portsmouth, Virginia. In recognition of his critical role in the initial start-up of the company in 1919 and his continued support for the ferry as Maryland state treasurer, the new vessel was christened *John M. Dennis*. Harrington, Dennis, and Sherman were present at the christening. This ferry, uniquely among those in the fleet in 1929, would go on to operate throughout the ferry's remaining years through 1952 and then served on the Delaware River well into the 1970s. Its twenty-three-year career was the longest of any ferry within the Claiborne-Annapolis Ferry Company (or its successors), though it remained second to the thirty-year career of BC&A's *Cambridge* on the Baltimore-Claiborne route.

Tolchester Steamboat Company Enters the Car-Ferry Business

The bankruptcy of the Peninsula Ferry Company in 1923 and that of the Baltimore and Eastern Shore Ferry Line Inc. in 1927 did not mean the end of competitive threats from new car-ferry operators. For years, the Tolchester Steamboat Company had provided an immensely popular excursion steamboat service from Baltimore to its amusement park and beaches at Tolchester on the Eastern Shore. Thousands of holidaymakers would step aboard one of their steamboats for the short trip across the Bay. The steamer *Louise* was especially popular with visitors and served on the route for four decades. But almost all passengers simply spent the day at Tolchester and then returned to Baltimore—there was minimal onward travel.

In 1925, Tolchester Steamboat Company decided to experiment with the ferry business and put on its Baltimore-Tolchester route the car ferry *Express*. This was an old steamboat, built in 1886 as *Robert Garrett* by Columbian Iron Works in Baltimore. It had seen decades of duty in New York Harbor. While technically a double-ender, the steamboat's sidewheels were not placed amidships, and thus the ferry handled well in open water in only one direction. It would have to turn around before backing into the slip at its destination. The tired *Express* also seemed accident-prone and repeatedly ended up in the repair yard rather than on the route.

Ferry captains were not the only ones puzzled by this design. Passengers also disliked the boxy, ungainly appearance of *Express*, greatly preferring the luxurious and romantic appeal of *Louise*. As author David C. Holly explains:

> *Louise*, beloved old matron, had steamed off each summer day bearing thousands of happy Baltimoreans bound for the beach and playground of Tolchester. *Express* was no substitute. She had broad decks: Baltimoreans disliked them. She had a level and enclosed ballroom and an orchestra; Baltimoreans longed for the slightly tilted floor and the view of the Bay from the *Louise's* dance floor. *Express* was boxy, bustling, and broad, and Baltimoreans hated her.[27]

Relatively few passengers seemed interested in using this route as a starting point for a journey across the Eastern Shore or to the ocean resorts. Auto traffic was disappointing. The freight business also never materialized. It was too hard for the line to compete against the linked rail operations in Love Point and (at least until 1928) at Claiborne. Competition from BC&A was fierce—and then the Great Depression hit. Finally, in 1932 the Tolchester Steamboat Company recognized the error of its thinking, pulled *Express* from the route, and returned to its lucrative excursion business.

Notes

1. "Capt. Higgins Takes Automobile on Short Submarine Voyage," *Salisbury Times*, September 15, 1930. The car was owned by Edward (Ned) Higgins, a captain on the Claiborne-Annapolis Ferry line. It was being driven off the ferry by his brother Daniel G. Higgins, the master of the *Gov. Emerson C. Harrington* on this trip. Both car and driver emerged from the water wet but otherwise unharmed.
2. Financial results for Claiborne-Annapolis Ferry Inc. were reported each year in the *Annual Report of the Maryland Public Service Commission*, Table No. 61. The reporting ended in 1932. However, the internal financial reports of the Claiborne-Annapolis Ferry Inc. are held in the Maryland State Archives.
3. "New Ferry Steamer," *Denton Journal*, December 26, 1925.
4. "State and Peninsula News," *Worcester Democrat* (Pocomoke City, MD), December 11, 1925.
5. "Double-End Ferry Boat Will Be Ready Next June," *Sun* (Baltimore, MD), April 21, 1926.
6. "The New Ferry Boat," *Denton Journal*, July 3, 1926.
7. "Bodkin Creek to Become Amusement Park," *Afro-American* (Baltimore, MD), July 9, 1927.
8. "New Excursion Venture Here Goes to Smash," *Afro-American* (Baltimore, MD), July 16, 1927.
9. Ibid.
10. "Leaking Excursion Steamer Sinks After Race to Land 990 on Board," *The Sun* (Baltimore, MD), July 25, 1927.
11. "1000 Are Saved," *Afro-American* (Baltimore, MD), July 23, 1927.
12. "Excursion Boat Sinks After 990 Land in Safety," *Sun* (Baltimore, MD), July 25, 1927.
13. Ibid.
14. "Ship's Sinking Was Foretold, Says Captain," *Evening Sun* (Baltimore, MD), July 25, 1927.
15. "Boat Unsafe When Walton Got It," *Sun* (Baltimore, MD), July 26, 1927.
16. "Excursionists Not Warned, Says Negro," *Evening Sun* (Baltimore, MD), July 26, 1927.
17. "Sinking of Excursion Boat Is Laid to Open Port Hole," *Sun* (Baltimore, MD), May 27, 1928.
18. "Summary of Casualties, Violations of Law, and Investigations for the Year Ended June 30, 1928, Third Supervising District, Local District of Baltimore, MD," in *Miscellaneous Annual Reports: Steamboat Inspection Service, July 1, 1927, to June 30, 1928* (US Department of Commerce, 1928), vol. 18, 143.

19. Letter from George H. Dawson, secretary of Claiborne-Annapolis Ferry Inc., to Charles C. Wallace, city solicitor for the City of Baltimore, August 8, 1927. Contained in the files of Mayor & City Council of Baltimore v. Claiborne-Annapolis Ferry Inc., Records of the Circuit Court No. 2 of Baltimore City, No 15822/197.
20. *Majestic*'s sunken hull was later refloated, and the vessel was reconfigured as a barge. It was later destroyed by fire off the Choptank River in May 1937.
21. "250,000 Bond Issue to Buy Ferry Is Approved by P.S.C.," *Sun* (Baltimore, MD), December 8, 1927.
22. Offer letter to Claiborne-Annapolis Ferry Inc. from Claiborne-Annapolis Ferry Company, August 8, 1927, Maryland State Archives, Public Service Commission Formal Case File, S245, MdHR No. 19816-2.
23. Meeting Minutes of the Claiborne-Annapolis Ferry Inc. Board of Directors, August 19, 1927, Maryland State Archives, Maryland Public Service Commission, MSA S245-2, MdHR 19816-2.
24. Meeting Minutes of the Annual Meeting of Stockholders, Claiborne-Annapolis Ferry Company, March 26, 1928, Maryland State Archives, Maryland Public Service Commission, MSA S245, MdHR 19816-3.
25. Meeting Minutes of the Claiborne-Annapolis Ferry Company Board of Directors, January 23, 1928, Maryland State Archives, Maryland Public Service Commission, MSA S245-3, MdHR 19816-3.
26. Financial results are reported (until 1932) in the *Annual Report of the Public Service Commission of Maryland.*
27. David C. Holly, *Steamboats on the Chesapeake: Emma Giles and the Tolchester Line* (Tidewater Publishers, 1987), 281.

X

Geography Strikes Back

Claiborne's status as the primary ferry/rail hub on the Eastern Shore was, as has been suggested earlier, an accident of history. The northern tip of Kent Island was a far better option for ferries coming from Baltimore. The western shore of Kent Island was a better choice for ferries coming from Annapolis. But since the original plan was to move railcars from Bay Ridge, south of Annapolis on the Chesapeake's western shoreline, Claiborne had been selected, and a complex rail, jetty, and terminal infrastructure had been built there. That decision had legs: for the next forty years, Claiborne remained the focus of the cross-bay steamers and ferries.

But in the end, geography won out. There was pressure, driven by prospective competitors, to shorten the Annapolis-Claiborne ferry trip, one that required ferries to navigate around Bloody Point at the southern tip of Kent Island to reach Claiborne. Prospective investors realized the potential opportunity of a shorter route and sought permission to operate a competing ferry from the Annapolis area to Kent Island directly. What resulted were lengthy administrative and bureaucratic battles between these various upstarts and the established Claiborne-Annapolis Ferry Company, with Kent Island at the center. In this, the Claiborne-Annapolis Ferry Company adopted the role of monopolistic incumbent, assuming that mantle from the declining Baltimore and Eastern Railroad (successor to the Baltimore, Chesapeake, and Atlantic Railway [BC&A]).

This confrontation played to the political savvy and connections of Emerson C. Harrington, the former governor of Maryland from the Eastern Shore. Harrington was well connected, prescient, and willing to do battle. He could see that Kent Island was a natural ferry destination and that his company's stranglehold on cross-bay ferry traffic was in jeopardy. One of the first things Harrington did at this point was to cultivate support from other political leaders in Queen Anne's County, where Kent Island is located. As General Manager B. Frank Sherman recalled afterwards:

> Politics was bound to creep in and, at times, the ferry was compelled to fight for its very existence. Queen Anne's County representatives in both the Senate and House were always friends of the ferry, and I sincerely hope and believe none of them ever regretted having given their assistance.[1]

Challenges from Kent Island

The first competitive threat emerged just months after the new Claiborne-Annapolis Ferry Company had been restructured. In August 1928, a group of New York investors proposed to establish a short, high-frequency, and low-cost connection at the point where the Chesapeake Bay was narrowest: between Sandy Point on the western side and Stevensville on Kent Island on the eastern side.[2] With long piers, the actual over-water distance covered would be only three miles, a fraction of the much longer distance to Claiborne.

Once again, emulating the practice of the Eastern Shore Development Steamship Company and the Claiborne-Annapolis Ferry Company itself, this new challenger sought to disrupt the existing monopoly by using new technologies employed on a new route. The nascent Bay Bridge Ferry Corporation proposed to employ advanced "electric ferries," meaning ferries that ran propellers via electric motors powered by diesel generators, as opposed to direct mechanical connections between the diesel engines and the propellers. Financing totaling $1.5 million had been obtained from brokers James G. White & Co. in New York. The effort was led by Aldace Walker, son of Harold Walker. The elder Walker was at that time a member of the board of directors of the Claiborne-Annapolis Ferry Company, suggesting a clear conflict of interest.[3]

No doubt Harrington and his general manager, B. Frank Sherman, considered this a serious threat, one requiring a serious response. They adopted a classic tactic: the best way to repel an invader was to occupy the critical ground first, in this case literally. To start, Harrington and Sherman would establish a new ferry line to Kent Island, build a new terminal, and then protest the licensing of any new competitor in order to protect the monopoly. Next, and less well publicized but even more decisive, Harrington and Sherman would preempt all new competitors by taking control of *all* potential terminal locations on the western side of Kent Island.

But it was vital to move quickly, before the competitors could get organized and secure approval from the Maryland Public Service Commission, the County Commissioners of Anne Arundel County, and the County Commissioners of Queen Anne's County. Suddenly, the Claiborne-Annapolis Ferry Company took great interest in farm property on Kent Island.

The first option, advanced by Sherman in 1929, was to shorten the Claiborne route by cutting a canal, at an estimated cost of $242,779,[4] through Kent Island farmland, creating a new terminal on the island for those passengers who were only interested in traveling that far. This would shorten the trip from Annapolis to Claiborne by eight miles and perhaps save half an hour on the crossing.[5] Legislation permitting the construction of a canal was proposed and then adopted by the Maryland legislature in March 1929.[6] The Claiborne-Annapolis Ferry Company was duly authorized that year to "dig, construct, and maintain a canal across Kent Island, in Queen Anne's County, from Eastern Bay to Chesapeake Bay."[7]

The Annapolis-Claiborne ferries would also stop at a new terminal built on the Chesapeake Bay side of the canal, allowing cars and passengers who did not want to go on to Claiborne to leave the ferry at Kent Island. This new terminal would thus preempt the efforts of the Bay Bridge Ferry Corporation to launch a competing service on this route. However, under this scenario, Claiborne would remain the primary hub on the Eastern Shore.

The proposal for the canal was put forward publicly not as an anti-competitive strategy but rather as a way (yet once again) to prevent Baltimore's eternal nemesis—Philadelphia—from taking over trade that rightly should be kept in Maryland. This was the same threat used in 1886 and again in 1916. As was reported at the time:

> Mr. Harrington said one of the main objects of the canal was to shorten the distance between the Eastern Shore and Baltimore, so that trade of the Eastern Shore which now goes to Philadelphia and Delaware might be diverted to Baltimore. He said his company would start a campaign to tell the people of the Eastern Shore that they coud carry their produce to Baltimore over the new route more quickly than they could send it to Wilmington or Philadelphia and to tell the shoppers that they would save money and time by going to Baltimore over the shorter route instead of to Philadelphia and Wilmington.[8]

In February 1929, the Claiborne-Annapolis Ferry Company acquired from T. Roland Carville a 283-acre farm between Price Creek on the Chesapeake Bay side of Kent Island and Long Creek on the other side.[9] Known in the community as Carvel Farm and internally within the ferry company as "Farm No. 2," this property was on the lower third of Kent Island, just north off a straight line drawn from Annapolis to Claiborne. The property bordered both the Chesapeake Bay and an inlet that connected to Eastern Bay, thus providing all of the property required for a canal.[10] This acquisition is entirely consistent with plans to build a canal to connect Annapolis and Claiborne more seamlessly.

But as the internal company name suggests, the Carvel Farm (Farm No. 2) was not the only property acquired. "Farm No. 1" was also acquired quietly in February 1929, but this had nothing to do

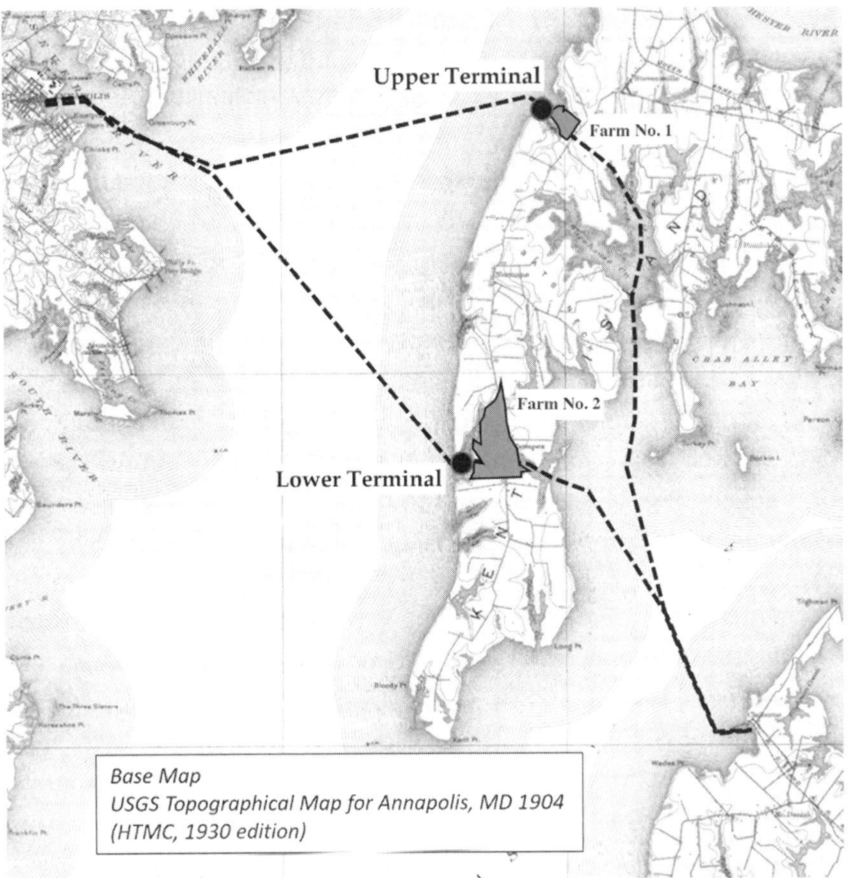

Map 7. Scenarios for Claiborne-Annapolis terminals and routes on Kent Island. Source: Base map is from US Geological Survey, detailed and annotated by the author.

with a canal. This property was farther north, just south of where the Chesapeake Bay Bridge now arrives on Kent Island.[11] This ninety-acre Broad Creek Farm did not extend all of the way to Eastern Bay, so it alone would be insufficient to cover the path required for a canal. Theoretically, one might acquire additional property to dig a canal and connect Upper Terminal to the headwaters of Warehouse Creek or Cox Creek, but this would still leave the Eastern Bay terminal quite a distance from Claiborne, and it would require navigation down shallow inland waters. Finally, Broad Creek Farm was hardly on a straight line between Claiborne and Annapolis. It would not save nearly as much time as the canal route through Carvel Farm.

However, the Broad Creek location would have served as an ideal place for the Claiborne-Annapolis Ferry Company—or a competitor—to build a ferry terminal on Kent Island itself. It would serve as a location to deposit or collect passengers and their vehicles near the community of Stevensville, adjacent to both rail and road lines onto the Eastern Shore. Indeed, when time came to build the Chesapeake Bay Bridge, this is almost the exact location chosen for its eastern starting point. It is entirely likely that Farm No. 1 was never seriously considered for a canal, but instead its acquisition was an effort to secure a potential Kent Island terminal location for a new cross-bay service—and to deny that same location to any potential future competitor. Given the announcement in 1928 by the Bay Bridge Ferry Corporation, such threats were not theoretical.

Both Farm No. 1 (Upper Terminal) and Farm No. 2 (Lower Terminal) were subject to detailed review by outside engineers led by Richard C. Hollyday. However, Hollyday's engineering study cast doubt on the viability of both the Upper Terminal and Lower Terminal locations for a ferry wharf. As he reported to the company's management in August 1929:

> An examination was made of the shores, shingle and [outcroppings] and boulders were observed which lead to the conclusion that possibly [outcroppings] and boulders may be found at no great depth below the water surface. There is also deep water with shoaler water further out, indicating that there are forces of nature at work causing a changing of water bottom elevations. Both of these indications are unfavorable.[12]

The engineer suggested an alternative for Upper Terminal, one a bit farther south and designated internally as the "Normans" location or "Farm No. 3."[13] Accordingly, just three weeks after the engineering report was submitted, the ferry company proceeded to acquire sixty-five acres of land in this area, the property known at

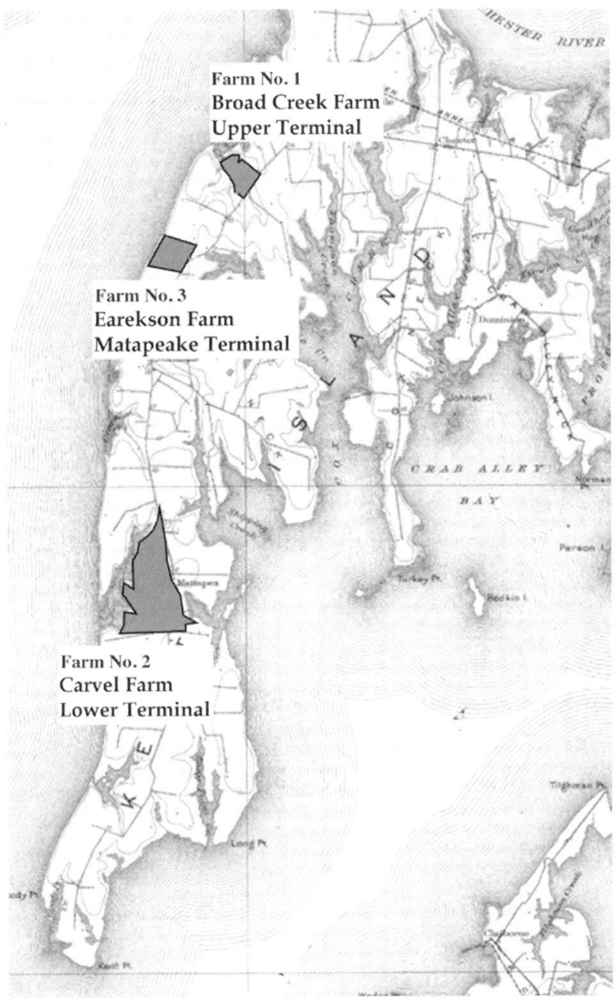

Map 8. Three farms acquired by the Claiborne-Annapolis Ferry Company in 1929. Source: Base map is from US Geological Survey, detailed and annotated by the author.

the time locally as The Earekson Farm. This was only positioned as a replacement for Upper Terminal, not as a substitute for Lower Terminal at the proposed canal's entrance through Carvel Farm.[14] The acquisition of Farm No. 3 would also deny any new competitor access to the one location on this part of Kent Island endorsed by the engineers as suitable for a major ferry terminal.

Although both the canal option (Farm No. 2) and the new

ferry-line option (Farm No. 3) were considered in the early days of 1929, the discussion began to shift away from the former and toward the latter. In the minutes of the ferry company's board meeting on August 12, 1929—one at which Hollyday presented an oral report on his engineering studies prior to the issuance of his written report the following day—the word "canal" does not even appear. Instead, the discussion is entirely around the logistical issues in constructing a ferry terminal on the western side of Kent Island at Farm No. 3. The decision to abandon the canal project in favor of a new ferry line was solidified a few weeks later when, at the company board meeting on August 30, the discussion centered on how to communicate to local authorities the decision to "abandon the canal project which had been considered and establish in lieu thereof a ferry terminal on the Island at the 'Normans' site." After discussion, the following resolution was approved by the board:

> That, if proper arrangements can be made with the County Commissioners of Queen Anne's County, a ferry route be established between Annapolis and the point designated as "Normans" by the Engineer on Kent Island.[15]

The result of those discussions in Queen Anne's County concluded with the abandonment of the canal project, although it is unclear whether this decision was driven by the commissioners, or accommodated by the commissioners based on the preference expressed by the ferry company. As the corporate board minutes report:

> President Harrington reported that the motion of the last meeting in regard to negotiations with the County Commisioners of Queen Anne's County was carried out by having the Commissioners request the abandonment of the Canal Project and the establishment of a ferry service between Annapolis and the terminal site selected by the Company. This is set forth in the contract signed by the County Commissions and the Ferry Company.[16]

Thus, the canal was never built and ferries to Claiborne would still have to make the long journey around Bloody Point.[17] Instead, "Normans" became the location that would serve as the eastern terminus of a new ferry line from Annapolis.[18] It would soon be known as Matapeake.

The Claiborne-Annapolis Ferry Company was in a hurry. The new ferry line needed to become a *fait accompli* in order to preempt potential competition. Construction started immediately. A new road was being laid from that location to Stevensville, connecting to existing roads from Kent Island to points east. This plan for the shorter ferry line was revealed publicly in January 1930, when Harrington announced that direct ferry service between Annapolis and Kent Island for the first time would begin in June of that year.[19] In this way, the Annapolis-to-Matapeake ferry service was born.

Permission for the new ferry to Matapeake was received from the Maryland Public Service Commission (PSC) on June 5, 1930—just a few weeks after the application was made.[20] This is further illustration of Harrington's continued political influence. Similar applications by potential competitors took months or years for adjudication.

Preparations were made for a gala opening, but the weather was less supportive. The grand opening on July 1, just in time for the busy holiday weekend, was interrupted by sheets of rain and a driving wind, forcing spectators and dignitaries to seek shelter in their automobiles. Speeches were called off. As was reported at the time:

> As the last float of the pageant passed the reviewing stand, the black clouds, which had been gathering since early afternoon, opened up and a blanket of water descended, turning costumed pageant participants, gaily dressed women and immaculately garbed men into just so may wet bedraggled humans.[21]

However, the adverse weather did not interfere with the arrival of *John M. Dennis*, the newest and most advanced vessel in the Claiborne-Annapolis Ferry fleet.

While many celebrated the new route, and its promise of a much faster journey to the Eastern Shore, observers in Claiborne must have seen the writing on the wall. Once the Matapeake terminal was in place, that shorter route would likely emerge as the primary destination of Annapolis ferries, with Claiborne, for the first time in four decades, relegated to second-tier status.

While all this was happening, the Claiborne-Annapolis Ferry Company still had to fend off continuing competitive threats from the Bay Bridge Ferry Corporation, but it was now in a far stronger position to do so. Aldace Walker and his investors were not dissuaded from the scheme just because the Claiborne-Annapolis Ferry Company had announced its new route to Matapeake. In April 1930, the Bay Bridge Ferry Corporation formally proposed the creation of its new cross-bay ferry, this one bypassing Annapolis as well as Claiborne. The new route would involve a direct connection between Stevensville on Kent Island and Sandy Point, directly opposite on the western side. This would create a faster connection than Harrington's new Annapolis-Matapeake line, just months away from inauguration. Application for the competing line was made to the Maryland PSC.[22] In May 1930, Harold Walker, Aldace's father, resigned from the board of directors of the Claiborne-Annapolis Ferry Company, removing any conflict of interest.[23]

Harrington and his company had prepared well for this battle, and it would be over before it really got started. The agreement Harrington had struck in 1929 with Queen Anne's County, when establishing the Matapeake ferry, had a specific provision that meant the county could not grant . . .

> . . . any other franchise, permit or authorization to any corporation or individual for the purpose of operating a ferry from Kent Island to Anne Arundel County, Maryland, so long as the Claiborne-Annapolis Ferry Company, or its assigns, rendered adequate service from said Kent Island to Anne Arundel County, Maryland.[24]

Accordingly, the county denied the application of the Bay Bridge Ferry Corporation. That company then appealed the decision to the courts and lost. It further appealed to the Maryland Court of Appeals—and lost again. In the end, it took until 1934 for the Maryland PSC to finally rule on the proposal, at which point the application was summarily "dismissed without prejudice."[25]

Challenges from Chesapeake Beach

A similar competitive threat had also emerged farther south, in a county without any non-compete clause negotiated with the Claiborne-Annapolis Ferry Company. The Chesapeake Beach Railway was keen to create a new ferry line connecting Chesapeake Beach with a new terminal at Trippe (Tripp's) Bay, on a peninsula in Dorchester County about ten miles west of Cambridge, where Harrington had his home. (In the mid-twentieth century, the name Trippe's Bay was generally shortened to Tripp's Bay.) Chesapeake Beach was the location of a popular resort with rail connections to Washington, DC, and ferry connections to Baltimore. However, passenger revenue on their lines was in decline as the automobile age reached full blossom. Thus, the leadership of the railway looked for new sources of revenue.

The presumed answer was a new ferry line. It would exploit the earlier efforts of another group of investors to petition the Maryland PSC for permission to operate a ferry service in the same area. Having failed to secure PSC permission, these investors joined hands with the Chesapeake Beach Railway for another attempt. This proposed link would provide a quicker route to Ocean City, bypassing Kent Island and Claiborne altogether. While centered on two large diesel car ferries, it was hoped the new service might even spur passenger traffic on the railway as passengers sought to bypass the longer Love Point rail connection from Baltimore.[26]

The plans for the new ferry line were made public in February 1931.[27] Promoters of the Chesapeake Beach Railway proposal pointed out that their trip to Ocean City would be ninety minutes shorter than Harrington's competing service. This threatened the Claiborne-Annapolis Ferry Company's monopoly on car ferries across the Chesapeake. Harrington's response to this challenge is perhaps the best example of how he would use legal tactics and bureaucratic maneuvering to delay, and ultimately derail, a competitor.

Harrington again pulled out the "we were here first" defense, but this time the controlling authorities were different and his argument did not persuade. Chesapeake Beach Railway had already applied to the federal Interstate Commerce Commission (ICC) and had received ICC's approval for their new ferry line on July 1, 1930. The Claiborne-Annapolis Ferry Company then sought to derail or delay the new ferry line by dragging the matter into court and requesting an injunction.[28]

Harrington argued that the Maryland PSC should make the decision whether to authorize the new ferry line, not the ICC. Given that Harrington himself, as governor, had appointed one of the three PSC members (J. Frank Harper) and that his running mate in 1915 (and successor as governor) Albert C. Ritchie had appointed the other two (Harold W. West and Steuart Purcell), Harrington might have expected a friendlier reception at the PSC than at the ICC. The case ultimately went to the US Supreme Court where, on April 11, 1932, the court ruled in favor of Chesapeake Beach Railway against the Claiborne-Annapolis Ferry Company.[29] The ICC authorization provided to the Chesapeake Beach Railway was reaffirmed. Harrington had lost the first round in the battle to protect his franchise.

Harrington's ferry company did not give up the fight, however, and decided to go after the financing for the new competitor. The next step was to object to an application filed by the Chesapeake Beach Railway to the federal Reconstruction Finance Corporation (RFC) for a $425,000 loan to finance the new ferry line. Again, Harrington attempted to derail the competitor by taking his protest to the RFC. Again, he lost: the loan was approved on May 18, 1933. But Harrington was tenacious. The Claiborne-Annapolis Ferry Company renewed its protest just two months later, challenging the basis by which the Chesapeake Beach Railway had applied for the loan and arguing, again, that the matter should be referred to the Maryland PSC.[30] But once again, Harrington lost.[31]

In 1933, Congress passed a law changing the approval authority for these projects from the RFC to the Public Works Administration (PWA). This forced the Chesapeake Beach Railway to reapply for the loan before the new agency, and it gave Harrington yet another chance to frustrate the potential competitor. Once more, Harrington argued that the matter should first be resolved by the Maryland PSC rather than by federal authorities. The approval process for the loan was held up as the courts went through the various legal filings.

In the end, the delays and bureaucratic reshuffling did the trick. The ICC's original authorization for the project required that the construction of the new ferry line be started by November 1, 1933—later extended by two weeks to November 16. But since the Chesapeake Beach Railway still had not yet received PWA approval for its requested $425,000 loan, in large part due to legal maneuvering by the Claiborne-Annapolis Ferry Company, it was not in a position to begin work on the new terminals.

The railroad did not reapply for re-authorization from the ICC. Instead, it argued its original application was still valid. In the end, the Chesapeake Beach Railway lost that battle. There was no further extension to the original authorization, and no loan. The time period for the initial authorization had lapsed, and the Chesapeake Beach-Trippe's Bay ferry line was never established. It had taken three years, but aggressive action by the Claiborne-Annapolis Ferry Company had once again upended a competitive threat.[32] By March 1935, the Chesapeake Beach Railway, in financial distress, was even forced to abandon some of its existing railroad network.

While Harrington was fighting these battles, a longer-term threat had also reappeared, one that would ultimately lead to the demise of the ferry company. Interest in a bridge across the Chesapeake Bay reemerged in 1929, and the Chesapeake Bay Bridge Commission was formed in 1931 to study the options, the preferred of which was a Baltimore-area crossing from Hart Island to Tolchester Beach.[33] (Hart Island and Miller Island are now known as

Hart-Miller Island after a dike was established between the two peninsulas in 1981.) However, the plan was for private investors to fund the construction, and securing the required capital proved a challenge. The bridge plan was put on hold—for the time being. The United States had, after all, just entered the Great Depression.

The Great Depression Hits

Just as the Claiborne-Annapolis Ferry Company was adapting to its new route structure and adding *John M. Dennis* to the fleet, the US economy tanked. The Great Depression had arrived. The slowdown started at the end of 1929 and continued through 1931. However, the real economic free-fall took place during 1932.

The results were evident in the operations of the company. In the early days of the Great Depression, overall company revenues continued to climb, spurred in part by the additional Annapolis-Matapeake route and the arrival of *John M. Dennis*. Revenues rose 16 percent in 1929 and another 16 percent in 1930. Revenue slipped a bit in 1931, down 1 percent, and then started falling off a cliff, dropping 18 percent in 1932 and another 17 percent in 1933. Net income dropped 64 percent in 1932 and another 26 percent in 1933.[34]

The Claiborne-Annapolis Ferry Company responded to the economic decline in a number of ways. Dividends to shareholders were suspended in 1930 and 1931, though reinstated at the end of 1932. In March 1932, company President Emerson C. Harrington took a pay cut from $12,000 per year to "only" $10,000. (This was still more than ten times the average worker's earnings in 1932.) General manager B. Frank Sherman volunteered to take a pay cut from $6,000 per year to $5,400. The company attributed this action to altruism:

> The Directors felt that this was a very unselfish sacrifice on the part of these two Officers, but upon being convinced of the sincerity of the proposal as a measure of economy, and for the good of the Company in a period of depression, a motion was duly made, seconded and adopted.[35]

In an effort to boost traffic, rates for vehicles were discounted. In January 1934, base rates for automobiles were cut by 25 percent, and categories were modified to allow more vehicles to qualify for the lowest possible rate. The steps worked: revenues rose again by 10 percent in 1934.

Meanwhile, the ferry company looked at ways to streamline operations and reduce costs. This attention was increasingly focused on the service to Claiborne, now being eclipsed by the more popular direct service to Matapeake.

Attention Shifts from Claiborne to Matapeake

When the Matapeake route opened in 1930, service from Annapolis to Claiborne continued as before. At first, Claiborne and Matapeake were treated as equals in the ferry operations. The Claiborne-Annapolis Ferry Company schedule for the summer season from 1930 to 1932 listed six round trips per day to both Claiborne and Matapeake. But then the pattern shifted as traffic fell during the Great Depression and motorists' preferences became clearer. The Claiborne-Annapolis Ferry Company responded by shifting its most critical resources—the ferries—from Claiborne to Matapeake. From 1933 to 1937, summer round trips from Claiborne averaged three per day, while daily trips from Matapeake rose from six per day in 1933 to nineteen per day in 1937.

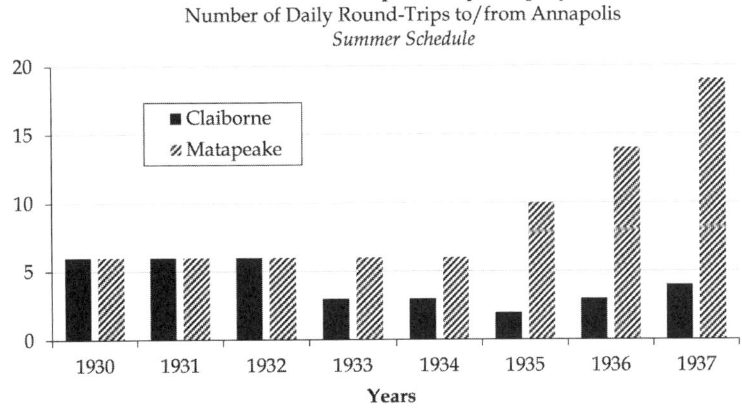

The shift in focus was just as apparent, if not more so, in the off-season schedule typically running from early September through late May. Whereas traffic used to back up on the approaches to Claiborne, those backups now occurred on the road to Matapeake, and the Claiborne ferry line was often sparsely occupied. The company reacted appropriately. By 1932 there were twice as many trips from Matapeake as there were from Claiborne. By 1935 Matapeake had three times as many, and by 1937 it had ten daily round trips versus only two for Claiborne.

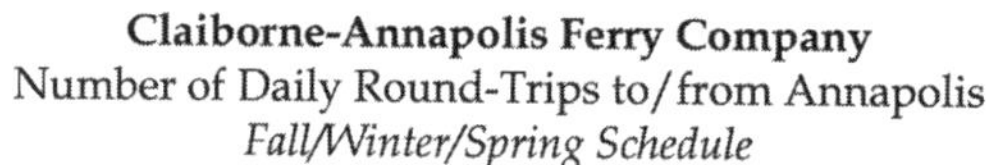

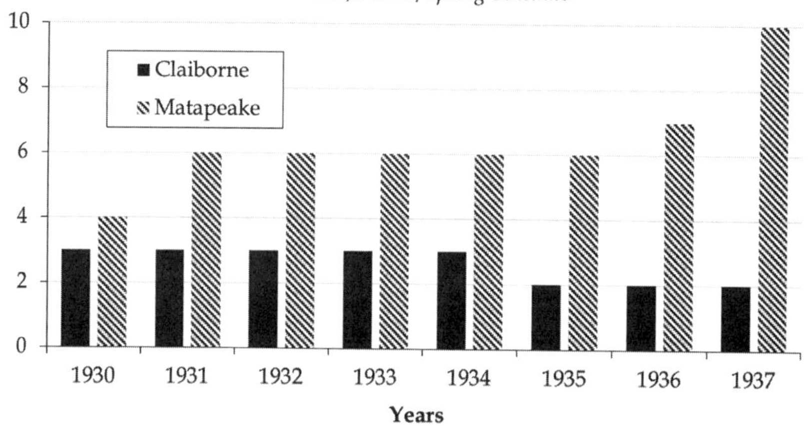

Claiborne had become the stepchild of the Claiborne-Annapolis Ferry Company. By 1936, the company assigned the two modern diesel double-ender ferries, *Gov. Albert C. Ritchie* and *John M. Dennis,* to the Matapeake run exclusively.[36] Claiborne was left for the most part with the old coal-fired sidewheel steamer *Gov. Emerson C. Harrington*, which, although technically a creation of the twentieth century, was more akin to relics of the nineteenth century. Even the name on the published schedules changed just a few years after the new terminal was built. What had been listed on the schedules as the Claiborne-Annapolis Ferry—"Claiborne" came first—was now the Annapolis-Claiborne-Matapeake Ferries.[37]

Claiborne had officially been demoted, part of a long decline that took place throughout the 1930s.

Threats Reappear and Harrington Again Emerges Victorious

In the mid-1930s, the Claiborne-Annapolis Ferry Company once again faced two forms of competition, the first from yet another proposed ferry line and the second from a potential bridge across the Chesapeake. Harrington, by this point, was used to dealing with potential threats by exploiting his considerable influence with Democratic legislators in Maryland. In a truly brilliant move, he exploited the new developments in a way that cemented the franchise of the Claiborne-Annapolis Ferry Company, while simultaneously providing a profitable exit path for himself and other shareholders, should the worst happen.

In 1929, the State of Maryland awarded to the Chesapeake Bay Bridge Company the franchise to build the bay bridge—if it could raise private capital for funding. In this it had failed once the United States entered the Great Depression and capital markets became skittish. If the bridge was to be built, an alternative source of capital was required.

Such an option emerged as the new administration of President Franklin D. Roosevelt sought to address mass unemployment, which had reached 24.9 percent in 1933.[38] The plan was to stimulate the economy with doses of public spending, including new infrastructure projects. In 1933, an application was made to the new Reconstruction Finance Corporation for a loan to fund the proposed Chesapeake bay bridge, but that application was rejected. In 1934, a similar application for financing was sent to the Public Works Administration but was refused. In both cases, federal authorities doubted that the State of Maryland was prepared to fund the maintenance and upkeep of a new bay bridge.[39]

Local Maryland legislators attempted to fill the gap in 1935. Both the Maryland Senate and the House of Delegates passed new legislation with four major provisions. First, they authorized the spending of $10 million to build a bridge. Second, they authorized the spending of not more than $1,200,000 for the purchase of the Claiborne-Annapolis Ferry Company—should the bridge be built. Third, they forbid any new ferry operations from being established within twenty miles of the proposed bridge route. Finally, the legislation established the Chesapeake Bay Bridge Authority to pursue the matter.[40]

The legislation had Harrington's skillful fingerprints all over it. It established state protection for his current monopoly (and that of the smaller Love Point ferry). It protected his financial interests against the threat of a new bridge by authorizing the state's purchase of the Claiborne-Annapolis Ferry Company should a bridge be built. Finally, it placed Harrington himself on the three-member board of the Chesapeake Bay Bridge Authority, where he could continue to use his influence to protect his ferry company. Harrington's personal participation was even specified in the legislation.

But the political winds were beginning to shift in Maryland, and not in a direction favorable to Harrington's preferred direction of travel. Albert C. Ritchie, colleague of Harrington, co-founder of the ferry company, and successor to Harrington as governor, had been in office for four consecutive terms starting in 1920. Nevertheless, his luck ran out when he ran for a fifth term in 1934. In an incredibly close election, Democratic candidate Ritchie was defeated by Republican Harry W. Nice. The intimate relationship between Harrington and Ritchie did not extend to Nice. The new governor was willing to sign the bridge legislation, but only if he was able to change the members of the Chesapeake Bay Bridge Authority. Specifically, he wanted Harrington off the board, and he got his way.[41] With that achieved, the bridge effort was able to move forward.[42]

Notably, the legislation passed in 1935 did not provide a source of funding for bridge construction and assumed that the federal government would provide the lion's share. The federal government expressed a potential willingness to kick in about half of the required sum if the State of Maryland could supply the rest.[43] In the end, Maryland struggled to do so.

One reason involved the location of the proposed bridge. The route proposed in the legislation is different from where the bridge was eventually completed in 1952. Through 1935, the various proposals envisioned a bridge farther north, running east from Baltimore to Middle River, then over to what is now Hart-Miller Island, and from there crossing the Chesapeake to the popular resort of Tolchester on the Eastern Shore. Marylanders accustomed to taking the ferry to cross from Kent Island to Annapolis did not support the idea of having to travel north through Baltimore to cross to the other shore and then driving farther south just to arrive at the destination they could now reach easily with the ferry.

The matter dragged on for a couple of years. Finally, President Roosevelt ended the debate in 1937 by vetoing any funding of a bay bridge, arguing that it would interfere with navigation of an important port associated with national security (Baltimore). His veto followed the recommendation of the War Department, worried that collapse of the bridge from bombing or sabotage could block vital travel of ships up and down the Bay.[44] Without the federal government's support, the plan for the bridge faded. (Years later, in 2024, the collapse of Baltimore's Francis Scott Key Bridge would affirm the potential risks to Baltimore Harbor of a bridge failure.)[45]

Harrington once again scored a victory through this whole process. Importantly, the 1935 legislation allowed his company to avert new competition anywhere near the proposed bridge route. This was soon put to the test. In 1936, the newly formed Maryland Bay Company sought permission from the Maryland PSC to operate a Sandy Point-to-Stevensville route, as had been proposed earlier in 1930 by the Bay Bridge Ferry Corporation.[46] The new company promised faster trips across the Bay and rates less than one-half of those charged by the Claiborne-Annapolis Ferry Company.[47] The land for the western terminal was in hand, already owned by William T. Emory, president of this potential new competitor. This property was just north of what would become Sandy Point State Park and was home to the Log Inn, a summer/fall hotel owned and operated by Emory.[48] Certainly, a ferry terminal at this location would boost business for his hotel.

Many business leaders on the Eastern Shore embraced this

new proposal, hoping to secure improved and lower-cost services across the Bay. Frustration had begun to grow with the Claiborne-Annapolis Ferry Company for what was seen as an inadequate schedule, high rates, and mediocre service. Once again, the competitive threat from Philadelphia was also cited as justification:

> Under present conditions of fixed and inconvenient schedule and many hours with no schedule at all and high rates, a very large volume of the business of the Eastern Shore, which should normally go to Baltimore, is being diverted to business centers to the north of our state with a consequent loss to Baltimore business interests. It seems ridiculous to compel the public to content itself with an eight-mile crossing out of the line desired by the traffic, as the Matapeake-Annapolis crossing is, when a three-mile crossing is available directly in the line desired by the traffic.[49]

Both the Claiborne-Annapolis Ferry Company (operating Annapolis to Matapeake) and the Baltimore and Eastern Railroad (operating Baltimore to Love Point) protested.[50] This proposal never made it through the PSC given the restrictions on new ferry services within twenty miles of the proposed bridge location.[51] It arose again a couple of years later but was put aside by an act of the Maryland legislature early in 1937.[52] Harrington had protected his franchise once again.

But the issue did not die forever. In October 1938, Harrington caught wind of investors pursuing yet another effort for a Sandy Point-Kent Island ferry, one that would compete with the Annapolis-Matapeake route offering a far shorter journey for most motorists.[53] The company's response was to revert back to the playbook of the late 1920s—to move to secure its incumbent position by taking control of the critical properties before a competitor could get started. As was reported in the minutes of the executive committee:

> No formal action was taken on these rumors, but it was suggested that the Company investigate carefully the

possibility of obtaining a suitable site for a ferry terminal at or near Sandy Point so as to be prepared to install a ferry service at that point if any popular demand for same should develop.

It was William T. Emory who had reemerged as a potential landowner of a new ferry terminal at Sandy Point. B. Frank Sherman was instructed by the company's executive committee to investigate the feasibility of securing this property to protect the Claiborne-Annapolis Ferry Company.[54]

Later, in the summer of 1940 when rumors of a new ferry or bridge to Kent Island accelerated, the company also investigated the possibility of acquiring the "much more feasible" site for a ferry terminal north of Matapeake: the farm owned by Dr. Charles S. Snyder. To obtain right of way over this property, the Claiborne-Annapolis Ferry Company was willing to trade away its Broad Creek Farm property ("Farm No. 1"), which the company knew was not suitable for a ferry terminal.[55] Given that it already owned the Matapeake site a few miles south, one can interpret this as another effort to deny a potential ferry terminal site to a potential competitor.[56] In the end, the transaction never took place.

The End of Cross-Bay Ferry Service to Claiborne

Not all of the attention in the late 1930s was focused on the Annapolis-Matapeake route. The year 1938 saw the second shoe fall when it came to Claiborne's status as a cross-bay ferry terminal. That year, the Claiborne-Annapolis Ferry Company decided to terminate all direct cross-bay service to Claiborne. The primary role of Claiborne as the eastern terminus for bay ferry traffic had begun to fade after 1930. Now its status as a cross-bay destination was disappearing altogether. The decisions in 1938 completely reversed the actions taken in 1886 that had established Claiborne in that capacity. Geography had finally struck back, though it had taken half a century to do so.

Pressure had been building for some time to find a way to serve

Claiborne without having to run ferries all of the way from Annapolis, given that the southeastern portion of Kent Island was fewer than five miles away from Claiborne and service to Kent Island was now well established. The urgency was compounded by continuing losses on the Annapolis-Claiborne route, offsetting the high profits earned on the Annapolis-Matapeake route. The company's board of directors had discussed this as far back as 1934:

> One suggestion was that the service to Claiborne be reduced to one round trip per day, and the idle time of this boat on this line be utilized in augmenting the schedule to Matapeake. Another suggestion was that the Company acquire a smaller boat and use it to operate a short-run service between Claiborne and the southern end of Kent Island, as a feeder to the Matapeake Line, and that both the "[John M.] Dennis" and "[Gov. Albert C.] Ritchie" be operated between Annapolis and Matapeake only.[57]

Initially, emerging plans for a Bay bridge put a hold on any fundamental restructuring of the ferry system, especially since, should the bridge be built, the ferry company would be acquired by the State of Maryland and shut down.

However, just as in 1929, the bay bridge proposals in the mid-1930s faded away by 1937, enabling the Claiborne-Annapolis Ferry Company to move forward on the new route. Plans were formalized in spring 1937 when B. Frank Sherman announced its proposal to create a faster shuttle service from Kent Island to Claiborne. Service on the new route was expected to start in August of that year and would replace the current twice-daily ferry between Annapolis and Claiborne. Another boat, *Mount Holly*, had been secured for the new shuttle route.[58] It would replace the aging *Gov. Emerson C. Harrington,* which was sold and then relocated to Pocomoke City for use as a restaurant.[59]

Mount Holly represented progress of a kind for the ferry system and its Claiborne passengers. It was somewhat newer, built in 1913 in Jacksonville, Florida, by the Merrill-Stevens Company.

Unlike *Gov. Emerson C. Harrington*, it was a double-ender and thus better suited for carrying vehicles. It also had a modern propeller system, unlike the old sidewheels on *Gov. Emerson C. Harrington*. However, it still used a coal-fired steam engine for power, unlike the modern diesels present in *Gov. Albert C. Ritchie* and *John M. Dennis* on the Matapeake route. This meant that the new, secondary service to Claiborne would remain slow and sooty.

The Claiborne terminal remained ready to go, but a new terminal needed to be built on Kent Island. Progress on this new, bare-bones terminal and wharf at Long Point was rapid. In June 1937, the Claiborne-Annapolis Ferry Company secured property on the Eastern Bay side of Kent Island.[60] The new Romancoke terminal and pier were under construction and almost complete just two months later in August.[61]

Meanwhile, the ferry for the Romancoke-Claiborne route was in Salisbury, being completely rebuilt. The new name for the ferry had been selected by unanimous vote of the board of directors: it was to be *Claiborne*.[62] (For a brief time, the first ferry to Claiborne—*Thames River*—was also supposed to be named in honor of Claiborne, but this never happened.) However, the decision to name the new ferry *Claiborne* was reversed three months later when the board concluded that "the name 'Gov. Emerson C. Harrington' should not be allowed to disappear from our fleet." The board then voted to abandon the name *Claiborne* and to rename *Mount Holly* as *Gov. Emerson C. Harrington II*.[63] The loss of status for Claiborne now even extended to the names of ferries.

The Claiborne-Annapolis Ferry Company's control over the new ferry steamboat and the new terminal did not extend to the full project, and thus start of the new shuttle route was delayed. The hold-up was on the ground. At that time there was no road linking the location of the new Romancoke terminal to the terminal at Matapeake. The State Roads Commission did not even begin taking bids for the contract for the new road until late September 1937. It was estimated it would take six weeks to finish the job, after which the ferry could start operations.[64]

The six-week prediction proved optimistic. Slow progress led to a postponement of the new shuttle route's opening to early January 1938.[65] In January, the opening was delayed until mid-February.[66] In mid-February, it was announced that the opening would take place in the spring.[67] In April 1938, it was announced that the road—which was supposed to have been built by mid-November 1937, would open in two weeks. The announcement followed a test run of *Gov. Emerson C. Harrington II* on the route. It took only thirty-seven minutes combined for the ferry trip from Claiborne to Romancoke and a drive over the unfinished road to Matapeake.[68] Finally, in May, the new road was ready and the new route could be formally opened.

The celebration on May 3, 1938, actually involved two new ferries for the company, as well as a new terminal. The Romancoke-Claiborne route was not the only one to see an addition to the route in 1938. The deferment of the bay bridge proposal, and the securing of the near-term future of the ferry system, also allowed expansion plans to proceed for the main Annapolis-Matapeake route. In 1937, the Claiborne-Annapolis Ferry Company placed an order for a new, all-steel ferry capable of operating in ice. (The year 1936 had been a tough one for operations on the Chesapeake Bay, which had frozen over.) This would create a fleet of four ferries, one coal-fired steamer on the shuttle run to Claiborne and three modern diesel ferries on the Annapolis-Matapeake route.

The new Matapeake ferry was named after Harry W. Nice, then serving as Maryland governor. It was constructed in Baltimore by the Maryland Drydock Company and was of a modern design: a double-ender with diesel engines. Unique within the ferry fleet, this new vessel was also strengthened for operations in ice. While officially part of the Claiborne-Annapolis Ferry Company, the new *Gov. Harry W. Nice* would not routinely service Claiborne. The only times it even visited Claiborne in service was during a two-week period in February 1943 when the Matapeake terminal had to be closed for dredging.

The celebration orchestrated for May 3 was complex, befitting this large expansion: the new terminal in Romancoke and two new ferries. The plan was for *Gov. Harry W. Nice*, on its maiden voyage as a Claiborne-Annapolis ferry, to carry a delegation of dignitaries from Annapolis to Claiborne, led by Emerson C. Harrington and

Baltimore Mayor Howard W. Jackson. There they would celebrate *Gov. Harry W. Nice* as well as the new Romancoke-Claiborne route and *Gov. Emerson C. Harrington II*. Once the new ferries were christened, the entire contingent would travel to Romancoke to continue the celebration there.

It did not go as planned. On the outbound trip from Annapolis, as the ferry was rounding Bloody Point, *Gov. Harry W. Nice* broke down with an overheated piston. It drifted helplessly within sight of the shore-based celebration party for two hours before the piston could be lifted. Finally, upon arriving in Claiborne (on seven cylinders rather than eight), the celebration continued. As reported at the time, the formal speeches were only part of the attraction:

> [T]he crowd for the most part was more interested in the splendid lunches furnished by the company. It was all free, including ice cream, punch, ginger ale, etc. . . . There was plenty to eat and drink, and no on went hungry or thirsty. . . . It was a great opportunity for the political candidates, who were out in force buttonholing friends and acquaintances, and getting heads together on political issues. . . . Altogether it was a gala day for everybody. Smiles and handshakes were the rule regardless of wether you were acquainted or not.[69]

The gala atmosphere may have been lost on the residents of Claiborne, who saw their relevance to the ferry operations diminished and the commercial viability of the town threatened.

From the standpoint of Claiborne travelers, the elimination of direct cross-bay service to Claiborne had both positive and negative effects. On the positive side, it actually reduced the time needed to get from Claiborne to Annapolis. It was faster to take a ferry to Romancoke, drive or take a bus to Matapeake, and take the ferry from there to Annapolis than it was to take the ferry from Claiborne to Annapolis. The route was far shorter, and the over-the-road portion operated at two or three times the speed of the ferries. The schedule was structured so that a ferry departure from Claiborne would connect with a ferry departing from Matapeake one hour later. Another positive is that the frequency of service increased. Instead of two ferries per day serving Claiborne, there would be six ferries per day, although this dropped to only five per day after June 1939. So, from the standpoint of travelers seeking to get to or from Claiborne, things had improved somewhat.

But the downside for the village itself was considerable. No longer would drivers seeking to cross between the Eastern Shore and urban areas on the western side travel through Claiborne. Once they were required to go to Matapeake, it would just be faster to start their Eastern Shore drive from there and bypass Claiborne altogether.

Even then, service on the Claiborne route was clearly subordinated to the needs of the primary Annapolis-Matapeake route. In February 1938, for example, service to Claiborne from Annapolis was suspended altogether for thirty days in order to fill a gap in the Matapeake route caused by the need to simultaneously take both *Gov. Albert C. Ritchie* and *John M. Dennis* out of service for repairs in drydock.[70]

Claiborne's golden era was over. Before 1930, Claiborne was the only Eastern Shore transit point on the ferry system. Before 1938, Claiborne was at least an option for direct cross-bay travel, especially for those heading to Easton, Oxford, or Cambridge (as opposed to Ocean City). Now Claiborne was just a sideline to the primary ferry operation. After 1938, it became incidental to most traffic crossing the Bay.

The loss of status was visible in the very structure of the town. It was at this time that the major hotel in Claiborne, the Bellfonte, shut its doors. Within months, the large wooden building suffered a major fire and was largely destroyed.[71] The commercial operations at the Claiborne Landing also ceased operations. Photos of the Sea Gull Inn in 1938 show a dilapidated building with rotting siding. The Al-Mar Inn across the ferry wharf had vanished a few years before. In town, Bergmann's Bakery would close by 1942, perhaps in response to anti-German sentiment after the United States entered World War II. Business at the local boarding houses fell, and some stopped hosting visitors altogether.

Change came as well to the Holy Innocents Chapel, which had served the community from 1879. St. Michael's Parish put the chapel building up for sale in 1940.[72] The ownership changed hands a few times after 1940, until the structure was gutted by fire in 1944.[73] However, the original 1889 bell from the Holy Innocents Chapel survived the fire and was sold in late 1944 to Holy Trinity Episcopal Church in Oxford, Maryland.[74] (It remains there today, suspended from the top of a wooden pier outside the church.)

Baltimore and Eastern Plays Catch-Up

The success of the Claiborne-Annapolis Ferry Company, especially after the introduction of its double-ender car ferries, made it clear that the old-fashioned railroad-centric model of the Love Point service was reaching an end. Railroads were diminishing in popularity. Cars were the future. It was time for the Love Point service to join the revolution.

The old *Cambridge*, which had started carrying passengers to Claiborne in 1894, was finally taken off the route and retired in 1929. *Cambridge* was replaced temporarily by the passenger steamer *New York*, borrowed from the PRR-owned New York, Philadelphia and Norfolk Railroad (NYP&N). This was hardly an upgrade, but a further example of how PRR sought to minimize costs on the Love Point route by employing steamers at the end of their service lives. *New York,* built by Harlan & Hollingworth in 1889, was a year older than *Cambridge*. It was not in service long.[75]

Major changes were to come in 1931. But there was a hurdle to be surmounted first. B&E was not quite sure whether it would be permitted to carry vehicles as well as passengers on the Love Point route. It was concerned about legislation making its way through the Maryland legislature that would require any new vehicular ferry service within B&E to be approved by the mayor of Baltimore and the Maryland State Roads Commissioner. Perhaps the B&E leadership saw how aggressively Harrington had defended his franchise from new entrants and did not want to be still another victim of his political maneuvering.[76]

B&E, and its parent PRR, had great plans for Love Point. The new ferry line would, for the first time, be able to carry vehicles on the Baltimore-Love Point run, matching the capability that had been offered by the Claiborne-Annapolis Ferry Company starting in 1919. It was not just the upgrade to car ferries they envisioned. B&E also launched a novel container service for the Baltimore-Love Point-Salisbury route, pioneering the multi-modal container shipping revolution of the 1950s.[77] Trains in Baltimore would offload cargo onto *Bucyrus*, a special steam-powered lighter. *Bucyrus* would ferry the containers over the Chesapeake to Love Point.[78] There, the containers would be offloaded onto trucks that would then haul them to Salisbury.[79]

Then, on May 16, 1931, the first double-ender arrived for the Love Point run.[80] This was *Philadelphia*, a steam-powered ferry famous for belching black smoke and fondly remembered as "Smokey Joe." Built in Chester, Pennsylvania, in 1899 and already thirty-two years old, it still marked a major improvement in the services offered to Love Point. No longer did Claiborne have a monopoly on car ferries to the Eastern Shore.[81] The threat this time was not from a poorly financed start-up, or a misdirected excursion company. The threat this time was from the Pennsylvania Railroad. It knew something about running ferries and had operated a steamer line to Love Point for twenty-five years.[82]

Philadelphia ("Smokey Joe"), while deeply associated with the Love Point service from 1931 through 1947, did not actually operate on the route across that entire interval. In 1934, *Philadelphia* was shifted to New York and replaced by the ferry *Pittsburgh* ("Smokey Joe Jr.").[83] *Pittsburgh* was similar to but smaller than *Philadelphia*. It was a double-ender steam-powered car ferry built by William Cramp & Sons in Philadelphia in 1896 and thus was well suited for use on the Love Point route.

The original "Smokey Joe," *Philadelphia*, made its celebrated return to Love Point in January 1938 and operated on that route for the next decade, belching black smoke, carrying cars, and rescuing stranded mariners.[84] But traffic on the Love Point rail line had continued to decline, and with *Philadelphia* back on the route enabling passengers to bring their automobiles, B&E decided it was time to shut down passenger service on the Love Point railroad.[85] The last passenger train ran on March 29, 1938. Almost twenty years after the creation of the Claiborne car ferries, the Love Point ferry had joined the automotive revolution.[86] Now, for the first time in forty-eight years, there was no way to get from Baltimore to destinations on Maryland's Eastern Shore by rail, either via Claiborne or Love Point.

Notes

1. From an untitled paper by B. Frank Sherman on the history of the Claiborne-Annapolis Ferry Inc., contained in his personal papers held by the Chesapeake Bay Maritime Museum. See B. Frank Sherman Papers, MS3, Series 1, Folder 1, p. 4. The paper is undated, but elsewhere there is a reference to "when this war is over," so it most likely was completed between December 1941 and August 1945.
2. "New Ferry Plan for Chesapeake," *Evening Journal* (Wilmington, DE), August 16, 1928.
3. "New Company Seeks Permit for Bay Ferry," *Evening Sun* (Baltimore, MD), May 10, 1930. Harold Walker was the former head of a major railroad and a general counsel of Superior Oil Company.
4. Meeting Minutes of the Claiborne-Annapolis Ferry Company Board of Directors, February 23, 1919, Maryland State Archives, Maryland Public Service Commission, MSA S245-3, MdHR 19816-3.
5. "Plan Shorter Ferry Route to Annapolis," *Salisbury Times*, February 27, 1919.
6. "Kent Island Ferry Canal Bill Passed," *Sun* (Baltimore, MD), March 27, 1929.
7. Horace E. Flack, ed., "Kent Island Canal" Ch. 577, Article 18, Sec. 1 in Code of the Public Local Laws of Maryland (King Bros. Inc., 1931), 4236. See also Maryland State Archives, Code of the Public Local Laws of Maryland, "Kent Island Canal," accessed January 2021, msa.maryland.gov/megafile/msa/speccol/sc2900/sc2908/000001/000377/pdf/am377–4236.pdf. The authorization was repealed in 1955.
8. "Kent Island Canal Planned by Ferry Firm," *Sun* (Baltimore, MD), February 14, 1929.
9. Queen Anne's County Circuit Court (Land Records), BHT 9, p. 0256, MSA_CE58_99. The creek extending into Carvel Farm is also referred to as Muddy Creek.
10. Meeting Minutes of the Claiborne-Annapolis Ferry Company Board of Directors, August 12, 1929, Maryland State Archives, Maryland Public Service Commission, MSA S245-3, MdHR 19816-3. The portion that connected to the Chesapeake was known as "Lower Terminal" within the company.
11. Queen Anne's County Circuit Court (Land Records), BHT 9, p. 0340, MSA_CE58_99. The purchase was made in the name of Henry P. Turner, a member of the board of directors of the Claiborne-Annapolis Ferry Company. It is recorded on the balance sheet of the company in 1929 as an asset of the company. Internally, this was known as "Upper Terminal."
12. Letter from Richard C. Hollyday, consulting engineer, to Emerson C. Harrington, president of the Claiborne-Annapolis Ferry Company, August 13, 1929, Maryland State Archives, Maryland Public Service Commission, MSA

S245-3, MdHR 19816-3. Note that "outcroppings" has been substituted for the actual word in the letter, which is excluded here because it involves the same term as a racial epithet.

13. Meeting Minutes of the Claiborne-Annapolis Ferry Company Board of Directors, August 12, 1929, Maryland State Archives, Maryland Public Service Commission, MSA S245-3, MdHR 19816-3.
14. Queen Anne's County Circuit Court (Land Records), BHT 10, p. 0128, MSA_CE58_100.
15. Meeting Minutes of the Claiborne-Annapolis Ferry Company Board of Directors, August 30, 1929, Maryland State Archives, Maryland Public Service Commission, MSA S245-3, MdHR 19816-3.
16. Meeting Minutes of the Claiborne-Annapolis Ferry Company Board of Directors, October 8, 1929, Maryland State Archives, Maryland Public Service Commission, MSA S245-3, MdHR 19816-3.
17. The company continued to own the two farms throughout the 1930s, selling them in conjunction with the sale of company to the Maryland State Roads Commission in 1941. They are referred to on the books of the company as "Farm No. 1" and "Farm No. 2." The State Roads Commission had no interest in owning these properties. Farm No. 1 was sold in December 1940 and was turned into a major housing development. See Queen Anne's County Circuit Court (Land Records), ASG 3. 0546, MSA_CE58_118. Farm No. 2 was sold in October 1941, and much of this was turned into Blue Heron Nature Preserve and Blue Heron Golf Course. See Queen Anne's County Circuit Court (Land Records), ASG 5. 0184, MSA_CE58_120.
18. Meeting Minutes of the Claiborne-Annapolis Ferry Company Board of Directors, August 30, 1929, Maryland State Archives, Maryland Public Service Commission, MSA S245-3, MdHR 19816-3.
19. "New Ferry Line Is Due to Be Started in June," *Sun* (Baltimore, MD), January 14, 1930.
20. Report of the Public Service Commission of Maryland for 1930, Case No. 3084, Order No. 15976, 115–16.
21. "Storm Halts Festivities at Ferry Opening," *Sun* (Baltimore, MD), July 2, 1930.
22. "New Company Seeks Permit for Bay Ferry," *Evening Sun* (Baltimore, MD), May 10, 1930.
23. "Ferry and Bus Line Plan to Be Fought," *Evening Sun* (Baltimore, MD), May 19, 1930.
24. Bay Bridge Ferry Corporation v. County Commissioners of Queen Anne's County, 160 Md. 398 (1931).
25. Report of the Public Service Commission of Maryland for 1934, Case No. 3081, Order No. 25335, 159.

26. Ames W. Williams, *Otto Mears Goes East: The Chesapeake Beach Railway* (Calvert Country Historical Society, 1981), 181.
27. "Bay Span Interest Turning to Ferry," *Sun* (Baltimore, MD), February 23, 1930.
28. "District Supreme Court Sits En Banc," *Evening Star* (Washington, DC), May 18, 1931.
29. Claiborne-Annapolis Ferry Co. v. United States, 285 US 382, 52 S.Ct. 440 (1932).
30. "Ferry Firm Seeks Rehearing on Loan," *Evening Star* (Washington, DC), July 9, 1933.
31. "I.C.C. Denies Rehearing to Ferry Company," *Sun* (Baltimore, MD), August 3, 1933.
32. David Guth, *Bridging the Chesapeake: A 'Fool Idea' That Unified Maryland* (Archway Publishing, 2017), 157.
33. "Broening's Secretary in Address Urges State Build Bay Bridge," *Salisbury Times*, February 8, 1930.
34. Financial results are based on Claiborne-Annapolis Ferry Co. financial statements as presented in the annual reports to shareholders. Maryland State Archives, Maryland Public Service Commission, MSA S245-3, MdHR 19816-3.
35. Meeting Minutes of the Claiborne-Annapolis Ferry Company Board of Directors, March 28, 1932, Maryland State Archives, Maryland Public Service Commission, MSA S245-3, MdHR 19816-3.
36. Meeting Minutes of the Claiborne-Annapolis-Ferry Company Board of Directors, April 24, 1936, Maryland State Archives, Maryland Public Service Commission, MSA S245-3, MdHR 19816-3. Technically, *Gov. Albert C. Ritchie* was two decades older than *Gov. Emerson C. Harrington*, but the former had been completely rebuilt and modernized in 1926.
37. The company name itself remained Claiborne-Annapolis Ferry Company. On the side of the ferries, the large label "Claiborne Annapolis Ferry" was replaced with "Claiborne Annapolis Matapeake Ferry." The published schedule used the name "Annapolis-Claiborne-Matapeake Ferries."
38. Calculated using data prepared by Stanley Lebergott, "Labor Force, Employment, and Unemployment, 1929–1939: Estimating Methods," *Monthly Labor Review* (US Bureau of Labor Statistics, July 1948), 51.
39. "Urged by Nice New Route to Eastern Shore," *Sun* (Baltimore, MD), January 26, 1935.
40. "Senate Endorses Bay Bridge Plan," *Sun* (Baltimore, MD), March 28, 1935. See also Chapter 330, *Laws of the State of Maryland Made and Passed At the Session of the General Assembly, Begun and Held at the City of Annapolis, on the Second Day of January, 1935*, and Ending on the First Day of April, 1935, (20th Century Printing, 1935), 743–59. Available through Archives of Maryland Online, Session Laws 1935, Volume 579.

41. "PWA to Accept Alteration in Bridge Set-Up," *Evening Sun* (Baltimore, MD), May 10, 1935. Since the PWA had already received the original proposal, its approval was required to change the board.
42. "Announces Move for Bay Span Loan," *Evening Sun* (Baltimore, MD), May 21, 1935.
43. "Bridge Group Decides to Ask RFC for Funds," *Sun* (Baltimore, MD), August 20, 1935.
44. "Bay Bridge Bill Meets with Veto," *News* (Frederick, MD), August 28, 1937.
45. "The Five Minutes That Brought Down the Francis Scott Key Bridge," *New York Times*, March 27, 2024.
46. "Denton Group Advocates New Ferry," *Denton Journal*, November 14, 1936.
47. "Firm Promises Fast, Low Rate Ferry Service," *Salisbury Times*, November 10, 1936.
48. "Says New York Bankers Will Finance New Ferry," *Journal-Every Evening* (Wilmington, DE), December 11, 1936.
49. Letter to the Public Service Commission from Calvert C. Merriken, president of the Chamber of Commerce of Denton, as quoted in "Backs Application for New Ferry Line," *Sun* (Baltimore, MD), November 13, 1936.
50. "The Claiborne Ferry Protests Another Ferry," *Easton Star-Democrat*, December 11, 1936; "Baltimore and Eastern Fights New Bay Ferry," *Salisbury Times*, December 2, 1936.
51. "Chesapeake Bay Bridge Project Up to Governor," *Evening Sun* (Baltimore, MD), March 30, 1935.
52. "House Kills Plan for New Ferry," *Sun* (Baltimore, MD), March 18, 1937.
53. Meeting Minutes of the Claiborne-Annapolis-Ferry Company Executive Committee Meeting, October 12, 1938, Maryland State Archives, Maryland Public Service Commission, MSA S245-3, MdHR 19816-3.
54. Meeting Minutes of the Claiborne-Annapolis-Ferry Company Executive Committee, November 3, 1938, Maryland State Archives, Maryland Public Service Commission, MSA S245-3, MdHR 19816-3.
55. Meeting Minutes of the Claiborne-Annapolis-Ferry Company Executive Committee, June 30, 1940, Maryland State Archives, Maryland Public Service Commission, MSA S245-3, MdHR 19816-3.
56. The issue became moot when the ferry company was taken over by the state the following year. However, the company's instinct was correct: Dr. Snyder's property would eventually be selected as the eastern landing place for the Chesapeake Bay Bridge.
57. Meeting Minutes of the Claiborne-Annapolis-Ferry Company Board of Directors, December 12, 1934, Maryland State Archives, Maryland Public Service Commission, MSA S245-3, MdHR 19816-3.

58. "Bay Ferries Plan Speedy Short Trips," *Salisbury Times*, April 30, 1937.
59. The restaurant venture did not succeed. In 1941, it was towed to Annapolis for use as a waterfront hotel. This ended in 1942 when the US Navy commandeered the waterfront for wartime activities. The floating hotel was left a derelict. After the war it was taken back to Pocomoke City for a second attempt there, which also failed. Finally, in 1949, the owners called it a day, dismantled much of the old ferry, and towed the hull to Baltimore for scrapping.
60. This was land owned by Dr. Theodore Cooke Jr. and his wife Kate C. Cooke. See Queen Anne's County Circuit Court (Land Records), ASG 3, p. 0565, MSA _CE58_118. The deed records a number of special considerations. Some land was conveyed to the State Roads Commission for road construction. The deed also restricts the activities on the land to the ferry terminal itself, and specifically precludes "amusement stands, eating or drinking booths or stands and similar uses or concessions."
61. "Speeding Up Improvements for the Ferry," *Easton Star-Democrat*, August 6, 1937.
62. Meeting Minutes of the Claiborne-Annapolis Ferry Company Board of Directors, June 3, 1937, Maryland State Archives, Maryland Public Service Commission, MSA S245-3, MdHR 19816-3.
63. Meeting Minutes of the Claiborne-Annapolis Ferry Company Board of Directors, September 17, 1937, Maryland State Archives, Maryland Public Service Commission, MSA S245-3, MdHR 19816-3.
64. "New Road Contract Let," *Easton Star-Democrat*, October 1, 1937.
65. "Shuttle Ferry Run Opens Next Month," *Salisbury Times*, December 13, 1937.
66. "Shuttle Ferry Starts Operating in a Month," *Salisbury Times*, January 25, 1938.
67. "To Suspend Claiborne Service in Thirty Days," *Easton Star-Democrat*, February 13, 1938.
68. "Thirty-Seven Minutes From Claiborne to Matapeake,"*Easton Star-Democrat*, April 1, 1938.
69. "Ferry Company Entertains a Large Crowd," *Easton Star-Democrat*, May 6, 1938.
70. "To Suspend Claiborne Service for Thirty Days," *Easton Star-Democrat*, February 18, 1938.
71. There have been various spellings of this hotel's name. When opened by Albert J. Wyatt and Mary E. Wyatt in 1923, it was called the Belfonte Hotel. When taken over by Mary Wyatt's sister Annie B. Card in 1926, the spelling changed to "Bellefont." When put up for sale in 1938, the spelling became "Bellefonte."
72. "For Sale: Chapel at Claiborne, Md.," Easton Star-Democrat, April 19, 1940.
73. Anna Ellis Harper, History of St. Michael's Parish (n.p., 1956), 33.

74. "County News Notes: Oxford," *Easton Star-Democrat*, December 22, 1944.

75. The exact date of replacement is unclear. The last public reference to *Cambridge* on this route was in March 1929. B&E published advertisements indicating an "important change" in the schedule in April 1929. The first reference to *New York* on the route is June 1929. The handover happened in that interval, though it is possible that service was suspended for that time. After leaving the Love Point service, *New York* was sold to William M. Mills. It was destroyed by fire in Staten Island on July 18, 1932.

76. See the April 7, 1931 entry in Christopher T. Baer's "PRR Chronology: A General Chronology of the Pennsylvania Railroad Company Predecessors and Successors and Its Historical Context," available at prrths.com/newprr_files/Hagley/PRR1937%204_15_15.pdf. As a hedge, PRR created another subsidiary, the Maryland Ferry Company, and sought approval for that subsidiary to operate a new car ferry from Baltimore to Love Point, apart from (and in parallel with) B&E's passenger service. See "Love Point Ferry Charter Is Sought," *Sun* (Baltimore, MD), April 8, 1931. Just as quickly as it had arrived, the Maryland Ferry Company then went away. The legislative threat to the B&E franchise evaporated, so the Maryland Ferry Company was effectively dissolved back into its parent, B&E, surviving until 1953 as a shell company. B&E was about to enter the car-ferry business.

77. "P. R. R. Announce New Transportation," *Harrisburg Telegraph*, April 17, 1931.

78. Official number of Bucyrus was 214411. The vessel was built in 1916 as *P.R.R. Lighter No 151* by Staten Island Shipbuilding in Port Richmond, New York.

79. "Announces New Freight Haul to Baltimore," *Salisbury Times*, April 17, 1931. Once *Philadelphia* entered service, the need for *Bucyrus* ended and it was taken off the route.

80. "New Ferryboat Here for Shore Service," *Evening Sun* (Baltimore, MD), May 16, 1931. Philadelphia had official number 150806.

81. "New Ferry Service Begins Next Week," *Journal-Every Evening* (Wilmington, DE), May 19, 1931.

82. The new Love Point operation brought with it new captains. The initial steamer, *Love Point*, was captained by William J. Taylor. Following Taylor was John A. Clark, who started on the route in 1906 and continued for more than a decade before retiring in 1922. Clark was followed by William A. Perry, who began his career aboard *Cambridge* and eventually rose to captain on *Westmoreland* in the early 1930s. He was replaced by Linwood P. Clifton, who captained *Pittsburgh* in the mid-1930s. Perhaps the most illustrious of all was Washington I. Woodall. His career on the steamer *Love Point* started back in 1906 as first officer. By the late 1920s, he was captain of *Cambridge*,

afterward transitioning in the mid-1930s to the first car ferry on that route, *Philadelphia*. Woodall set an amazing record for rescues on the Chesapeake Bay, saving many lives.

83. *Pittsburgh* had registration no. 150741 and was supplemented in the summers of 1936 and 1937 by *Maryland* ("Smokey Joe 3rd"). See "Smokey Joe 3rd Now to Ply Famed Route to Love Point," *Sun* (Baltimore, MD), July 30, 1936. On two occasions in the 1930s, the ferry *Pennsylvania* substituted for *Philadelphia* (April 1934) or *Pittsburgh* (June 1935) while the regular ferry was undergoing overhaul. *Maryland* (official number 204242) was built by Maryland Steel (later Bethlehem Steel) in 1906 and was 1,369 gross register tons (GRT). *Pennsylvania* (official number 150849) was slightly smaller at 1,352 GRT and was built in 1900 by John Roach & Sons at the Delaware River Iron Shipbuilding & Engine Works in Chester, Pennsylvania. *Maryland* and *Pennsylvania* were conventional steamers designed to carry passengers. Although reconfigured to carry some cars, these were not double-enders and were primarily oriented toward carrying tourists visiting Kent Island, or those remaining passengers interested in continuing their journey by rail. There are also various accounts in the media about the ferry *New Brunswick* having served on this route as a "Smokey Joe." However, no confirming references have emerged. *New Brunswick*, also operated by PRR, was busy moving passengers to/from Manhattan at the time.
84. "Smokey Joe Due Home Tomorrow," *Evening Sun* (Baltimore, MD), January 17, 1938.
85. Through service to Ocean City had already terminated after a massive hurricane in August 1933 washed away the wooden trestle bridge carrying the rail line across Sinepuxent Bay.
86. See the March 29, 1938, entry in Christopher T. Baer's "PRR Chronology: A General Chronology of the Pennsylvania Railroad Company Predecessors and Successors and Its Historical Context," available at prrths.com/newprr_files/Hagley/PRR1938%204_15_15.pdf

XI

Big Changes for Owners and Workers

The Claiborne-Annapolis Ferry Company did not make its decisions about ferries and routes in isolation. Intra-state ferries were regulated by the Maryland Public Service Commission (PSC). The company was increasingly under the spotlight and a subject of political controversy. These pressures, which built gradually in the mid-1930s, reached a crescendo at the end of that decade and were to have a major impact on the system in the early 1940s. In the end, the Claiborne-Annapolis Ferry Company would be dissolved, and Emerson C. Harrington would receive a very handsome payout.

One immediate catalyst for these new pressures had been the major swing in Maryland politics in 1934 when Republican Harry W. Nice eked out his narrow and somewhat surprising win over Democratic incumbent Albert C. Ritchie. For the first time in almost twenty years, and for the first time since the Claiborne-Annapolis ferry line was launched, Maryland had a Republican governor. While Democrats continued their control of the Maryland Senate and House of Delegates, Harrington's influence had begun to wane. Things might have improved slightly with the election of Herbert

R. O'Conor as governor, a Democrat who assumed office in January 1938. However, the decades-long special partnership between Emerson C. Harrington and Albert C. Ritchie had come to an end.

Public pressure began to build against the Claiborne-Annapolis Ferry Company based on three general issues. First was the sense that the company unfairly used its political connections to preempt competition, whether that be via a potential bay bridge or a new ferry line. The list of the vanquished competitors was considerable, starting with the Baltimore, Chesapeake and Atlantic Railway route to Claiborne, which was abandoned in 1924. Moreover, one after another, new entrants promising shorter routes and/or more modern equipment had to abandon their efforts when confronted by Harrington's opposition and political skill:

- Peninsula Ferry Company to Love Point (1922)
- Baltimore and Eastern Shore Ferry Line Inc. to Rock Hall (1927)
- Bay Bridge Ferry Corporation to Stevensville (1934)
- Chesapeake Beach Railway/Cambridge Ferry Company to Trippe's Bay (1935)
- Maryland Bay Company to Stevensville (1937)

Second was opposition to the annual operating subsidy of $23,000, raised from the original $18,000 when the additional Matapeake line was established. Provided to the company from Maryland taxpayers, and part of an annual $48,000 for ferry subsidies that also included the Baltimore-Tolchester ferry, the subsidy was seen by many as unnecessary and a waste of funds.

Third, around all of this was a sense that the company had become quite profitable, paying its managers excessive salaries and its shareholders excessive dividends, beyond what seemed appropriate given that it was a regulated public utility. Moreover, those great profits were not seen as being shared with the rank-and-file workers.

State Senator Harry T. Phoebus of Somerset County, a Republican, summarized the views held by many in the State of Maryland:

The minute that budget reaches the Senate, I am going to work night and day to see that the practice [of subsidies] is discontinued. There is no reason why the taxpayers of Maryland should be contributing the sum of $48,000 a year to the operation of paying enterprises—business that enable the respective companies to pay their officials high salaries.[1]

As we have seen earlier, Governor Nice had addressed the first issue—the ferry's habit of squashing competition—himself, demanding the resignation of Harrington from the Chesapeake Bay Bridge Authority as a condition for him signing the 1935 legislation advancing the plan for that bridge (including the potential purchase of the ferry company).[2] Harrington himself preempted the second controversy, in 1935, by voluntarily relinquishing the $23,000 annual subsidy.[3] The third issue—regarding excessive profits of this regulated utility—did not go away and continued to simmer for the next five years.

There were some in the legislature who believed the ferry system would better serve the interests of Marylanders if it were owned and run by the state itself, rather than a private company. After all, that was to have been the model all along when the ferry line was first proposed in 1916. Legislation passed in Annapolis in 1935 authorized the state to purchase the Claiborne-Annapolis Ferry Company for an amount not to exceed $1.2 million. The original intent was to compensate the company for the inevitable termination of its business should a bridge across the bay be built. However, even when that immediate scenario faded into the background, advocates of a state takeover used the 1935 legislation as a starting point for another takeover effort.

Apparently, serious discussions about a purchase of the Claiborne-Annapolis Ferry System were underway as far back as 1937. Legislation that year authorized the state government to conduct a financial audit of the company, as a precursor to its acquisition by the State of Maryland. The discussions were enabled by a ruling of the Maryland Attorney General that the 1935 legislation authorized the potential purchase of the ferry company—whether a bay bridge was built or not.[4] In fact, part of the reason the legislature shot down the idea of any new competing ferry was to avoid complicating the negotiations then underway between the state authorities and the Claiborne-Annapolis Ferry Company.[5]

Pressure to do something—build a bridge, allow competition, or take over the ferry company—was growing. Representatives from the Eastern Shore made clear their interest in securing cheaper service across the bay. In a telegram to the State Roads Commission in June 1938, W. G. Winterbottom of Cambridge, representing many commercial interests on the Eastern Shore, demanded lower rates. As was reported at the time:

> Its rates are at least double what they should be, he said, and the State either should make it reduce its rates or allow the Maryland Bay Company to operate the competing service it has proposed three times, unsuccessfully, to the Public Service Commission.[6]

At the same time, Winterbottom decried the proposed Hart Island–Tolchester bridge as a viable option. He concluded it was just too far north for their needs. If competition was not the answer, and a bridge to Tolchester was not acceptable, that led to only one alternative: a state takeover.

Hearings at the Public Service Commission

This was the environment when the Maryland PSC launched a hearing into the finances of the Claiborne-Annapolis Ferry Company in early 1940. The company tried to delay the hearings, suggesting they would interfere with negotiations around a potential purchase then underway.[7]

However, Harrington was about to meet his match: Joseph Sherbow, the People's Counsel of the Maryland PSC. Sherbow was one of the "bright young stars" in former Governor Ritchie's administration, later recalled as the "dean of public-utilities counsel in Maryland."[8] He had been appointed as an associate judge on the People's Court in 1929, dealing with civil issues and minor criminal offenses, and had held that role until 1936, when he assumed his responsibilities with the PSC. A battle was brewing, and as much as Baltimore, Chesapeake and Atlantic Railways' Willard Thomson had struggled to best Charles J. Fox back in 1906—the time of the steamer captains' strike—Harrington was about to confront an able foe in the form of Joseph Sherbow.

Sherbow's response to Harrington's delaying tactic was swift, direct, and apparently intended for public consumption:

> [The company is] merely seeking to put off the investigation to permit the stockholders to continue to reap their rich harvests from the high fares for bay ferry transporation. . . . [These returns came from] the rate payers, who have paid high and excessive rates from the Eastern to the Western shores of Maryland and return. These high and excessive rates have to a material extent retarded the development of a closer relationship between the people of the Eastern Shore and their neighbors across the bay.[9]

Other newspapers, after seeing the financial analysis of the Claiborne-Annapolis Ferry Company prepared by Sherbow, called the operation a "Gold Mine."[10]

There was legitimacy to Sherbow's declarations. In 1937, Emerson C. Harrington earned $10,000 in salary as president of the company, down temporarily from $12,000 before the Great Depression. General Manager B. Frank Sherman earned $5,400 and Secretary-Treasurer Charles M. Speicher earned $2,400.[11] These salaries put all of the executives in the top 6 percent of income earners in the United States that year, with Harrington clearly in the top 1 percent.[12] Moreover, since Harrington and Sherman (and likely Speicher) were stockholders, and since the company was paying dividends at that time, the total earned and unearned income for these company managers was even higher.

Sherbow led the charge in criticizing the excess profits earned by the ferry company, which operated as a regulated utility and at that point was a state-sanctioned monopoly. The ferry company had grown from a cash investment of only $7,500 in 1919, coupled with an additional sum of $71,000 put into the company in the early days for operating expenses.[13] When the company was restructured in 1928, it required an additional cash investment of $150,000, for total equity investments of about $228,500.

Yet by 1940, some $325,000 in dividends had been disbursed, with another $700,000 in profits put into reserves.[14] This happened at the same time the State of Maryland had contributed cash subsidies of $165,830 to the Claiborne-Annapolis Ferry Company, in addition to the $143,750 contributed to its predecessor, Claiborne-Annapolis Ferry Inc.[15] Other state contributions included $10,250 for maintenance work and $4,100 for the wharf at Claiborne. The state had also spent $188,635 building approaches and roads to connect the ferry terminals to the broader road system.[16] The total state commitment was $512,565. Given these expenditures, it was realistic to expect tough questions would be asked, as the state had invested over twice as much as the owners, but had earned a zero share of the profits.

In response, the ferry company insisted that its profits were not excessive, and it pointed out that it was in the process of reducing rates. Perhaps in an effort to deflect public criticism, the company dropped the fare for automobiles from $2.50 to $1.50. Passenger fares fell from $0.65 to $0.50. Sherbow at the PSC was not so easily appeased. He continued to apply pressure, publicly, on the company.

The PSC hearings in 1940 also had a direct bearing on the future of the Romancoke-Claiborne shuttle. Sherbow reported that the shuttle had been losing money, that passenger use was declining, and that it was a drag on overall company earnings. If the Claiborne service were to be abandoned, the rates on the main Annapolis-Matapeake service could then be lowered. Sherbow's comments led to panic in Claiborne, and the ferry company had to issue a response to reassure Claibornites that there was no plan to discontinue that service.[17]

State officials also put forward major changes in Annapolis, shortening the route (and making it more convenient for Baltimore drivers) by moving the western terminus from Annapolis to Sandy Point, farther north along the coast and several miles closer than downtown Annapolis to the thriving Matapeake terminal. This would finally implement the short ferry route proposed by the Bay Bridge Ferry Corporation in 1930 and the Maryland Bay Company a few years later—both of which had been shot down following pressure from the Claiborne-Annapolis Ferry Company. The loss of service to Claiborne would be offset (for non-Claibornites, at least) by expanding the available nighttime operations out of Matapeake.[18]

It appeared increasingly that external forces would be dictating the future course of the Claiborne-Annapolis Ferry Company and its services to Matapeake and Claiborne.

Ferry Workers Organize

Harrington and his colleagues faced pressure from another source around this same period, this time from within the company. The workers at the Claiborne-Annapolis Ferry Company were about to join a union.

Ferry operations had evolved substantially in the 1930s, but one thing that changed little was the workforce. Employment by the Claiborne-Annapolis Ferry Company (and the Love Point ferry) proved lucrative in the challenging economic times that applied in the first part of that decade. Ferry jobs were protected during the Great Depression—the ferries kept running and the jobs kept paying. The strike by licensed deck officers in 1906 had resulted in improved compensation across the industry, at least for those licensed masters, first officers, and second officers. Particularly for communities on the Eastern Shore, where other occupations tended to evolve toward farming or oystering, a job with the ferry brought with it prestige and a solid middle-class income.

Nowhere is this more adequately demonstrated than in the experience of the Higgins family of Talbot County. The ferry was an important part of the life of this family, and the family was an important contributor to the Claiborne-Annapolis Ferry, and the community of Claiborne more broadly. Three Higgins brothers worked as captains on the ferry line: Daniel, Gardner, and Edward (Ned). Gardner's son John (Jack) Higgins also served as ferry captain, and Daniel's son, also named Daniel, worked the ferry during his summer breaks from college. A cousin, Howard M. (Pat) Higgins, was a first officer.

The Higgins family was fortunate to have had steady employment during the Great Depression, and they often shared their good fortune with those who were down on their luck. The Higgins family recalls how Daniel, who unlike many in Maryland enjoyed a steady paycheck, would often bring a stranger to dinner, someone who was penniless or homeless and who Daniel had encountered on his last ferry run back to Claiborne.[19]

The Higgins brothers were captains, at the top of the pyramid when it came to jobs on the ferries. Captains were respected professionals, requiring extensive training and experience, and who were licensed by state officials. The hours were long and often involved overnight stays away from home. But by the standards of the time, these jobs were also reasonably well paid. In 1939, a captain on the Claiborne ferry line earned $2,100 per year.[20] This salary meant that a captain earned more than 90 percent of all workers in the United States in 1939, at a time when overall median wage and salary income was only $954 per year.[21] The only employees earning more were President Harrington at $12,000, General Manager Sherman at $6,000, and Secretary-Treasurer Speicher at $2,600. (The temporary pay cuts these leaders had taken during the Great Depression had been reversed by 1939.) Other licensed maritime workers were also well paid. This included chief engineers ($1,800) and first officers ($1,350). An annual wage of $1,350 put first officers above 75 percent of the US workforce in 1939.

A second group consisted of unlicensed workers on the ferry. Able seamen earned $780 and ordinary seaman earned $720, which was below the median wage income for US workers. Specialized trades earned slightly more: carpenters ($1,000), pursers ($900 to $1,200), fireman ($1,000), and assistant engineers ($960). This third group also included land-based personnel such as ticket agents ($900 to $1,800) and watchmen ($720 to $900).

What these first two categories of jobs had in common is that they were filled exclusively by white men. Black workers, both men and women, were limited to lower-paid jobs, all earning well under the US median income. These positions included cooks ($540 annual pay), maids ($420 to $520), and porters ($400). Only one Black worker identified with the ferry earned close to the US median income in 1939, a waiter with income of $900 (potentially earned from multiple jobs).

While at least some of the ferry workers were handsomely paid, that income came at a sacrifice. For captains as well as crews, work on the ferry was arduous. The workday lasted thirteen hours, from when the ferry started up in the morning until it ended in the evening. The work week was six days. Benefits were nonexistent: no pension, no medical coverage, no paid vacation, no overtime pay, no paid holidays. During the height of the Great Depression, in the early 1930s, ferry workers probably considered themselves fortunate, even with the grueling conditions. But as the economy started growing again in the late 1930s, and as unemployment fell, pressure for change emerged.

Given the relatively low income and tough working conditions of most ferry workers, it might not be surprising to learn that they were seen as a target-rich environment for union organizers. The first union to represent the workers at the Claiborne-Annapolis Ferry Company arrived in 1940, exploiting the frustration that had been building within the workforce for some time. The economy had rebounded from the Great Depression, and the rewards to senior executives and shareholders at the company had grown. But wages had grown only modestly over the years. There is an account, for example, of Captain Daniel Higgins engaging in an intense argument with the general manager (and Claiborne neighbor), B. Frank Sherman, over the disparity in incomes between the line workers and the managers of the company.[22]

Things had changed since 1906, when Willard Thomson could

simply reject any need to engage a union in labor negotiations, even when his workers had joined a union. The election of Franklin D. Roosevelt as president in 1932, and his reelection in 1936, had ushered in a more conducive environment for union organizing. The National Industrial Recovery Act of 1933 established the legal rights to collective bargaining for union employees. The Wagner Act of 1935 required employers to negotiate in good faith with any union that was supported by a majority of workers. The American Federation of Labor (AFL) and the (then separate) Congress of Industrial Organizations (CIO) asserted themselves more aggressively in labor matters, including heightened use of labor strikes.

In August 1940, while the owners of the company were negotiating its sale to the State of Maryland, and while managers were dealing with Joseph Sherbow and a combative PSC, this new challenge emerged in the form of the International Longshoremen's Association (ILA), part of the AFL. The union claimed to have signed up fifty-seven of the seventy eligible employees via a "card-check" process.[23] This included three of the four captains, meaning that at least two of the Higgins brothers were involved, and possibly all three.[24]

The company had no choice but to acknowledge the new reality, as it did in a letter to the ILA leader, Captain Josiah A. Cox. The letter, drafted on August 19, 1940, conceded "that your Association has been authorized to represent a majority of our employees" and committed to entering "into discussions with your Association."[25]

The union demands—characterized by the union as "low in comparison with our agreements elsewhere," included the following:[26]

- An eight-hour working day
- A $10 per month increase in pay for licensed personnel: masters first mates, engineers, and so forth
- A $5 per month increase in pay for unlicensed personnel: able seamen, ordinary seamen, oilers, cooks, porters, ticket agents, maids, watchmen, and so forth
- Two weeks of vacation with pay

- Five paid days off for national holidays, or compensating pay if those days are worked
- Time-and-a-half pay for overtime and for Sundays

Discussions began immediately between the ILA and the Claiborne-Annapolis Ferry Company, with B. Frank Sherman leading the team for the company. Sherman adamantly refused to accept the demand for an eight-hour day, most likely because the ferries operated on a thirteen-hour schedule and this would complicate staffing procedures and almost double the number of workers required. Other union demands were rejected, including those related to sick leave and paid vacation. In the end, the negotiations lasted only ten days, and the following agreement was struck on August 29, 1940:[27]

- Five-day work week for all employees (down from six days)
- Thirteen-hour workday between 7:00 a.m. and 9:00 p.m., excluding cooks, waiters, maids, and porters (It is worth noting that these positions were typically the ones held by Black workers at the ferry.)
- Time-and-a-half for overtime work
- Closed shop (e.g., all employees were forced to join the union)
- Effective September 1, 1940

The union accepted these terms but was not finished. One of the first acts of the new union was to initiate a federal investigation of pay practices under the Fair Labor Standards Act. The investigation resulted in the Claiborne-Annapolis Ferry Company providing back pay of $3,600 to the ten ferry employees working on land and thus covered by the act. (Those working at sea were classified as seaman and were exempted under the Fair Labor Standards Act.[28])

The agreement to adopt a "closed shop" meant that all eligible employees were forced to join the union. Local 1510 of the ILA represented the licensed maritime workers, such as captains and engineers. Local 1603 represented the unlicensed workers, who accounted for perhaps 70 percent of the total workforce. It was a time of change. The union had arrived. Coal had been replaced by diesel fuel (with one exception). Propellers had replaced side-wheels. Claiborne had been supplanted by Matapeake. And even bigger changes were on the horizon.

The State Takes Over

The fate of the Claiborne-Annapolis Ferry Company was decided in 1940 when the State Roads Commission completed negotiations for the takeover of the company.[29] This returned the ferry to its original concept: a state-run service for the residents of and visitors to Maryland. Envisioned way back in 1916, it had evolved as a privately run company only because the state lacked adequate funding to acquire its own ferry outright.

Placing a value on the company was a complex exercise. Most of the value was tied up in the four operating ferries: *Gov. Harry W. Nice*, *John M. Dennis*, *Gov. Albert C. Ritchie*, and *Gov. Emerson C. Harrington II*. The PSC engaged an engineer to calculate replacement value, net of accumulated depreciation, and this led to a valuation of $989,000. A consultant hired by the Claiborne-Annapolis Ferry Company valued the ferries at $1,260,900.[30] The company valued its business as a whole at $1,902,743. Discussions continued in early 1940, and by June the government's estimate had risen to $1,038,310.[31]

There was pressure on the ferry company to accept an offer. Joseph Sherbow and the PSC had great power here: the PSC was both the agent valuing the business and the entity that helped determine the ferry company's prosperity via the PSC's ability to set rates for passengers and vehicles. Sherbow was perfectly willing to play hardball. In May 1940, the PSC ordered a 40 percent reduction in passenger rates charged by the ferry company for its Annapolis-Matapeake service. The estimated reduction in passenger fees of $54,000 would cut company profits by a third.

Harrington and his board gave in and agreed to sell. Agreement was finally reached on the change of ownership on November

19, 1940. The negotiated price was $1,020,000 plus whatever the declared value of inventory was on the date of closing, ultimately leading to a final tally of $1,024,000. The operation was to be run by the Maryland State Roads Commission and financed by an issue of bonds guaranteed by the state. We had come full circle: Joseph B. Seth's vision in 1886 of using municipal bonds to fund a cross-bay ferry had finally been realized, some fifty-four years later.

The sale of the Claiborne-Annapolis Ferry Company was executed formally during a meeting of the company stockholders just one week later. Of the 60,000 shares outstanding, 56,000 were represented in the meeting, and those shares were voted unanimously in favor of the transaction.[32] The per-share value of the transaction was about $17.07.[33] This equates in 2024 dollars to about $400 per share, leading to an overall valuation of the enterprise in 2024 dollars of $22 million. The Harringtons (Emerson C., wife Mary, sons Emerson Jr. and William, and daughter Mary Truitt) realized $195,867 in proceeds, or about $4.3 million in 2024 dollars. Harrington, who earlier had declared, "I do not want to make a dollar on this Ferry," had exited with a bundle of them.[34]

The formal handover took place on June 10, 1941. The Claiborne-Annapolis Ferry Company was dissolved, and the operations were assumed by the newly created Chesapeake Bay Ferry System. Harrington left his role as president. However, B. Frank Sherman transitioned to the new ferry operation, continuing his long-standing role as general manager.

It was less clear what would happen to the union workforce at the end of a ninety-day transition period that started June 10. The original plan was for the 109 workers in the Claiborne-Annapolis Ferry Company to join the Maryland State Classified Service upon qualifying for the State Merit System. They would receive the same wages as they did before the handover and, in addition, would for the first time qualify for a pension. At the end of the ninety-day transition period, they would be under normal regulations for state employees, called the Merit System.[35] The role of the ILA, representing the workers for less than a year, was uncertain. Because the State of Maryland did not have a unionized workforce, it was initially assumed that workers at the company who belonged to a union would have to resign from that union.[36]

Not surprisingly, the union balked at this arrangement. In July, Local 1603 of the ILA, representing about sixty unlicensed workers at the ferry, threatened to call a strike. The workers they represented were concerned about whether they would have jobs at the end of the ninety-day transition period, and they wanted the union to be recognized as the bargaining agent. Local 1510, representing the licensed workers, was worried about the same issues.[37] The strike in July was averted when the State of Maryland promised to initiate discussions on the subject.

That peace did not last long. Upset that the promised conference on wages and working conditions had yet to meet, a strike took place on the morning of August 23, 1941. The crew for the ferries in Matapeake showed up on time but then refused to man the boat for the first trip at 7:25 a.m. The strike lasted only six hours and ended when the State Roads Commission committed to working with the union.[38]

The commission capitulated to the union demands in November 1941, approving a 15 to 16 percent increase in base wages for the 120 workers of the Chesapeake Bay Ferry System, although there was still no premium for overtime. The State Roads Commission formally agreed to recognize Locals 1603 and 1510 as bargaining agents for each worker individually—but not collectively. This sidestepped state restrictions on collective bargaining with organized labor.[39]

The stage had been set for the next decade or more. However, global events were about to intercede. The new Chesapeake Bay Ferry System, with its unionized workforce, was about to enter the Second World War.

Notes

1. “Plans to Fight Subsidies for Two Ferries,” *Sun* (Baltimore, MD), January 6, 1935.
2. “Nice Reported in Control of Bay Span Board,” *Evening Sun* (Baltimore, MD), May 9, 1935.
3. “Nice Accepts Ferry Subsidy Surrender,” *Evening Sun* (Baltimore, MD), January 16, 1935.
4. “Starting With One Boat, $18,000 Subsidy, Ferry Line Is Valued Over Million,” *Sun* (Baltimore, MD), March 26, 1937.
5. “House Kills Plan for New Ferry,” *Sun* (Baltimore, MD), March 18, 1937.
6. “Says Shore Wants Fast, Cheap Ferry,” *Sun* (Baltimore, MD), June 3, 1938.
7. “Ferry Company Asks Delay on Hearing on Rate Structure,” *Salisbury Times*, January 17, 1940.
8. “Joseph Sherbow, Powerful Lawyer and Judge, Dies,” *Sun* (Baltimore, MD), December 17, 1979.
9. “Ferry Company Asks P.S.C. to Defer Hearing,” *Evening Sun* (Baltimore, MD), January 22, 1940.
10. “‘Gold Mine’ Revealed as Probe Opens,” *Salisbury Times*, January 22, 1940.
11. “Starting With One Boat, $18,000 Subsidy, Ferry Line is Valued Over Million,” *Sun* (Baltimore, MD), March 26, 1937.
12. In 1937, the median income for US workers was $723 overall and only $671 for Maryland. Only 5.6 percent of US workers earned as much or more than the $2,400 paid to Speicher. In all likelihood, both Sherman and Harrington were in the top 1 percent of workers when it came to annual wages and salaries. Since both were shareholders and the company was paying dividends, their total income was likely even higher. See Max J. Wasserman and John R. Arnold, “Old-Age Insurance: Covered Workers and Average and Median Taxable Wages in 1937,” *Social Security Bulletin 2*, no. 1 (January 1939): 3-8.
13. “Admits Ferry Stock Value Grew 1,400%,” *Sun* (Baltimore, MD), March 6, 1940.
14. “Ferry Company Asks P.S.C. to Defer Hearing,” *Evening Sun* (Baltimore, MD), January 22, 1940.
15. “Behind the News: The State Gets Its Ferry,” *Evening Sun* (Baltimore, MD), November 14, 1940.
16. “Challenges Ferry Company to Refute Charge,” *Sun* (Baltimore, MD), February 1, 1940.
17. “Denies Plan to Abandon Ferry Shuttle Service,” *Sun* (Baltimore, MD), January 12, 1940. The issue arose again later that year, as a change in ownership seemed imminent. It was revealed that state officials, who would take over

management upon a sale, were considering the abandonment of the Claiborne line altogether.

18. "Plan Changes in Operation of the Ferry," *Easton Star-Democrat*, November 22, 1940.
19. Interview with Daniel G. Higgins III, grandson of Captain Daniel G. Higgins. This interview relayed stories told by Captain Higgins's son, Daniel Jr.
20. The 1940 US census asked respondents to identify their occupation and to list their earned income for the year 1939. About fifty workers at the ferry company can be identified within the census, and their reported income forms the basis of the compensation data provided here. This represents perhaps two-thirds of the ferry workforce at the time.
21. US Department of Commerce, Bureau of the Census, *Sixteenth Census of the United States: 1940, Part 1: General Characteristics* (Government Printing Office, 1943). Income statistics are from Chapter 7 "Wage and Salary Income in 1939, Table 1," 11.
22. Interview with Daniel G. Higgins III. The date of this argument is unknown, but it could very well have correlated with interest by the ferry workforce in union representation.
23. The "card check" process is not an election in which workers vote (anonymously) on whether or not to join a union. The union simply goes door to door and requests workers to endorse a union. If enough do so, the union is authorized to represent the workers. Some suggest that union intimidation can play a role in the card-check process, creating a distorted result.
24. "Seeks Closed-Shop Ferry Agreement," *Evening Sun* (Baltimore, MD), August 20, 1940. There were four captains known to be working at the Claiborne-Annapolis Ferry in 1940: Daniel Higgins, Gardner Higgins, Edward Higgins, and Merle Dawson. Dawson's draft card for October 1940 makes this clear. It is possible that Thomas Woolford also worked for part of 1940—his date of retirement is uncertain, although his application for Social Security did not take place until May 11, 1942, just after his seventieth birthday.
25. The draft of the letter was included in the Meeting Minutes of the Claiborne-Annapolis Ferry Company Executive Committee, August 19, 1940, Maryland State Archives, Maryland Public Service Commission, MSA S245-3, MdHR 19816-3.
26. "Seeks Closed-Shop Ferry Agreement," *Evening Sun* (Baltimore, MD), August 20, 1940.
27. Meeting Minutes of the Claiborne-Annapolis Ferry Company Board of Directors, September 6, 1940, Maryland State Archives, Maryland Public Service Commission, MSA S245-5, MdHR 19816-9/10.
28. "Ferry Company Voluntarily Pays Men $3600," *Easton Star-Democrat*, January24, 1941.

29. “Behind the News: The State Gets Its Ferry,” *Evening Sun* (Baltimore, MD), November 14, 1940.
30. “Valuations of 4 Four Ferry Boats Differ,” *Easton Star-Democrat*, March 15, 1940.
31. “PSC Orders Passenger Fare Cut on Ferries,” *Evening Sun* (Baltimore, MD), May 29, 1940.
32. “Ferry Sale Consummated,” *Easton Star-Democrat*, November 29, 1940.
33. The company had no long-term debt in 1940. It had fully paid off all bonds and similar debt by 1934.
34. *The Claiborne-Annapolis Ferry*, an open letter to company shareholders, from Emerson. C. Harrington, March 22, 1921, Maryland Public Service Commission, MSA S245-1, MdHR 19816-1. A reasonable calculation is that between 1928 and 1941, Harrington and his immediate family realized annual salaries, annual dividend payments, and a one-time acquisition payout from the Claiborne-Annapolis Ferry Company of about $206,000. This total would be worth about $9 million in 2024 dollars.
35. “State Classifies Ferry Employees,” *Sun* (Baltimore, MD), June 19, 1941.
36. “Plan Changes in Operation of the Ferry,” *Easton Star-Democrat*, November 22, 1940.
37. “State Ferry Crew Strike Threatened,” *Evening Sun* (Baltimore, MD), July 23, 1941.
38. “Strike on Bay Ferries Is Ended,” *Salisbury Times*, August 23, 1941.
39. “120 Employees on Ferry to Get Raises,” *Sun* (Baltimore, MD), November 28, 1941.

XII

The Last Decade

The Chesapeake Bay Ferry System took over operation of the Annapolis-Matapeake and Romancoke-Claiborne ferry routes just in time for the US entry into World War II. The war was going to have a direct effect on the ferry routes and the terminals they served. It also led to continued reductions in the quality of service at Claiborne, including multiple attempts to shut down that line entirely. The little village of Claiborne, which had been put on the map by a planned railroad ferry, and which had entered its golden era with the Annapolis-Claiborne car ferry, was now seen as an unprofitable distraction. The village would escape time and time again from efforts to remove it from the Chesapeake Bay Ferry System. These efforts were driven not by financial investors in distant cities, but rather by Claiborne's new nemesis, Maryland's own State Roads Commission in Annapolis.

Challenges to Romancoke-Claiborne Service

On January 16, 1942, it was announced that the State Roads Commission would terminate the Romancoke-Claiborne ferry line, because "the business of this route was so inadequate as to cause a considerable loss each day." The announcement provided only two weeks' notice, with the service to be withdrawn starting February

1. Because a coal-fired steam-propelled ferry was not seen as fit for the Annapolis-Matapeake service, *Gov. Emerson C. Harrington II* would be laid up and presumably sold. A local newspaper reported that "the doom of Claiborne was sure after the State Roads Commission bought the Ferry lines, indeed it is surprising that Claiborne has been used this long."[1]

Unsurprisingly, this decision did not sit well with residents and merchants of Talbot County, and a campaign to reverse the decision was organized by State Senator A. Raymond Marvel, who represented that county. Just three days before the planned withdrawal, a stay of execution was issued by the governor: Herbert R. O'Conor decided on January 28 to overrule his State Roads Commission and to continue the Claiborne service. He reported that "civic and citizens groups had pledged themselves to effect an increase in the use of the ferry service" and that "the roads commission would watch the ferry's receipts closely in the next few months to ascertain whether more persons use the service."[2] It was going to be a challenge. Throughout the entire month of February, after the locals had pledged to expand use of the Claiborne line, total receipts on the Romancoke-Claiborne service amounted to only $440, versus over $27,000 for the Annapolis-Matapeake line.[3]

The State Roads Commission continued its campaign in an attempt to reverse the governor's decision, hoping to enlist the broader public in its efforts. It was time to engage the number-crunchers in an effort to build a stronger economic argument. An auditor's report released publicly in April 1942 confirmed that the Romancoke-Claiborne service was hemorrhaging money. Total receipts for the twelve-month period ending June 30, 1942, was projected at $13,704. Direct operating costs (including provisions for the annual overhaul of the ferry) were $48,146, which meant the ferry lost money every time it sailed. Moreover, the indirect costs (overheads, debt service, etc.) apportioned to the Romancoke-Claiborne line added another $29,825 in costs, though to be fair, it is not clear how much of this indirect cost would vanish if the line were terminated. The bottom line offered by the auditor, nonetheless, was that the Romancoke-Claiborne service was losing $63,176 per year.[4]

Even these auditors' results failed to deliver a knockout punch in the effort to shut down the Claiborne service. Governor O'Conor would not reverse his decision. Despite the negative financial report, ferry service to Claiborne continued. Round one had ended, and Claiborne emerged a survivor.

Ironically, Claiborne's role was elevated in early January 1943 when issues on the boat channel into Matapeake meant that, temporarily, it could not be used as a ferry terminal. The Chesapeake Bay Ferry System was forced instead to reestablish the long-abandoned Annapolis-Claiborne route. For once Claiborne had the service of the modern ferry *Gov. Harry W. Nice*, as well as seeing the return of *John M. Dennis* to the Annapolis-Claiborne route.[5] The downside was that the Chesapeake Bay Ferry System also suspended the Romancoke-Claiborne service. The changes lasted only two weeks: by January 15, things had returned to normal.[6]

Round two in the campaign to close the Claiborne service took place in October 1943. In a novel approach, the State Roads Commission threatened to increase rates on the primary line to Matapeake unless it was allowed to discontinue the Romancoke-Claiborne service. Chairman Ezra B. Whitman indicated that fares would have to rise twenty-five cents per automobile and five cents per person if the Claiborne service continued. This was a transparent attempt to build popular support elsewhere in the state to shut down the Claiborne service. The outrage from other areas might counterbalance pressure coming from Talbot County to continue the service.[7] It was announced that service to Claiborne would end November 1.

The reaction was predictable. Civic groups and politicians pushed back and convinced Governor O'Conor that a ten-point "Intact" plan would reverse the deficient performance of the Romancoke-Claiborne line. They also argued that at a time of wartime rationing, it would be foolish to ask Claiborne drivers to go so far out of their way to get to Matapeake when gasoline would be conserved by using the shorter route via Romancoke. (The Claiborne-Romancoke ferry did not burn gasoline or diesel, but instead used abundant coal as its fuel.)

Once again, just a few days before the scheduled termination of service, Governor O'Conor issued his second stay of execution. He announced that the Claiborne line would continue at least through the end of the canning season in 1944, though rates on that line (only) would be increased. He also announced that *Gov. Emerson C. Harrington II*, serving the Romancoke-Claiborne route, would be overhauled and its coal-burning steam engine replaced with modern diesels.[8] The State Roads Commission had swung again but once more failed to deliver a knockout punch. Round two was over, and Claiborne was still standing.

But the commission had not given up. If the argument about financial losses did not work in round one, and the argument about rate increase did not work in round two, there was still one argument to make in the third round: the line was not safe.

In early 1944, the commission engaged its own engineers in a study of the Claiborne ferry terminal, backed up by a report by its insurer, the Royal Indemnity Company. Their conclusion regarding the Claiborne terminal was that "there is danger of sudden collapse." The defects, according to the report:

> ... are such that there is a serious hazard of sudden collapse of the approach deck and transfer bridge under motor vehicle load; or extensive damage to an incoming ferry in the event of failure of the fending pile clusters and slip structure.[9]

Although it might be possible to rebuild the terminal at a cost of $63,000, the report continued, the issue was moot because wartime rationing meant the critical construction materials would not be available. Therefore, the commission announced that the Romancoke-Claiborne service would terminate immediately, on March 15.

George T. Harrison, a leader of the local community, and the owner of a major seafood packing operation down the road from

Claiborne, sought to protect the Claiborne service. He immediately raised objections to the decision:

> I don't suppose the people of Talbot County have ever been shocked any more than when they read in *The Sun* this morning the notice of intention to take off the Romancoke-Claiborne ferry beginning Saturday. They stated it would cost $63,000 to fix the pier and that creosote timber and piling could not be obtained at this time. Our company (the Tilghman Packing Company, Tilghman, Md.) has bought a lot of creosoted lumber to fix up their docks and bulkheads lately.

Harrison argued, moreover, that he was aware of a company that could furnish the required materials quickly and that a reputable contractor had estimated the cost of repair to the terminal at only $9,000.[10]

Criticism was also launched at the State Roads Commission from other directions. Why had the commission not reviewed the condition of the terminal earlier? If, as claimed, 98 percent of the timber was original, then the deterioration would not have happened in just the past few months. Why had no repairs been made before reaching this point? As a *Sun* editorial reported, "We hope the commission, having failed to rid itself of the ferry because it did not make money, is not now using a roundabout way to reach its goal."[11]

It may be that the State Roads Commission pushed so hard in this case that its credibility was undermined. Credible estimates to repair the dock came in from suppliers and ranged from $18,195 to $28,000—far below the commission estimates. Governor O'Conor began to push back on the commission decision-making process.[12]

The State Roads Commission had swung a third time—and missed. On April 24, the governor announced that the Claiborne terminal would be rebuilt and that service to Romancoke would start up again as soon as the reconstruction was complete.[13] While the service had been suspended, a similar upgrade effort would take place in Romancoke.[14] Meanwhile, service to Claiborne would be suspended.

It took a year for the work to be completed. It was not until March 30, 1945, that ferry service resumed between Claiborne and Romancoke.[15] But when it did, it encountered the:

> . . . new terminal, of thoroughly modern construction, and including not only the new landing slip but new bulkheads and a fine new road approach. Built at a cost of more than $40,000, its substantial construction gives ample assurance of the continuing operation of this transportation system which is so vital to Talbot County.[16]

The State Roads Commission had failed in three attempts in three years to shut down the Claiborne ferry service. Indeed, the Romancoke-Claiborne run would even outlast the Annapolis-Matapeake line, but not without yet another long interruption. *Gov. Emerson C. Harrington II* needed a complete rebuild, including the delayed replacement of the antiquated steam engine with diesel motors. Such a rebuild had not been possible during the war, given that shipyard priority was focused on warships and ocean-going cargo ships. But after the war's end, the time had come. *Gov. Emerson C. Harrington II* was withdrawn from service December 10, 1945. The promise was that it would return to service in April 1946.[17] That promise got the month right. It just got the year wrong.

Annapolis Terminal Moves to Sandy Point

While the drama was playing out regarding the future of service to Claiborne, there were other issues affecting the primary Annapolis-Matapeake service.

Since the late 1920s, there had been an effort by several investors to create a shorter ferry line to Kent Island departing out of Sandy Point, rather than Annapolis. This made sense. Such a route would cut the distance covered by the ferry in half. For many drivers, the need to travel downtown to Annapolis to catch the ferry also added substantial driving time. The Claiborne-Annapolis Ferry Company had successfully driven away any efforts to build a terminal at Sandy Point. It took the Japanese Empire to finally make that change happen.

The attack on Pearl Harbor led to a massive expansion of the US Navy. Warships were being launched by the hundreds. The number of uniformed personnel rose from 119,088 before the war to 3,405,525 by its end.[18] But without trained officers, the ships would add little to the US ability to wage war. Consequently, there was need to expand the US Naval Academy in Annapolis, which bordered the ferry wharf at the end of King George Street.

The Naval Academy wanted that land for growth and, when it came to such things during the war, what the Naval Academy wanted, they generally got. The ferry wharf finally had to move to Sandy Point, though there had been pressure for decades for such a relocation. Construction of the new terminal was started in late 1942, with expectations of it being completed by year-end.[19] There were inevitable delays. It took until the following year for the terminal, the steel loading bridge, and the adjacent roadways to be completed. Finally on November 1, 1943, the new ferry terminal opened, almost a year behind schedule.[20] But the new terminal would prove immensely popular once traffic returned to normal after the war ended.

Post-War Boom

During the first years of the war, ferries *Gov. Harry W. Nice*, *John M. Dennis,* and *Gov. Albert C. Ritchie* had been busy shuttling between Matapeake and Annapolis (later Sandy Point). Passenger loads had risen steadily during the war, from 527,665 in 1942 to 642,314 in 1945.[21]

The ferry system suffered a blow when, in 1944, *Gov. Albert C. Ritchie* failed a federal safety inspection. This ferry had revolutionized service between Annapolis and Claiborne back in 1926. Although it had been thoroughly upgraded before entering that service, including replacing an old steam engine with diesel motors, the "bones" of the ferry still dated back to its construction in 1883. By March 1944, it was over sixty years old and deemed to be structurally unsafe.[22] Repairs would be expensive, impractical in wartime, and probably a waste given the age of the ferry. The answer, therefore, was to take it out of service forever and sell it for scrap. Service on the Sandy Point-Matapeake route had to be reduced. When one of the two remaining ferries on that route had to go into overhaul in early 1945, the Romancoke-Claiborne service would be suspended and *Gov. Emerson C. Harrington II* used on the Matapeake run.[23]

The ultimate answer was a new ferry. In May 1944, the State Roads Commission recommended the expenditure of approximately $1,000,000, covering both the purchase of a new ferry and related work on ferry terminals. A bond issue of $1,500,000 to cover these costs was advanced in 1945, along with the notification that the new ferry would be named after Governor Herbert R. O'Conor. In addition to the new ferry, the bond would finance the rebuilding of the single-slip Matapeake terminal into a modern two-slip facility and the expansion of the Sandy Point terminal from one to two slips. Each slip would be equipped with modern electric "bridges" to connect the ferry to the roads, of the sort introduced at Sandy Point in 1943.[24] (The smaller Romancoke and Claiborne terminals had been rebuilt the previous year but remained primitive by comparison.)

The new ferry was built in Baltimore, at the Maryland Drydock Company. It was to be the longest ferry in the fleet, though less in total volume (GRT) than the ferry it replaced, *Gov. Albert C. Ritchie*. (It was also smaller than *Groton*, the ferry originally acquired in 1889 to launch service to Claiborne, which instead was consumed by flames on the trip from Connecticut.) While the hull was launched in May 1946, post-war strikes at the plants resulted in completion of the engines being delayed for many months. The originally scheduled August 1946 delivery date came and went. Finally, in February 1947, *Gov. Herbert R. O'Conor* was ready for service.[25] It could carry eight hundred passengers and seventy-four automobiles on each trip. Its interior featured comfortable seating—still segregated for white and Black passengers—and a kitchen to serve passengers on the short trip. (It was said the kitchen served "the world's best hot dogs and the world's worst coffee."[26])

Delays did not only affect the Sandy Point-Matapeake line. There were similar delays in the reengining and overhauling of *Gov. Emerson C. Harrington II*. The original plan was to return the ferry to service in April 1946, but this was delayed more than a year due to problems with strikes at engine suppliers. This meant that Claiborne was without ferry service of any kind from March 1944 to March 1945 (for replacement of the terminal at Claiborne) and from December 1945 until April 1947 (for upgrades to *Gov. Emerson C. Harrington II*).

The arrivals of the new *Gov. Herbert R. O'Conor* and the upgraded *Gov. Emerson C. Harrington II* were just in time. The Chesapeake Bay Ferry System was undergoing a post-war boom. Annual passenger traffic rose from 600,000 in 1944 to almost double that by 1950.[27] *John M. Dennis* and *Gov. Harry W. Nice* would have struggled to move that many passengers, making the 1947 arrival of *Gov. Herbert R. O'Conor* especially welcome.

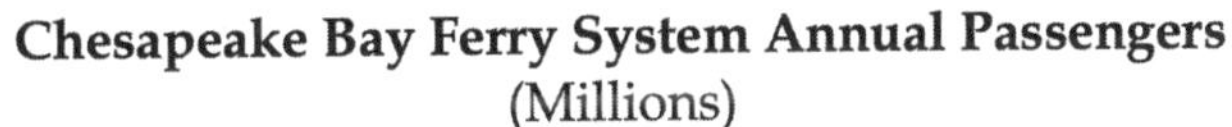

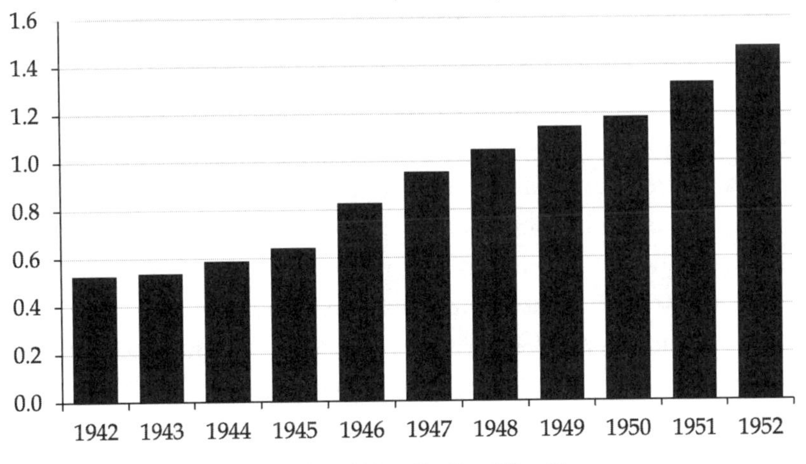

But the post-war boom was not equally distributed. Traffic rose hugely on the Sandy Point-Matapeake connection as war-weary civilians and demobilized personnel longed for days of fresh air and pleasant diversions to be found at ocean resorts. In contrast, by 1951, only 1.7 percent of passenger traffic on the Chesapeake Bay Ferry System was using the Romancoke-Claiborne line. The upgraded *Gov. Emerson C. Harrington II*, with new diesel engines, provided good service on that route—too good, perhaps. On busy weekends, when traffic on the Matapeake line overwhelmed the three ferries available there, the Claiborne service would again be suspended and the upgraded *Gov. Emerson C. Harrington II* was placed instead on the Sandy Point-Matapeake route.[28]

Demand was so great that an effort was made to secure a fourth ferry for the Matapeake route. This was *Eastern Bay*, built in 1927 in Camden, New Jersey, as *Frederick Pierce*. Smaller than *Gov. Herbert R. O'Conor*, it could carry thirty-five cars and 450 passengers, about half the load of the larger ferry. It was used to supplement the other three ferries on that line during busy travel holidays. The new ferry entered service in July 1948 but did not serve long under that name. In April 1949, the Maryland State Senate passed a resolution asking the State Roads Commission to rename *Eastern Bay* as *B. Frank Sherman*. This was done to honor the general manager of the Chesapeake Bay Ferry System who had served in that role since 1941, and the same role in the preceding Claiborne-Annapolis Ferry Company, since 1925. Indeed, Sherman had begun his career with the Claiborne-Annapolis Ferry Company the very first day operations started in 1919. The renaming of the ferry corresponded with Sherman's thirtieth anniversary with the ferry system.

With the new ferries came changes in personnel. Long-serving Captain Thomas M. Woolford retired about the time the State took over the ferry system. He had been with the ferry line since 1921 and had the special role of commanding all three diesel ferries when introduced into the fleet: *Gov. Albert C. Ritchie* (1926), *John M. Dennis* (1929), and *Gov. Harry W. Nice* (1938).[29] All three Higgins brothers stayed with the line until the end, extending their already impressive tenure and association with the ferry line. Edward

Higgins captained *John M. Dennis* through its last voyages in 1952. His brothers Daniel and Gardner shared duties on *Gov. Emerson C. Harrington II* on its trips between Claiborne and Romancoke. The last to leave the system was Edward, who served as the port captain for the fleet of inactive ferries as they awaited their fate. That role ended in early August 1953, and Edward himself died just a few weeks later, still a young man.

End of the Love Point Ferry

The post-war boom of the Chesapeake Bay Ferry System was not shared with the lingering Love Point line, still operated by the Baltimore and Eastern Railroad. On August 31, 1947, the old ferry *Philadelphia* made its final run from Baltimore to Love Point. On the line since 1931 (except for the period of 1934 to 1937), "Smokey Joe" had developed a strong following. But the Love Point operation could no longer compete with the high-frequency and fast operations of the Chesapeake Bay Ferry System, and in the end, it was not an operation worth saving. Long-serving Captain Norman C. Taylor was in charge during the last voyage of *Philadelphia* in 1947. Service between Baltimore and Love Point had ended after forty-five years.

The forces leading to the termination of the Love Point line did not affect that line in isolation. Ferries everywhere were seen as old-fashioned, slow, and inconvenient. They were relics of an earlier era. Lines of automobiles waiting for their turn on the Sandy Point-Matapeake run often ran a mile or more during busy holiday or summer weekends. Marylanders wanted a cross-bay bridge instead. The era of the cross-bay ferry was about to come to an end.

Notes

1. "Claiborne Ferry to Romancoke Withdrawn," *Easton Star-Democrat*, January 16, 1942.
2. "Romancoke Ferry to Be Continued, O'Conor Says," *Salisbury Times*, January 28, 1942.
3. "Ferry System's Income," *Sun* (Baltimore, MD), April 10, 1942.
4. "Auditor Tells of Romancoke Ferry Route," *Easton Star-Democrat*, April 24, 1942.
5. "Md. Bay Ferry Service Cut; One Line Runs," *Journal-Every Evening* (Wilmington, DE), January 2, 1943.
6. "Claiborne Ferry Will Resume Schedule," *Easton Star-Democrat*, January 15, 1943.
7. "This Week's News," *Sun* (Baltimore, MD), October 3, 1943.
8. "Romancoke Ferry to Be Continued," *Sun* (Baltimore, MD), October 29, 1943. The cost of coal for the ferry had become considerable, and the replacement with diesels promised cost savings.
9. "Claiborne-Romancoke Ferry Ordered to Close for Safety," *Journal-Every Evening* (Wilmington, DE), March 17, 1944.
10. "Ferry Closing Was Delayed," *Sun* (Baltimore, MD), March 18, 1944.
11. "A New Reason for Stopping the Claiborne Ferry," *Sun* (Baltimore, MD), March 18, 1944.
12. "Gov. O'Conor Urges Study of Ferry Plea," *Journal-Every Evening* (Wilmington, DE), April 21, 1944; "Talbot Countians Want Ferry Service Resumed," *Journal-Every Evening* (Wilmington, DE), April 17, 1944.
13. "Claiborne-Romancoke Wharf to Be Rebuilt; Ferry To Resume," *Journal-Every Evening* (Wilmington, DE), April 29, 1944.
14. "Romancoke Terminal to Be Finished Dec. 1," *Salisbury Times*, October 12, 1944.
15. "Romancoke Ferry Line to Resume Operation on Friday," *Journal-Every Evening* (Wilmington, DE), March 28, 1945.
16. "The Claiborne Ferry Will Be Resumed Today," *Easton Star-Democrat*, March 30, 1945.
17. "Claiborne-Romancoke Ferry Service to Be Discontinued Until April," *Denton Journal*, December 7, 1945.
18. John Darrell Sherwood, "Winds of War, Winds of Change: The U.S. Naval Academy During the World War II Era," *Naval History and Heritage Command*, January 23, 2025, history.navy.mil/browse-by-topic/heritage/naval-academy/usna-wwii.html.
19. "Ferry to Sandy Point May Be Opened Nov. 1," *Easton Star-Democrat*, October 29, 1943.

20. “New Terminal for Ferry Hailed,” *Journal-Every Evening* (Wilmington, DE), November 2, 1943.
21. Basic financial data for the Chesapeake Bay Ferry System is provided in the annual Maryland Manual publications issued by the State of Maryland.
22. “Ferry Repairs Cut Trips,” *Evening Sun* (Baltimore, MD), March 20, 1944.
23. “Claiborne Ferry Out for 6 Weeks,” *Sun* (Baltimore, MD), February 18, 1944.
24. “Bill Would Authorize New State Ferry Boat,” *Salisbury Times*, February 24, 1945.
25. “New Ferry Named for O’Conor Goes into Service Tomorrow,” *Evening Sun* (Baltimore, MD), February 21, 1947.
26. As reported by the daughter and the grandsons of B. Frank Sherman in an interview with the author in 2022.
27. Traffic data for the CBFS were provided in an annual publication by the Maryland government titled *Maryland Manual*. See, for example, B. Frank Sherman, “Chesapeake Bay Ferry System,” *Maryland Manual 1951–52* (20th Century Printing, 1952), 98.
28. See, for example, “Traffic Flow ‘Not Extreme,’” *Sun* (Baltimore, MD), July 2, 1950.
29. Other captains had emerged, including two brothers. Merle R. Dawson served as first mate under Woolford on *Gov. Albert C. Ritchie* in the late 1920s, received his master’s certificate in 1928, and took over as captain of that ferry in the mid-1930s. He signed up for military service afterward and spent a career running harbor operations for the US Army. His younger brother, Wilbert E. Dawson, became a captain on the line, ultimately operating the new *Gov. Herbert R. O’Conor* in 1948. Frank P. Conway took over operation of *Gov. Harry W. Nice* in the late 1940s. Finally, Joseph P. Marshall, who was a master mariner with an unlimited license—able to operate any vessel of any size on any ocean—stepped in as needed, commanding at one time or another all of the ferries in the CBFS fleet, including the newly acquired *Eastern Bay* (later *B. Frank Sherman*) in 1948.

XIII

Like a Wake

The Claiborne-Annapolis Ferry Company, under the leadership of Emerson C. Harrington, had managed to prevent direct competitors on its ferry lines throughout the 1920s and 1930s. By clever maneuvering, Harrington had protected his monopoly. In the end, the challenge came not from another ferry line, but from a bridge.

Attempts to build a bridge had surfaced before, most notably in the late 1920s (derailed by the Great Depression) and in the mid-1930s (vetoed by President Roosevelt). Both had envisioned a bridge running from east of Baltimore, over Hart-Miller Island, and then connecting to the Eastern Shore at Tolchester.

In 1938, legislation authorizing a bridge at a new location, between Sandy Point and Kent Island, was passed in the Maryland legislature. But this went nowhere as the nation geared up for World War II. Upon the war's end, interest in the bridge was renewed, and in 1947, new legislation promoted by Governor William Preston Lane Jr. (who succeeded Herbert R. O'Conor as governor in 1949) led to the start of construction.

The new bridge route almost duplicated the Sandy Point-Matapeake ferry line, and it was well understood that this ferry route would be shut down once the bridge opened. And so, when the new bridge finally opened on July 30, 1952, the Sandy Point-Matapeake ferry ceased operations, ending decades of cross-bay steamer and ferry operations.

Not everyone wanted to see the new Gov. William Preston Lane Jr. Memorial Bridge (the Chesapeake Bay Bridge) succeed. Retired Captain James R. Corkrin, who had piloted steamers on the Bay for sixty years, penned an article shortly after the bridge opened, making it clear that:

> I have no desire to visit the bridge or even see it. I don't think it will be there long anyway: just let the bay ice up and good the way it used to and it will be mowed down like a blade of grass.[1]

The bridge, in fact, was not completed without an incident directly tied to the ferry system. On July 7, just a few weeks before the new bridge opened, *John M. Dennis*, under the command of Edward (Ned) Higgins, suddenly veered off course as it approached Sandy Point and rammed one of the bridge supports. Officially, the cause was identified as a snapped steering cable, though such cables were inspected weekly to make sure they were not prone to failure. Higgins family lore has suggested another explanation, but one that has never been proven: the lore suggests Ned Higgins was not always sober while on duty and such might have been the case that day.[2] While the bridge survived without damage, *John M. Dennis* suffered a gash in the hull, and twenty passengers were banged up in the collision. Ferry and bridge met, and bridge emerged victorious. It was a perfect metaphor. The victory was made complete a couple of weeks later when the Sandy Point-Matapeake line of the Chesapeake Bay Ferry System was shut for good. The ferries serving that route were dispatched to Kent Island and laid up, awaiting sale.

The eventual fate of the Romancoke-Claiborne route was less clear since the new bridge did not compete with that route at all. Local supporters campaigned to keep that line intact. Claiborne residents had managed to stave off previous threats to cancel ferry service, especially in the years 1941 to 1946. But this effort was doomed to fail. The State of Maryland gave those supporters until the end of the year to show the route could break even. To no one's surprise, it did not. On December 31, 1952, the last ferry of the Chesapeake Bay Ferry System finished its round trip to Claiborne and left service, forever.

It was hardly the time and place for a festive New Year's Eve celebration. The weather was cold and rainy, perfect for the occasion. Sleet pummeled the steel roof of the ferry, drowning the normal sounds of the diesel engine humming and the waves splashing. That last ferry run, aboard the *Gov. Emerson C. Harrington II*, was captained by John ("Jack") Higgins, son of Gardner Higgins and nephew of Daniel and Edward Higgins, both of whom were on board for this last, sad trip. Also on board was the one individual who embodied the history of ferry operations out of Annapolis and Claiborne: B. Frank Sherman.

The ferry era was over. Reporter George Bowen of the Associated Press succinctly captured the atmosphere: "it was like a wake."[3]

Notes

1. James R. Corkrin, ". . . When the Bay Itself Was a Bridge," *Sun* (Baltimore, MD), September 14, 1952.
2. According to Daniel G. Higgins III, family lore has it that Ned Higgins might have been impaired. He had a reputation for drinking. However, no such impairment is suggested in the official accounts.
3. "Last Ferry Trip Like a Wake," *Evening Sun* (Baltimore, MD), January 1, 1953.

XIV

Legacy of the Claiborne Ferries

The steamers and ferries have been gone for seven decades. The village of Claiborne remains, an isolated and friendly community of retirees, local workers, and artists. The primary legacy of the Claiborne ferries for the village of Claiborne is the village itself—it was born out of the decision in 1886 to create a rail line across the Chesapeake from Bay Ridge to the vacant land in Talbot County, off Eastern Bay's Broad Cove.

The other visible reminder of Claiborne's past as a transportation nucleus is on the waterfront: the infrastructure that once supported competing ferry operations. The original earthen, stone, and wooden ferry wharf for the Baltimore and Eastern Shore Railroad, built between 1886 and 1890, remains but has decayed over time. Cars are no longer allowed to drive its length, but anglers still use it as a convenient spot when spin-casting for rockfish. The train terminal and wooden pier have long collapsed or been dismantled, though the outline is clearly visible via the pilings that have persisted. The skeleton of the 350-foot extension to the original stone breakwater, built in 1912, remains visible at low tide. Any evidence of the oyster houses that once adjoined the railroad jetty has long vanished, except for the stories that persist in oral histories and local legend.

The Baltimore, Chesapeake and Atlantic Railway steamers stopped in 1924, along with the steam locomotives.[1] The tracks are long gone, removed around 1938. The train terminal itself was disassembled in 1934 and rebuilt at Navy Point in the nearby town of St. Michaels, where it did duty for years as a packing plant for canning operations. Later, it was taken over by the Chesapeake Bay Maritime Museum where it sits today as the Small Boat Shed.

On the other side of Broad Cove is Claiborne Landing, the concrete and asphalt wharf last used by the Chesapeake Bay Ferry System through 1952. Built originally in 1911 for the Eastern Shore Development Steamship Company, it was expanded in 1919 for the first ferries of Claiborne-Annapolis Ferry Inc. It was upgraded again in 1926 to accept the new double-ender *Gov. Albert C. Ritchie*. The original terminal building was replaced by a larger one around 1931. In 1944, the wharf had been declared unsafe in an attempt to scuttle the Romancoke-Claiborne line, but with the unintended result that the wharf was substantially upgraded in 1944 and 1945. After it was taken over by the Talbot County Parks & Recreation Department, an additional upgrade was completed in 1978, which yields the landing we see there today. There is ample parking for boat trailers, a ramp for launching small craft, a few slips where locals can tie up their boats, and a tide-measuring station operated by the National Oceanic and Atmospheric Administration.

The wind continues to blow across Broad Cove. In the past, it would have been used to power bugeyes, skipjacks, or schooners harvesting the Bay's bounty, or otherwise engaged in commerce. In current times, the windy days make it a popular site for parachute surfers, exploiting for fun those Eastern Bay breezes that in the past were harnessed for work. In calm evenings, this same visage offers dramatic sunsets. In spring and autumn, a cluster of Claiborne residents occupy the site for their twice-weekly morning yoga sessions.

The village of Claiborne itself has never thought of itself a wealthy community, and the locals long ago mastered the art of reuse of old structures. The initial car-ferry terminal, replaced in 1931, was moved a couple of blocks away and became a private home in the village of Claiborne, where it remains today almost directly opposite the Village Hall. The larger replacement ferry terminal was likewise moved around 1953 and became a private home adjacent to the ferry landing, where it also stands today. It has just been sold to a new owner in the spring of 2025, and we will have to see whether the structure remains or is replaced.

The Sea Gull Inn, located at Claiborne Landing in the 1920s and 1930s, was moved inland to a farm in nearby Bozman, Maryland.[2] It survives there to this day, expanded into a caretaker's residence. Bergmann's Bakery is now a private residence, as is the former Claiborne General Store. The homes of B. Frank Sherman, Daniel Higgins, and Gardner Higgins remain much as they were and serve as private homes. The former Claiborne Supply Company evolved into the local post office. Since that closed in the mid-1980s, that structure has reverted to a private residence. A simple stroll down Claiborne Road presents physical evidence of the village's past commercial fervor—and its current domestic peacefulness.

Some change has taken place. The Bellfonte Hotel, rebuilt as a lodging house and residence after the 1938 fire, was torn down and replaced by a modern home a few years ago. Miracle House stopped providing tuberculosis-free lodging for Baltimore's youth in 1944, after the new vaccine made it redundant. Most of it burned down in 1954; today the land is used for private homes. Claiborne Hall burned down on Palm Sunday in 1956. Maple Hall was torn down just a few years ago and replaced by a modern home. Little Haven-on-the-Bay remains, reverted to its original role as a stately private estate.

Other evidence of the village's illustrious past have vanished. The gas stations are gone. The water tower that served as the village's water supply when the railroad left town was removed during or after World War II. The railroad turntable, located on the outskirts of the village, was disassembled in the 1920s, though it is said some remnants can still be found today in the woods outside Claiborne. The coal storage facilities are gone, though the shoreline just south of Claiborne still features piles of coal ash, accumulated in the days when coal-fired steamers would need a place to drop off that ash.

And what of the boats that served on these routes? Most have long vanished, though one lasted until May 2022. This was the former *Gov. Emerson C. Harrington II*, which, after years of service on the Romancoke-Claiborne route, was transferred to Lake Champlain where it performed another *seventy* years of service under the name *Adirondack*. Fondly remembered by locals as *Adi*, it was taken out of service in 2021 and tied up. Scrapping began the following May and was completed on Staten Island, New York.

Two other ferries that operated under the Chesapeake Bay Ferry System (but never really served Claiborne) remain today.[3] The former *Gov. Herbert R. O'Conor* is afloat in Fanny Bay, British Columbia, where it serves as a floating support base for local scallop farmers. The former *Gov. Harry W. Nice* is aground off a private parcel on Kentron Island, Washington, and is slowly decaying. Both ferries served decades in the fleet of Washington State Ferries, the former as *Rhododendron* and the latter as *Olympic*.

While most of the ferries have been scrapped or lost to fire or storms, some remnants remain. Outside the Claiborne Village Hall rests a large anchor, one of those from the first Claiborne-Annapolis ferry, *Gov. Emerson C. Harrington,* which served from 1919 to 1937. Inside that village hall one can find the stool upon which Captain Daniel Higgins sat for years as he skippered the ferries to and from Claiborne. The ship's bell from *B.S. Ford*, which originally served Claiborne from Baltimore in 1891, is in the collection of the Chesapeake Bay Maritime Museum in St. Michaels. That bell is just one item in the museum's impressive collection of artifacts from the ferry operations across the Chesapeake. While Holy Innocents Chapel burned in 1944, its bell also survives today at a church in nearby Oxford.

Finally, the memory lives on in the slogan of the little village of Claiborne, proclaimed with a mixture of pride, humor, and irreverence—so typical of the residents. Claiborne declares that it remains "Waiting for the Second Coming of the Ferry."

Technically, however, it would be the sixth coming of the ferry. . . but who's counting?

Notes

1. A small gasoline-powered railcar operated on the tracks until 1928.
2. This is the recollection of Judge John C. North Jr. of St. Michaels, Maryland. His grandparents operated the Sea Gull Inn. The initial name of the restaurant was Ye Ferry Inn. It was renamed Sea Gull Inn in 1920 when taken over by the North family.
3. Technically, neither *Gov. Herbert R. O'Connor* nor *B. Frank Sherman* should be thought of as part of the Claiborne-Annapolis Ferry since (1) they never served Claiborne, (2) they never served Annapolis, and (3) they were never owned by the Claiborne-Annapolis Ferry Company.

Appendices

A

Overview of Claiborne and Competing Ferry Operations

Claiborne was served by a number of scheduled steamboat ferry operations between 1867 and 1952. This included services to Tilghman Creek in 1867 (Samuel Ogle Tilghman with *Balloon*) and from 1877 to 1887 (Richard Dodson with *Olive*).

Service to the new Claiborne terminal on Broad Cove started in 1890 with the short-lived Bay Ridge service of the Baltimore and Eastern Shore Railroad (B&ES), which shifted service to Baltimore in 1891 and then was taken over by the Baltimore, Chesapeake and Atlantic Railway (BC&A) in 1894. A competing service from Annapolis to Claiborne existed from 1912 to 1916 with the Eastern Shore Development Steamship Company (ESDSC). In 1919 the Claiborne-Annapolis Ferry Inc. (CAFI) began service with car ferries between those two communities. In 1930, the Claiborne-Annapolis Ferry Company (CAFC) (which acquired Claiborne-Annapolis Ferry Inc. in 1928) created an additional line to Matapeake and in 1938 shifted the Claiborne service from Annapolis to Romancoke. All of this was taken over by the State of Maryland in 1941 and renamed the Chesapeake Bay Ferry System (CBFS). Service from Annapolis was shifted to Sandy Point in 1943, and the entire operation ended in 1952.

Meanwhile, the competing Love Point service was initiated by the Queen Anne's Railroad (QARR) in 1902, before being acquired by the Maryland, Delaware and Virginia Railway Company (MD&V), a subsidiary of BC&A, in 1905. That service was transitioned to another subsidiary, the Baltimore and Eastern Railroad (B&E), in 1924, which then took over all former BC&A operations in 1928.

Other steamboat or diesel cross-bay ferry operations existed for periods of time in this period, designed to bring travelers to connecting rail service or roadways, as opposed to excursions to specific Bay resorts. Two operations started in the early 1920s and ended almost as quickly: the Peninsula Ferry Company (PFC) service from Baltimore to Love Point and Queenstown, and the Baltimore and Eastern Shore Ferry Line Inc. (B&ESF) service from Bay Shore (outside Baltimore) to Rock Hall and Queenstown. The Tolchester Ferry Company ran excursions to its resort in Tolchester Beach—outside the scope of this analysis—but also operated a car ferry for ongoing travelers for a brief time in the late 1920s and early 1930s.

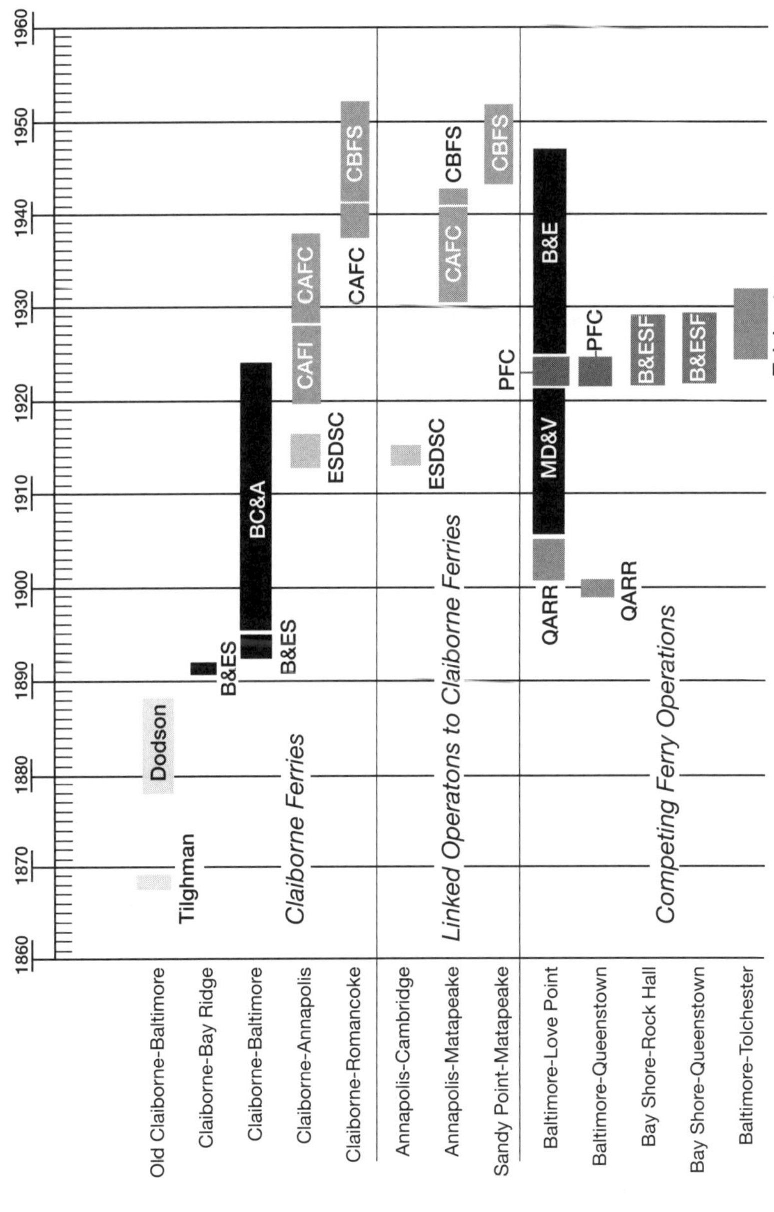

Scheduled Steam or Diesel Ferry Service to Claiborne and Competing Locations (Excludes Excursion Steamer Services and Seasonal Operations)

B

Evolution of Relevant Pennsylvania Railroad Companies

From 1894 through 1924, the Pennsylvania Railroad (PRR) had a controlling interest in the Claiborne ferry and rail operations. It also controlled a very large number of other ferry operations across and up/down the Bay.

The *modus operandi* of the company was centered on three principles, tailored for investments in a high-risk industry such as rail transport or ferry operations. The first principle was to wait until a rail or ferry company was immersed in bankruptcy and then acquire the assets from the receiver at discounted rates. This would pass the cost of the original investment onto shareholders and bondholders of the original company, who would often lose everything in the process. The second principle was to achieve effective control of subsidiary operations without actually having to put the subsidiary's associated debt on the parent company books. In this way, should the subsidiary go under, the PRR would be insulated from those losses. The third was to avoid competition at all costs, even if it meant temporarily depressing profits while the company engaged in brutal fare wars.

PRR has long dominated rail transportation on the Delmarva Peninsula, and its investments in ferry and rail operations were designed to support and protect that monopoly. This began with the effective takeover of the Baltimore, Chesapeake and Atlantic Railway Company (BC&A) in 1898 and the similar takeover of the Queen Anne's Railroad Company (QARR) in 1905. In both cases, the acquisitions were paired with investments in ferry services across and up/down the Bay.

BC&A's passenger ferry service to Claiborne ended in 1924, leaving only the rail connection (mostly freight), which was abandoned in 1928. Meanwhile, the Love Point ferry, along with a dozen or so other ferry routes around the Chesapeake, remained under the Maryland, Delaware and Virginia Railway Company (MD&V) until the company went bankrupt in 1923 and was taken over by the newly organized Baltimore and Eastern Railroad Company (B&E). In 1928 the remaining PRR operations were split into two. B&E took over the rail operations and the single ferry route to Love Point but divested all of its other ferry operations. Those other ferry operations were subsumed into the Baltimore and Virginia Steamboat Company.

It is sometimes written that the transfer of remaining rail assets from BC&A to B&E was a rare example of a subsidiary taking over the parent company. In reality, the parent company was dissolved, leaving only the two subsidiaries, one aligned with the Love Point ferry and rail operation and one running all other steamboat operations on the Chesapeake. The largely inconsequential rail operations on the McDaniel-Easton line were added to the B&E portfolio.

Ownership Structure Over Time of Integrated Steamer/Rail Lines

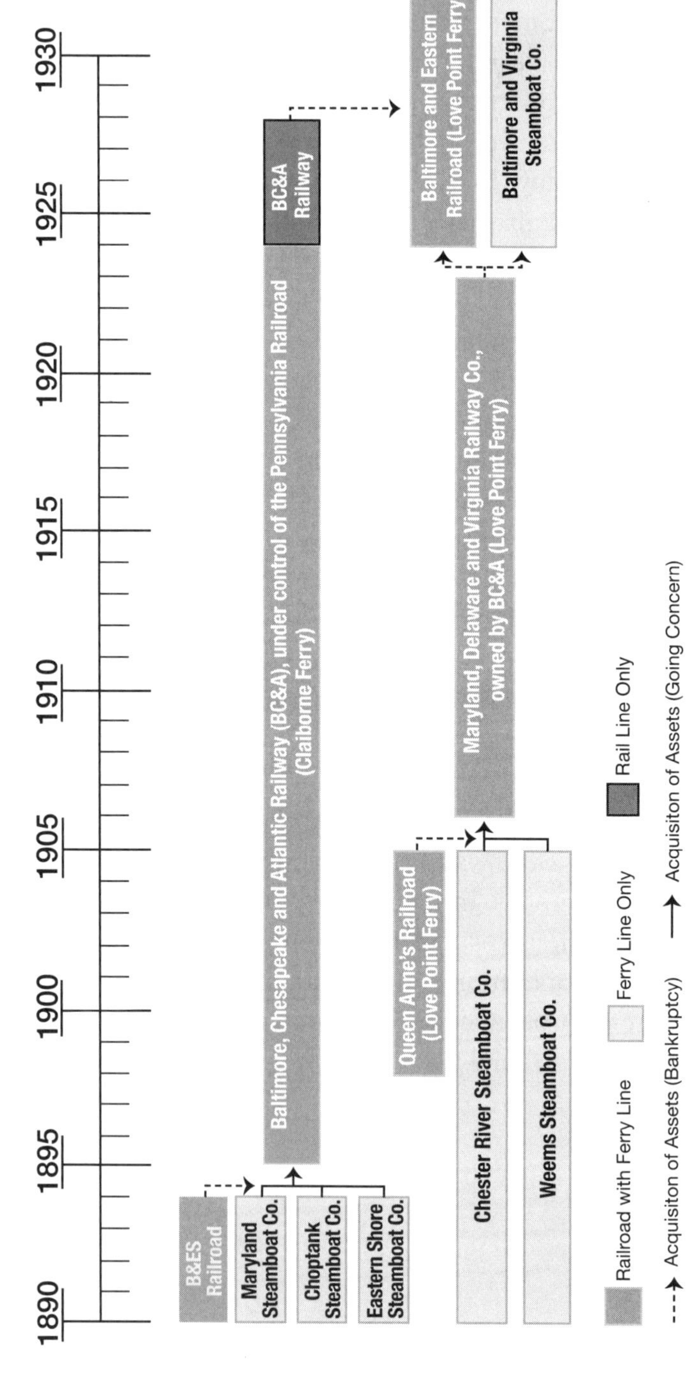

C

Particulars on Steamers and Ferries Related to Claiborne*

Samuel Ogle Tilghman

Vessel	Routes	Built	Particulars
Balloon No. 2032	Baltimore-Claiborne Jun 1867–Aug 1867	1839 Devine Burtis Brooklyn, NY	Wood Steamboiler with sidewheels 328 GRT; 160 ft LOA

Richard S. Dodson

Vessel	Routes	Built	Particulars
Olive No. 19306	Baltimore-Claiborne May 1877–Aug 1887	1869 John L. Porter (at Atlantic Iron Works) Norfolk, VA	Wood Steam boiler with propeller 288 GRT; 121 ft LOA

*In the tables that follow, GRT = gross register tonnage and LOA = length overall.

Eastern Shore Development Steamship Company

Vessel	Routes	Built	Particulars
Atlantic No. 111059 Formerly *Ruth*	Annapolis-Claiborne May 1912–Dec 1912	1894 (as *Ruth*) George A. Gilchrist Rockland, ME	Wood Steam boiler with propellers 143 GRT; 117 ft LOA
Texas No. 106635 Formerly *Augusta*, *Vivienne*, *Toinette*, *Laurita*, *Crescent*	Cambridge-Bellevue May 1912 (briefly) Annapolis-Cambridge May 1912–Dec 1912 Annapolis-Claiborne Dec 1912–Apr 1916	1889 as (*Augusta*) Herreshoff Bristol, RI	Wood Steam boiler with propellers 116 GRT; 105 ft LOA
City of Milford No. 202913	Annapolis-Cambridge Dec 1913–Dec 1914	1906 Abbott Shipbuilding Milford, DE	Wood Steam boiler with propellers 264 GRT; 127 ft LOA
York River No. 126516 Formerly *Corsair*	Baltimore-Cambridge Jan 1915–Apr 1916 Annapolis-Claiborne Sep 1915 (briefly)	1888 (as *Corsair*) Joseph Provencher East Providence, RI	Wood Steam boiler with propellers 143 GRT; 85 ft LOA
Mermaid No. 203233	Annapolis-Claiborne Sep 1915 (briefly)	1906 J.M. Bayles & Son Port Jefferson, NY	Wood Gas with propellers 56 GRT; 63 ft LOA
A.J. McIntosh No. 210143	Tilghman-Cambridge Jan 1913–Feb 1913	1912 Elco Bayonne, NJ	Wood Gas with propellers 78 GRT; 55 ft LOA

Vessel	Routes	Built	Particulars
Gen. J.A. Dumont No. 86521 Formerly *James F. Freeborn, USS Nansemond, USRC Wm. H. Crawford*	Unclear if this steamer was ever put into service by this company	1862 (as *James F. Freeborn*) Lawrence & Foulks Williamsburg, NY	Wood Steam boiler with sidewheels 309 GRT; 145 ft LOA

Baltimore and Eastern Shore Railroad Company

Vessel	Routes	Built	Particulars
Groton No. 85482 Formerly *Charles J. Osborn*	Not in service; burned and sank on transit to Chesapeake	1873 (as *Charles J. Osborn*) Henry Steers Brooklyn, NY	Wood Steam boiler with sidewheels 1,421 GRT; 253 ft LOA
Tockwogh No. 145523	Bay Ridge-Claiborne Aug 1890–Nov 1890	1889 William Skinner & Sons Baltimore, MD	Wood Steam boiler with sidewheels 457 GRT; 166 ft LOA
Thames River No. 24870	Bay Ridge-Claiborne Nov 1890–Oct 1891*	1871 Henry Steers Brooklyn, NY	Wood Steam boiler with sidewheels 882 GRT; 183 ft LOA

*Intermittent service during this interval with frequent absences

Vessel	Routes	Built	Particulars
Olive No. 19306	Bay Ridge-Claiborne Dec 1890–May 1891*	1869 John L. Porter (at Atlantic Iron Works) Norfolk, VA	Wood Steam boiler with propellers 288 GRT; 121 ft LOA
B.S. Ford No. 3045	Baltimore-Claiborne Oct 1891–Jan 1892 Jun 1892–Oct 1892 Jun 1893–Aug 1893	1877 Harlan & Hollingsworth Wilmington, DE	Iron Steam boiler with sidewheels 418 GRT; 165 ft LOA
Tangier No. 135049	Baltimore-Claiborne Feb 1892–May 1892 Nov 1892–Apr 1893 Sep 1893–Apr 1893	1875 Harlan & Hollingsworth Wilmington, DE	Iron Steam boiler with sidewheels 681 GRT; 170 ft LOA
Maggie No. 90013	Baltimore-Claiborne Apr 1893–Jun 1893 May 1894–Jun 1894*	1869 Harlan & Hollingsworth Wilmington, DE	Iron Steam boiler with sidewheels 606 GRT; 164 ft LOA
Helen No. 95094	Baltimore-Claiborne Jul 1893–Aug 1893	1871 Harlan & Hollingsworth Wilmington, DE	Iron Steam boiler with sidewheels 550 GRT; 150 ft LOA

*Intermittent service during this interval with frequent absences

Baltimore, Chesapeake and Atlantic Railway Company

Vessel	Routes	Built	Particulars
Cambridge No. 126668	Baltimore-Claiborne Jun 1894–May 1924	1890 William E. Woodall & Co. Baltimore, MD	Iron/Wood Steam boiler with propellers 834 GRT; 165 ft LOA
Tred Avon No. 145390	Baltimore-Claiborne Jun 1894–May 1924	1884 William E. Woodall & Co. Baltimore, MD	Wood Steam boiler with propellers 677 GRT; 151 ft LOA
Joppa No. 76576	Baltimore-Claiborne Feb 1923–Mar 1923*	1885 Harlan & Hollingsworth Wilmington, DE	Iron Steam boiler with sidewheels 608 GRT; 190 ft LOA

*Only as temporary substitute for damaged *Cambridge*

Claiborne-Annapolis Ferry Inc.

Vessel	**Routes**	**Built**	**Particulars**
Gov. Emerson C. Harrington No. 145885 (formerly *Thomas Patten*)	Annapolis-Claiborne Jun 1919–Dec 1927	1901 (as *Thomas Patten*) T.S. Marvel & Co. Newburgh, NY	Steel Steam boiler with sidewheels 875 GRT; 202 ft LOA
Gen. Lincoln No. 130126 (formerly *Nahant*)	Annapolis-Claiborne Jul 1920–Jul 1922	1878 G. Pierce Chelsea, MA	Wood Steam boiler with sidewheels 398 GRT; 160 ft LOA
Majestic No. 96688 (formerly *Happy Day*)	Annapolis-Claiborne Apr 1923–Sep 1926	1903 Lewis Nixon Elizabeth, NJ	Steel Steam boiler with sidewheels 717 GRT; 202 ft LOA
Gov. Albert C. Ritchie No. 130262 (formerly Newburgh)	Annapolis-Claiborne Jul 1926–Dec 1927	1883 (as *Newburgh*) Ward, Stanton & Co. Newburgh, NY	Steel Diesel engine with propellers 797 GRT; 194 ft LOA

Claiborne-Annapolis Ferry Company

Vessel	Routes	Built	Particulars
Gov. Emerson C. Harrington No. 145885 (formerly *Thomas Patten*)	Annapolis-Claiborne Jan 1928–Sep 1937 Annapolis-Matapeake Jul 1930–Jun 1936	1901 (as *Thomas Patten*) T.S. Marvel & Co. Newburgh, NY	Steel Steam boiler with sidewheels 875 GRT; 202 ft LOA
Gov. Albert C. Ritchie No. 130262 (formerly *Newburgh*)	Annapolis-Claiborne Jan 1928–Jun 1936 Annapolis-Matapeake Jul 1930–Jun 1941	1883 (as *Newburgh*) Ward, Stanton & Co. Newburgh, NY	Steel Diesel with propellers 797 GRT; 194 ft LOA
John M. Dennis No. 228683	Annapolis-Claiborne Jun 1929–Jun 1936 Annapolis-Matapeake Jul 1930–Jun 1941	1929 Spear Engineers Portsmouth, VA	Steel Diesel engine with propellers 889 GRT; 215 ft LOA
Gov. Harry W. Nice No. 237285	Annapolis-Matapeake May 1938–Jun 1941	1938 Maryland Drydock Co. Baltimore, MD	Steel Diesel with propellers 773 GRT; 198 ft LOA
Gov. Emerson C. Harrington II No. 211156 (formerly *South Jacksonville, Mount Holly*)	Romancoke-Claiborne May 1938–Jun 1941	1913 (As *South Jacksonville*) Merrill-Stevens Co. Jacksonville, FL	Steel Steam boiler with propellers 319 GRT; 130 ft LOA

Chesapeake Bay Ferry System

Vessel	Routes	Built	Particulars
Gov. Albert C. Ritchie No. 130262 (formerly *Newburgh*)	Annapolis-Matapeake Jun 1941–Oct 1943 Sandy Point–Matapeake Oct 1943–Mar 1944	1883 (as *Newburgh*) Ward, Stanton & Co. Newburgh, NY	Steel Diesel engine with propellers 797 GRT; 194 ft LOA
John M. Dennis No. 228683	Annapolis-Matapeake Jun 1941–Oct 1943 Sandy Point–Matapeake Nov 1943–Jul 1952	1929 Spear Engineers Portsmouth, VA	Steel Diesel engine with propellers 889 GRT; 215 ft LOA
Gov. Harry W. Nice No. 237285	Annapolis-Matapeake Jun 1941–Oct 1943 Sandy Point-Matapeake Nov 1943-Jul 1952	1938 Maryland Drydock Co. Baltimore, MD	Steel Diesel engine with propellers 773 GRT; 198 ft LOA
Gov. Emerson C. Harrington II No. 211156 (formerly *South Jacksonville, Mount Holly*)	Romancoke-Claiborne Jun 1941–Mar 1944 Apr 1944–Dec 1945 Mar 1946–Dec 1952 Sandy Point-Matapeake Jul 1950–Aug 1950*	1913 (As *South Jacksonville*) Merrill-Stevens Co. Jacksonville, FL	Steel Steam boiler with propellers (through Dec 1945) Diesel engine with propellers (After Mar 1946) 319 GRT; 130' LOA

Vessel	Routes	Built	Particulars
Gov. Herbert R. O'Conor No. 251646	Sandy Point-Matapeake Feb 1947–Jul 1952	1946 Maryland Drydock Co. Baltimore, MD 21624	Steel Diesel engine with propellers 937 GRT; 218 ft LOA
Eastern Bay (prior Feb 1950) *B. Frank Sherman* (after Feb 1950) No. 226194 (formerly *Frederick Pierce, Westchester, North Jersey*)	Sandy Point-Matapeake Jul 1948–Jul 1952	1926 New York Shipbuilding Camden, NJ	Steel Diesel electric with propellers 406 GRT; 146 ft LOA

*Intermittently on busy weekends

D

Fate of the Claiborne Steamers and Ferries

The following pages present a short summary of the fate of steamers and ferries associated with Claiborne after they left that service. Please note that in some cases dates are approximate. For example, transactions recorded in the 1925 *Merchant Vessels of the United States* could have taken place between July 1, 1924, and June 30, 1925.

Abbreviations Used

B&ES Baltimore and Eastern Shore Railroad Company. Formed in 1886 and began operations in 1890; declared insolvent in 1891 and placed under receiver; assets auctioned in 1894.

BC&A Baltimore, Chesapeake and Atlantic Railway Company. Formed in 1894 (different shareholders than B&ES); acquired B&ES assets out of bankruptcy in 1894; entered bankruptcy in 1928; assets acquired by Baltimore and Eastern Railroad Company (Love Point ferry and railroad) and Baltimore and Virginia Steamboat Company (other ferries).

ESDSC Eastern Shore Development Steamship Company. Formed in 1911 and began operations in 1912; declared bankrupt in 1916; assets sold at auction in 1916.

CAFI Claiborne-Annapolis Ferry Inc. Formed in 1919; taken over by CAFC in 1928; shareholders in CAFI and CAFC largely the same.

CAFC Claiborne-Annapolis Ferry Company. Formed in 1927 by similar shareholders to those within CAFI; acquired by State of Maryland in 1941.

CBFS Chesapeake Bay Ferry System. Formed in 1941 and acquired assets of CAFC; terminated operations in 1952 and assets sold off by 1954.

Early Steamer Operations to Claiborne

Ferry	Operators	Subsequent Fate	
Balloon	Tilghman	1867	Removed from service; owner sued
		1870	Sold at sheriff's auction January 1870
		1871	Sold to Dialogue & Wood in Camden, NJ
		1872	Destroyed by fire October 29, 1872 while tied up at wharf
Olive	Dodson B&ES	1891	Removed from service on Claiborne route; sold to Suffolk and Carolina Railway Company based out of Norfolk
		1903	Sank in storm (possible tornado) in Chowan River with 17 killed on February 16, 1903
		1904	Wreck raised; rebuilt and renamed *Hertford*
		1914	Laid up; eventually abandoned in Elizabeth City, NC
		1924	Sank at its berth in May 1924

Baltimore and Eastern Shore Railroad Company

Ferry	Operators	Subsequent Fate	
Groton	B&ES	1889	Destroyed by fire off the Atlantic coast from Assateague Island, VA, on November 30, 1889, while in transit to Baltimore; all crew saved by *Thames River*
Thames River	B&ES	1891	Removed from service and laid up in Baltimore October 10, 1891
		1896	Purchased by H. Clay Tunis; converted for use as a lumber barge
		1898	Renamed *John R. King*; operating from Norfolk
		1905	Converted to scow; renamed *Virginia H. Hudson*; based in Newark, NJ
		1906	Foundered in storm off Hereford, NJ, on September 15, 1906; all crew rescued
B.S. Ford	B&ES	1893	Removed from Claiborne service; returned to other ferry operations in Chesapeake Bay
		1930	Acquired by Mary E. Mitchell in Baltimore and converted to a barge
		1958	Acquired by Calvin Baumgartner and used in grain trade between Norfolk and Baltimore
		1960	Foundered in Honga River near west side of Hoopers Strait (Dorchester County in Maryland)
Tangier	B&ES	1927	Sold for breaking up; instead, converted to tanker and renamed *Suburban*; owned by Petroleum Storage Corporation; relocated to New York
		1935	Sank at pier in Kill Van Kull on March 3, 1935; raised
		1942	Reported as abandoned

Ferry	Operators	Subsequent Fate	
Maggie	B&ES	1894	Removed from Claiborne service; returned to other ferry operations in the Chesapeake
		1913	Acquired by William Whitehurst & Company for salvage in February 1913
		1914	Hull towed to Norfolk for scrapping in May 1914
		1915	Scrapped
Helen	B&ES	1894	Removed from Claiborne service; returned to other ferry operations in the Chesapeake
		1929	Converted to a tanker and relocated to New York
		1941	Scrapped

Baltimore, Chesapeake and Atlantic Railway Company

Ferry	Operators	Subsequent Fate	
Cambridge	BC&A	1924	Transferred from Claiborne route to Love Point route
		1929	Taken off Love Point route
		1930	Acquired by new owners in New York, NY; deployed as excursion steamer
		1940	Scrapped
Tred Avon	BC&A	1924	Removed from Claiborne service
		1929	Reclassified as a freighter
		1930	Sold to Refinery Transportation Corp.; vessel home port in Baltimore
		1931	Sold to Robert W. Bottomley
		1932	Sold to Stoney Creek Improvement Co.
		1941	Reported as abandoned; some sources report scrapped in 1939
Joppa	BC&A	1929	Removed from service and laid up
		1930	Acquired by Alwynn Wootten of Victor Lynn Transportation Line
		1934	Rebuilt as tanker in Salisbury
		1935	Renamed *City of Salisbury*
		1941	Sold to USA Navigation Company
		1945	Transferred to US Army as transport *Col. Henry R. Casey*
		1946	Declared surplus and put up at auction by War Shipping Administration
		1947	Purchased by F. C. Sears; once again named *City of Salisbury*
		1950	Sold to owners in Mexico; likely broken up in Mexico in 1950

Eastern Shore Development Steamship Company

Ferry	Operators	Subsequent Fate	
Atlantic	ESDSC	1912	Removed from Claiborne service after accident; sold to Booz Brothers Inc. shipyard
		1918	Acquired by US Navy; reamed USS Atlantic (ID 3268)
		1920	Reclassified as ferryboat YFB-3268; sank at moorings on November 25, 1921; refloated
		1921	Declared unfit for service and sold to Harry Hitner & Sons in Philadelphia
		1925	Foundered in Cooper River, SC, on September 10, 1925
Texas	ESDSC	1916	Sold by US Marshals at auction to Faranholt & Meredith Company on November 11, 1916
		1922	Owned by Southern Oil & Transport; being refitted for proposed service in Central America
		1923	Sold by US Marshals at auction to Elizabeth City Iron Works & Supply Company in Elizabeth City, NC
		1929	Converted to a lumber barge; out of documentation;
		1931	Burned to the waterline on May 27, 1931; scrapped afterwards

Ferry	Operators	Subsequent Fate	
City of Milford	ESDSC	1915	Sold to John W. R. Crawford
		1918	Sold to George Wever; sold by Wever to Bluefields Fruit Company; converted to a steam tub by Booz Brothers Inc.; renamed *San Juan*; acquisition by US Navy contemplated and assigned pennant SP-3306 but acquisition did not happen happen before the end of World War I
		1919	Transited Panama Canal; used as steam tug in Nicaragua; subsequent fate unknown
York River	ESDSC	1916	Sold by US Marshals at auction to Lyman Stevens on November 11, 1916
		1919	Sold to Electric Welding Company in Baltimore
		1919	Sank at Baltimore Dry Dock & Ship Building Co.; towed to Westport and beached
		1922	Out of documentation; reported as abandoned
A.J. McIntosh	ESDSC	1914	Burned and destroyed in Annapolis on October 3, 1914
Mermaid	ESDSC	1916	Sold by US Marshals at auction to William H. Valliant
		1925	Reclassified as yacht; removed from US merchant ship register
		1927	Reported as yacht owned by George L. Shearer
		1932	Out of documentation; reported as abandoned

Claiborne-Annapolis Ferry Inc. and Follow-On Enterprises

Ferry	Operators	Subsequent Fate	
Gov. Emerson C. Harrington	CAFI CAFC	1937	Removed from service to Claiborne; purchased by Clinton K. Duncan on December 3, 1937; towed to Pocomoke City and converted to restaurant; engines removed and reclassified as a barge
		1940	Sold to Everett Smith; moved to Annapolis for use as hotel
		1941	Access to hotel curtailed by expansion of US Naval Academy; laid up as derelict for duration of war
		1946	Purchased by Rosco Bailey and taken to Pocomoke City for use as a hotel and nightclub
		1949	Partially scrapped; hull towed to Baltimore for final scrapping
Gen. Lincoln	CAFI	1922	Removed from service in July 1922 after major accident on July 2, 1922; put up for sale
		1924	Sold January 1924; renamed *Indian Head* out of Baltimore
		1929	Sold March 1929; renamed *Mayflower* operating out of Norfolk
		1933	Passengers riot during cruise; ferry taken out of operation
		1935	Listed as abandoned; subsequent fate unknown

Ferry	Operators	Subsequent Fate	
Majestic	CAFI	1926	Removed from Claiborne-Annapolis service in September 1926
		1927	Sank at pier while on excursion voyage in Baltimore (all 1,000 aboard were able to escape); CAFI abandons wreck
		1928	Raised in April 1928; salvaged and converted to a barge
		1932	Caught fire in Schuylkill River in July 1932; fire extinguished and all crew escaped
		1937	Destroyed by fire at mouth of Choptank River on May 5, 1937; crew rescued
Gov Albert C. Ritchie	CAFI CAFC CBFS	1944	Failed annual federal inspection and condemned as structurally unsafe; removed from service
		1945	Sold to Marine Industries Ltd. for scrapping; scrapped in Sorel-Tracy, Quebec
John M. Dennis	CAFC CBFS	1952	Laid up by Chesapeake Bay Ferry System
		1953	Sold to Delaware River Ferry Company; renamed *Delaware*; used on Chester-Bridgeport route
		1968	Sold to private owner; relocated to Deal Island Harbor in August 1968 with plans to convert ferry into a restaurant
		1974	Caught fire while being scrapped in Deal Island Harbor; remains scrapped

Ferry	Operators	Subsequent Fate	
Gov. Harry W. Nice	CAFC CBFS	1952	Laid up by Chesapeake Bay Ferry System
		1954	Sold to Washington (state) Toll Bridge Authority; renamed *Olympic*
		1997	Removed from service; sold to Darrell McNabb on Bainbridge Island; renovation effort contemplated but never completed
		2010	Sold to private owner; relocated from Bainbridge Island to Kentron Island; run aground there
		2024	Still aground on Kentron Island, WA, in deteriorating condition
Gov. Emerson C. Harrington II	CAFC CBFS	1952	Laid up by Chesapeake Bay Ferry System
		1954	Sold to Lake Champlain Transportation Company; moved to Lake Champlain; renamed *Adirondack* and used for ferry service
		1970	Diesel engines replaced as part of a major overhaul
		2021	Removed from service and laid up
		2022	Scrapping underway

Chesapeake Bay Ferry System

Ferry	Operators	Subsequent Fate	
Gov. Herbert R. O'Conor	CBFS	1952	Laid up by Chesapeake Bay Ferry System
		1954	Sold to Washington (state) Toll Bridge Authority; renamed *Rhododendron*
		2012	Withdrawn from service
		2013	Sold as support vessel for scallop farming in Fanny Bay, British Columbia
		2024	Still afloat in Fanny Bay
Eastern Bay / *B. Frank Sherman*	CBFS	1952	Laid up by Chesapeake Bay Ferry System
		1954	Sold to Commonwealth of Virginia; renamed *Chesapeake*; placed on Old Point to Willoughby route as a reserve ferry
		1958	Transferred to Scotland-Jamestown line after Hampton Roads Bridge-Tunnel completed in 1957
		1967	Removed from service and laid up
		1968	Reported as out of documentation; possibly scrapped in 1979

Bibliography

Ferries, Steamboats, and Steamboat Lines

Burgess, Robert H. *Chesapeake Circle*. Cornell Maritime Press, 1965.

Burgess, Robert H., and H. Graham Wood. *Steamboats Out of Baltimore*. Tidewater Publishers, 1968.

Dayton, Fred Erving, and John Wolcott Adams. *Steamboat Days*. Frederick A. Stokes Company, 1925.

Denny, William J. *Days of Gratitude: A Brief History of a Chesapeake Steamboat and the Town Named After Her*. American Literary Press, 2007.

Hain, John Antonio. *Side Wheel Steamers of the Chesapeake Bay 1880–1947*. Glendale Press, 1947.

Heyl, Erik. *Early American Steamers, Volume II*. Edwards Brothers, 1956.

Holly, David C. *Chesapeake Steamboats: The Steamboat Era, 1813–1963 on the Chesapeake*. Tidewater Publishers, 1994.

Holly, David C. *Chesapeake Steamboats: Vanished Fleet*. Tidewater Publishers, 1987.

Holly, David C. *Steamboat on the Chesapeake: Emma Giles and The Tolchester Line*. Tidewater Publishers, 1987.

Holly, David C. *Tidewater by Steamboat: A Saga of the Chesapeake*. Johns Hopkins University Press, 1991.

Pickens, Steven J. *Crossing Puget Sound: From Black Ball Steamer to Washington State Ferries*. Arcadia Publishing, 2006.

Shaum, Jack. *Lost Chester River Steamboats: From Chestertown to Baltimore*. Arcadia Publishing, 2015.

Shaum, Jack. *122 Years on the Old Bay Line*. Arcadia Publishing, 2022.

Shaum, Jack. "The Steamboats of Chesapeake Bay." *Bugeye Times* 41, no. 4 (Winter 2016–2017).

Simmons, Clara Ann. *Chesapeake Ferries: A Waterborne Tradition 1636–2000.* The Maryland Historical Society, 2009.

Tigner, James A. Jr. *Steamboat Days on the Chesapeake: Betterton and Tolchester Beach*. Schiffer Publishing, 2009.

Railroads

Baer, Christopher T., William J. Coxey, and Paul W. Schopp. *The Trail of the Blue Comet: A History of the Jersey Central's New Jersey Southern Division*. The West Jersey Chapter of the National Railway Historical Society, 1994.

Dickon, Chris. *Images of Rail: Eastern Shore Railroad*. Arcadia Publishing, 2006.

Hayman, John C. *Rails Along the Chesapeake: A History of Railroading on the Delmarva Peninsula, 1827–1978*. Marvadel Publishers, 1979.

Poore, Douglas. *Abandoned Railroads of Delmarva.* Arcadia Publishing, 2021.

Poore, Douglas. *Railroads of Delmarva: A Pictorial History*. Arcadia Publishing, 2020.

Treese, Lorett. *Railroads of the Eastern Shore*. History Press, 2021.

Williams, Ames W. *Otto Mears Goes East: The Chesapeake Beach Railway*. Calvert County Historical Society, 1981.

General Regional History

Brugger, Robert J. *Maryland: A Middle Temperament 1634–1980*. Johns Hopkins University Press, 1988.

Corddry, Mary. *City on the Sand: Ocean City, Maryland, and the People Who Built It*. Schiffer Publishing, 2011.

Crenson, Matthew A. *Baltimore: A Political History*. Johns Hopkins University Press, 2017.

Dickson, Preston J. *Talbot County: A History*. Tidewater Publishers, 1983.

Driggs, Margaret Barton. "Claiborne." In *Last Hotel: Eastern Shore Summers & a Vanished Way of Life*. Chesapeake College Press, 1985.

Footner, Karen M. *Neavitt: Chesapeake Charm*. Historical Society of Talbot County, 2011.

Guth, David W. *Bridging the Chesapeake: A 'Fool Idea' That United Maryland*. Archway Publishing, 2017.

Hoxter, Nick. *A Walk Back in Time: Kent Island Remembered in Pictures*. Pavsner Press, 1997.

Keiser, R. Jerry, and Barbara Thomson Lewis. *Talbot County: Images of America*. Arcadia Publishing, 2006.

McWilliams, Jane Wilson, and Carol Cushard Patterson. *Bay Ridge on the Chesapeake: An Illustrated History*. Brighton Editions, 1986.

Roundtree, Helen C., and Thomas E. Davidson. *Eastern Shore Indians of Maryland and Virginia*. University of Virginia Press, 1997.

Schley, David. *Steam City: Railroads, Urban Space, and Corporate Capitalism in Nineteenth-Century Baltimore*. University of Chicago Press, 2020.

Schoch, Mildred C. *Of History and Houses: A Kent Island Heritage*. Queen Anne Press, 1982.

Sullivan, John C. *Old Ocean City: The Journal and Photographs of Robert Craighead Walker, 1904–1916*. Johns Hopkins University Press, 2001.

Vitabile, Christine. *Around St. Michaels: Images of America*. Arcadia Publishing, 2007.

Wennersten, John R. *The Oyster Wars of Chesapeake Bay*. Eastern Branch Press, 2007.

Reference Materials

Annual Report of the Public Service Commission of Maryland. Publishers vary by year:

Years 1910 to 1912: Sun Job Printing Office, 1911 to 1913.
Years 1913 to 1915: Kohn & Pollock, 1914 to 1916.
Year 1916: Thomas & Evans Printing, 1917.
Years 1917 to 1922: Kohn & Pollock, 1918 to 1923.
Years 1923 to 1924: Day Printing, 1924 to 1925.
Year 1925: Kohn & Pollock, 1926.
Year 1926: The Industrial Printing, 1927.

Merchant Vessels of the United States, Government Printing Office. The responsible issuing organization varies over time:

Department of the Treasury, Bureau of Statistics, vols. 1 (1869) to 15 (1883).

Department of the Treasury, Bureau of Navigation, vols. 16 (1884) to 34 (1902).

Department of Commerce and Labor, Bureau of Navigation, vols. 35 (1903) to 44 (1912).

Department of Commerce, Bureau of Navigation, vols. 45 (1913) to 64 (1932).

Department of Commerce, Bureau of Navigation and Steamboat Inspection, vols. 65 (1933) to 67 (1935).

Department of Commerce, Bureau of Marine Inspection and Navigation, vols. 68 (1936) to 73 (1942).

Department of the Treasury, Bureau of Customs, 1943 to 1966.

Department of the Treasury, United States Coast Guard, 1967 to 2020.

Baer, Christopher T. *PRR Chronology: A General Chronology of the Pennsylvania Railroad Company Predecessors and Successors and Its Historical Context.* Pennsylvania Railroad Technical & Historical Society. Available online at prrths.com.

Poor, Henry Varnum. *Poor's Manual of Railroads of the United States,* vols. 23 to 58. Poor's Railroad Manual, 1890 to 1924.

First-Hand Accounts

Bryan, Margaret, Chris, and Mark, interviewed August 31, 2022. Margaret is the daughter of B. Frank Sherman, the general manager of the Claiborne-Annapolis Ferry Company and the Chesapeake Bay Ferry System from 1925 to 1952. He also worked as a station manager from the ferry's inception until promoted to general manager. Chris and Mark are grandsons of B. Frank Sherman. The Bryans also shared their extensive personal records and photographs from B. Frank Sherman's time in the ferry company.

Guthrie, Trudy, exchange of emails during 2022–2024. Trudy is the granddaughter of Emerson C. Harrington and shared information about family history.

Higgins, Daniel C. III, interviewed August 13, 2022, with follow-up email exchanges. Dan is the grandson of Daniel C. Higgins, the senior captain of the Claiborne-Annapolis Ferry and its successor, the Chesapeake Bay Ferry System. His grandfather worked on the ferry during its full existence from 1919 to 1952. Dan also shared photos and records of his father's career. Dan's two great uncles, Gardner and Edward (Ned), were also captains on the ferry line, as was his uncle John (Jack).

Hon. North, John C. Jr. John was a long-time resident of Talbot County and a retired judge. Universally known as Judge North, he was very active in preserving the maritime heritage of his community, and he happily shared his knowledge with this author. His grandparents operated the Sea Gull Inn at the Claiborne ferry wharf from about 1920 until the late 1930s. Sadly, Judge North passed in September 2025, shortly before his 95th birthday and one month before this book was published.

Price, Jacqueline. Jacqueline is the daughter of Captain Jack Higgins of the Chesapeake Bay Ferry System. She is the granddaughter of Gardner Higgins, who worked for the Claiborne-Annapolis Ferry Company and the Chesapeake Bay Ferry System. Jacqueline shared her father's papers and photographs, which included Gardner's personal logbook from 1920 and 1921.

Index

References to illustrations, maps, or figures appear in italics

About the author

Martin J. Bollinger is a retired management consultant who spent thirty years advising senior executives of the aerospace, defense, and maritime industries on issues of business and corporate strategy. Mr. Bollinger has been writing on topics related to maritime history for over two decades. While searching for a new project, he stumbled upon Claiborne's largely forgotten heritage as a major regional transportation hub, which was the inspiration for *When Claiborne Bridged the Chesapeake: The Rise and Fall of the Ferry Era*.

Other books by the author:

From the Revolution to the Cold War: A History of the Soviet Merchant Fleet from 1917 to 1950

Warriors and Wizards: The Development and Defeat of Radio-Controlled Glide Bombs of the Third Reich

Stalin's Slave Ships: Kolyma, the Gulag Fleet, and the Role of the West (translated into Polish and French)

About the publisher

The Maryland Center for History and Culture (MCHC) collects, preserves, and interprets the history, art, and culture of Maryland within the broader United States. By exploring multiple perspectives and sharing national stories through the lens of Maryland, MCHC inspires critical thinking, creativity, and community. Founded in 1844 as the Maryland Historical Society, MCHC is the oldest continuously operating cultural institution in the state. MCHC Press has been publishing for over 150 years, offering dynamic, vibrant insights into all areas of Maryland history. We publish the *Maryland Historical Magazine*, a semiannual, peer-reviewed journal, as well as historical monographs and companion volumes to our collections and exhibitions.